Psychological Fingerprints

Lifestyle Assessments and Interventions

FIFTH EDITION

DANIEL ECKSTEIN, PH.D.
CAPELLA UNIVERSITY
ADLER SCHOOL OF PROFESSIONAL PSYCHOLOGY

ROY KERN, ED.D.
GEORGIA STATE UNIVERSITY

KENDALL/HUNT PUBLISHING COMPANY
4050 Westmark Drive   Dubuque, Iowa 52004

Cover images ©2002 PhotoDisc., Inc.

Contents

Chapter 4—Lifestyle Interpretive Skills   79

Chapter 5—Reorientation   143

One of a Kind

There are two basic ways to get to know people, one from the outside and the other from the inside.

Looking at people's personalities from the outside, we compare each person to someone else to determine how they are the same and how they are different. Most personality assessment tools in psychology take this approach. They ask the respondent to answer a set of questions, and then they compare the answers to those of hundreds or thousands of others to find out which ones they resemble. The respondent is then put into categories based on these similarities. Examples are the Minnesota Multiphasic Inventory (MMPI),[1] the 16PF,[2] the NEO—FFI,[3] and the BASIS-A.[4]

We know the value of each approach in the process of science and in particular psychology; however, I am pleased that the authors have been able to integrate both approaches in their book so as to benefit from the clinical as well as the more objective scientific assessments to acquire important knowledge on a person's psychological fingerprint or lifestyle.

From the Outside

Technically, the approach represented by these examples is called "nomothetic" or "naming." The nomothetic approach could be thought of as having "Rumplestiltskin" assumptions. In the fairy tale, the elf Rumplestiltskin lost his power once he had been named. Likewise, the naming and categorization of flora and fauna by Linnaeus in the early 19th century made it possible for Darwin to remove some of the mystery of the biological sciences.

Today, advances in statistics and the capacity for computers to process large numbers of nomothetic observations have made it possible for researchers to draw complex conclusions such as "If you score X, you are Y% more likely to do/have A than someone who scores Z." These conclusions can help to remove the mystery in making predictions about groups of people and in indicating diagnostic categories. They also "look" very scientific in that they may be presented in tables and numbers and pass tests of reliability and validity, just like sciences that are considered more legitimate, such as biology and physics.

As compared with the inside approach, however, nomothetic, or "outside," approaches have two shortcomings, one theoretical and one personal.

Nomothetic Shortcoming #1

The theoretical problem is one that social psychologists and sociologists have pointed out for decades: human behavior is very much influenced by the social field and by one's definition of the situation. No matter who is watching—my dog's behavior when he comes to a fire hydrant is always the same. Needless to say, that is not the case with human beings. Part of the charm of dogs and other pets is that they don't craft their behavior to impress us, or to avoid disgusting us, unless of course a person has trained them to appear to do so.

Even less does a rock skip across the water to fulfill the expectations of the person throwing it. But a person might, if she could skip across water. Because human beings survive only by the support of others and come to be fully human only through interaction with others, it is our nature to orient ourselves to our social situation as we perceive it. If we think formality is demanded, we may comply or rebel, but whatever we do is in reference to the situation. To conclude that we know a person, when all we know are his answers to questions in a testing situation, is to ignore a part of what makes humans human.

The fact that nomothetic assessment removes the person being assessed from his social context is a major shortcoming.

Nomothetic Shortcoming #2

The other shortcoming of the nomothetic approach is that people feel they are not treated personally—as unique individuals. To understand this shortcoming, I ask you to imagine being informed of a score you received on an assessment, say the BASIS-A: "Hello, _____ (fill in your name). You scored in the 95th percentile of the "Going Along" scale of the BASIS-A."

Your first response might be, "What does that mean?" Knowing that, most psychologists do not reveal raw scores to those whom they have assessed. Instead, they interpret the scores, which means that they guess what they mean. Even though these guesses may look very authoritative because they are written up in a "Psychological Report," they are *guesses* because of the principle stated above: a person's behavior is influenced by one's interpretation of the situation. The psychologist who has assessed you knows for sure only the score, not what you *meant* by your answers.

As a result of the score you have received and the guesses made about it by your assessor, you may be given a diagnosis, or recommended for a certain kind of treatment, or told what kind of career fits people "like you." You might respond, "I feel like I'm just a number or a label." Indeed, it was responses like these to nomothetic vocational assessments that prompted Les White and me to develop the Work Style Assessment that appears in the Appendix to this volume.

The personal, subjective shortcoming of the nomothetic approach is that individuals are not treated *as individuals*, as unique as we all think we are. In Chapter 4 of this volume, the authors state, "Each man [sic] is unique, and that is the beauty of the individual."

We know that we are like others in some ways, but we feel disrespected, or even violated, when our uniqueness is ignored.

From the Inside

The other way to get to know people is from the inside. This book offers several assessment approaches which avoid both shortcomings of the nomothetic approach. Lifestyle assessment is based on this approach to getting to know people, one that is technically called "idiographic," as in one's "unique idiom." In this approach, the assumption is made that each person has a unique history and perspective, a unique fingerprint. Each of us is recognized as one of a kind.

Because the principle of idiography, or uniqueness, is a basic assumption in the philosophy of Alfred Adler, it is little wonder that this book is based on Adlerian psychology. Indeed, another name for Adlerian psychology is "Individual Psychology" in English. The English translation "individual" misses the connotation that Adler intended in German: psychology of the whole, integrated, and unique person.

Many psychologists have been willing to pay the price of the nomothetic approach in order to gain scientific legitimacy. Gathering and analyzing quantitative data requires us to ignore context, unique history, and subjective perspective. During much of the past century, this was not considered too high a price in psychology because the dominant trends were psychoanalysis and behaviorism. Psychoanalysis was interested in intrapsychic phenomena, in the conflicts inside a person, so social context was irrelevant. Behaviorism did take into account one's environmental history, but this was a mechanistic, stimulus-response approach that ignored subjectivity. Neither insisted on including both context and subjectivity.

In assuming that social embeddedness and subjective creativity account for individual uniqueness, along with holism and goal-directedness, Adlerian psychology joined with social psychology in representing an alternative to the dual hegemony of psychoanalysis and behaviorism. As we enter a new millennium, cognitive psychology has begun to appreciate the need to study context, history and emotions, in addition to "pure" thinking.[5] And social constructivists[6] have begun to recognize how people co-create their reality. In effect, mainstream clinical psychology is catching up with an Adlerian perspective[7] in insisting on a contextualized, embodied, subjective perspective.[8]

However, there still remains the argument that nomothetic assessments are the only ones that are truly scientific. If the only way to assess from the inside was an informal conversation, then this argument might have merit. Does the very subjective bias that makes each of us unique also make it impossible to validate an idiographic assessment? A long history of the development of idiographic, or qualitative, methods[9] yields the answer "No," although we must look outside mainstream psychology for most of that history.

In my own studies in anthropology and sociology, an idiographic approach was necessary. Cultural anthropologists who wanted to understand a society that had been isolated from Western contact could not give the society a questionnaire—they could not even speak the language of the people they wanted to work with. So they let the people be their teacher. For example, their ability to get a drink of water when they asked for it in the indigenous language was proof of their being able to understand and use the language. An approach called "ethnomethodology" was what anthropologists used to discover the uniqueness of new (to them) societies.

I submit that Adler's approach to understanding personality, the Lifestyle Assessment which Eckstein and Kern have presented in many of its variations, is like an ethnomethodology of an individual. We could call it "psychomethodology." The idiographic approach this represents may seem unusual in a narrow psychological context, but in the wider context of all the social sciences, it is at home as part of a long and rich tradition.

Psychomethodology

Like ethnomethodology and other qualitative approaches, psychomethodology does have methods for controlling for bias on the part of the researcher or assessor. Two major ones are triangulation[10] and iteration (or reflexivity[11]).

In learning a new language where there are no dictionaries and no translators, an ethnomethodologist seeks several sources of information. He checks what one informant tells him against what he observes and then checks that against what another informant reports. Using a metaphor from surveying, this is a check on one's observations which qualitative researchers have called "triangulation." If different perspectives yield pretty much the same information, the ethnomethodologist can be more certain that the observations are reliable.

Likewise, the psychomethodologist, using one of the assessment methods presented in this volume, collects overlapping data, such as a description of a client's siblings, as well as a rating of the children in a family on traits such as "intelligence" and "rebellious." These are two different ways of asking for the same information. If those two data points support each other, then the assessor can better rely on their accuracy. When I teach Lifestyle Assessment, I suggest that students look for at least two different points of convergence before guessing at the patterns of a client's Lifestyle. For example, if the client describes her older brother as "a bookworm" and also rates him as highest on "intelligence," these two bits of information support the observation that the client saw her brother as the smart one in the family constellation.

"Iteration," or "reflexivity" has to do with trying one's conclusions in real life. An ethnomethodologist cannot be sure her knowledge of a new language is acceptable until she can carry on a conversation with native speakers and be understood. If she asks, "May I have a drink of water?" and a native speaker gives her a handful of straw, she knows at least some of her conclusions about the language are invalid.

A psychomethodologist uses a similar validation technique when she guesses, "Your older brother was the smart one, so you specialized in being sociable." This remains a guess until the client affirms, "Yes, that's right." This is in keeping with the Adlerian assumption of equality, that the client is the expert on her life. Only after iteration, or feeding back of information and getting assent, does the psychomethodologist conclude that she understands a part of how the client trained herself to approach life—that is, her Lifestyle.

Iteration, or back-and-forth checking, is necessary because each of us is one of a kind. Each of us, in a sense, speaks a private language full of meanings that only we know. The methods of anthropology and sociology, developed to understand unique social patterns, are crucial if we want to get to know someone from the inside in their one-of-a-kind uniqueness.

BOTH AND . . .

I believe that idiographic methods are crucial to a full and respectful assessment of individuals—or couples, families, or groups, for that matter. But I am not presenting an either-or argument. Nomothetic assessment recognizes another truth about human beings—that we are alike in many ways, and that we are like some others in some ways. The sophistication of statistical techniques in analyzing quantitative data represents a significant contribution.

The BASIS-A described in this volume by one of its developers, Roy Kern, is a nomothetic assessment tool based on Adlerian theory. When scores from the BASIS-A correspond with idiographic interpretations made as part of a more traditional Lifestyle assessment, we can better rely on those interpretations. The BASIS-A can lend triangulated evidence to our conclusions. Thus, the most effective approach to assessment combines the strengths of both nomothetic and idiographic tools.

I commend the authors of this book for including both kinds of assessment tools. In their selection and their writing, they demonstrate breadth and balance.

I particularly appreciate their encouragement of new applications of Lifestyle Assessment. The Work Style Assessment (see Appendix) is an example of an application designed specifically to be used in workplace and career-oriented settings. It is my hope that readers of this book will seek other ways to apply the tools presented in these pages and to make their own unique contributions to the development of Lifestyle assessment. Karl Marx said, "Philosophers merely interpret the world. The point, however, is to change it." Clinical psychology, counseling, social work, and Adlerians following the predilection of Alfred Adler help people overcome suffering and live their lives more fully. In addition to the assessment tools presented in these pages to help professionals understand people, I am pleased that the coauthors conclude with a chapter on "Reorientation," or how to use that understanding to facilitate positive change.

I have relied on previous versions of this work for many years in teaching Adlerian psychology and assessment. I welcome this completely revised and integrated volume as a much-needed contribution to understanding people and to helping them change.

Linda Page, Ph.D.
President, Adler School of Professional Psychology, Toronto

Endnotes

1. Hathaway, S. R., and McKinley, J.C. (1989). *Minnesota Multiphasic Personality Inventory-2 (MMPI-2): Manual for Administration and Scoring.* Minneapolis, MN: University of Minnesota Press.

2. Institute for Personality and Ability Testing, Inc. (1991). *Administrator's manual for the Sixteen Personality Factor Questionnaire (16PF).* Champaign, IL: Author.

3. Costa, Jr., P.T., and McCrae, R.R. (1992). *NEO PI-R professional manual: Revised NEO Personality Inventory (NEO PI-R) and NEO Five-Factor Inventory (NEO-FFI).* Odessa, Fl:

4. Curlette, W.L., Wheeler, M.S., and Kern, R.M. (1997). *BASIS-A Inventory technical manual.* Highlands, N.C.:

5. Mahoney, M.J., and Gabriel, T.J. (1987). Psychotherapy and cognitive sciences: An evolving alliance. *Journal of Cognitive Psychotherapy, 1,* 39-60.

6. Maines, D.R. (2000). The social construction of meaning. *Contemporary Sociology: A Journal of Reviews, 29,* 577-584.

7. Watts, R.E. (2000). Entering the new millennium: Is Individual Psychology still relevant? *Journal of Individual Psychology, 56,* 21-30.

8. Stiles, W.B. (1995). Stories, tacit knowledge, and psychotherapy research. *Psychotherapy Research, 5,* 125-127.

9. Flick, V. (1998). *An introduction to qualitative research: Theory, method and applications.* London: Sage.

10. Denzin, N.K. (1978). *The research act: A theoretical introduction to sociological methods.* New York: McGraw-Hill.

11. Denzin, N.K., and Lincoln, Y. S. (Eds.). (1994). *Handbook of qualitative research.* Thousand Oaks, CA: Sage.

The "Troubling" Aspect of One's Strengths

If you would like to know how you make trouble for yourself, think about your strengths. What is the style that takes you to your successes? Play around in your mind with those beliefs that manifest themselves in your lifestyle and take you to your successes, and you can take a giant step towards understanding how you make trouble for yourself. Consider the husband who was attractive to his young wife because he was such a decisive young man, who now is dominating his wife by excluding her from decision making. Consider the mother who promised herself she would "always be there" for her children and not be neglectful as her own parents had been, whose effusive giving of attention and service helps render her children helpless and dependent.

Many psychologists and other therapists have understood the pervasive influence of the private logic of one's lifestyle since Alfred Adler and subsequent teachers of Adlerian Psychology have brought it to their attention. There is no greater asset available to therapists and mental health counselors than the ability to understand behavior from a holistic point of view, and bring to the conscious level of clients the belief system the client uses to deal with the challenges of life.

Therapists and teachers of therapists need look no further than this remarkable compendium of lifestyle theory and technique for his or her text, guide, and reference. I congratulate my dear friends, Daniel Eckstein and Roy Kern, for this thorough and much needed contribution to the holistic interpretation of behavior.

Francis X. Walton, Ph.D.
Private practice of psychology
Past president, North American Society for Adlerian Psychology.

Columbia, SC

Introduction

There are many terms that a counselor applies to the systematic assessment of a client's life experience, i.e., life-script, re-occuring recovering themes, lifestyle personality attributes, personality, and typologies. The authors have chosen the title "Psychological Finger-prints" because both physical and psychological etchings have a number of similar characteristics. We believe that understanding lifestyle of an individual is like looking at a person's unique fingerprints. No two are the same.

The child is born with a set of fingerprints but they are very vague. He or she is also born into a family (community). Psychological fingerprints (life) begins to develop. As the child grows, this becomes more obvious—the personal psychological fingerprints becomes stable and predictable. This is the method that each of us in a unique and also predictable manner utilizes for solving life's problems. Despite differences in each of the major theories, clinicians typically attempt both to "discover" the client's fingerprints from which specific interventions for how to be most helpful can evolve. Indeed, Fiedler[1] found that experienced therapists as a group of different theoretical schools were more alike than were beginning therapists of the same theoretical approaches. We all have psychological fingerprints which are one's characteristic of dealing with life's problems.

The goal for the helper is not one of *changing* the psychology fingerprints; instead interventions are for *helping* them to use it more effectively. For example, consider the case of a male adolescent juvenile offender. He prided himself with his skills in breaking into and robbing houses. He was skillful enough not to do this on *any* house. Rather, he only selected the houses with the largest "protected by —— Company" signs prominently displayed on the front lawn and/or at the door. Alas, although he was skilled enough to break and enter homes, his undetected escape techniques were not as refined. Nonetheless, upon his release he was hired as a consultant by the one of the very security companies in which he had successful disarmed their protection devices. So his basic "style" did not change—what did change was the socially and personally creative useful adaptation of the style.

This book is directed toward various ways of discovering the individual's psychological fingerprint/lifestyle and for providing the clinician with therapeutic interventions for enhancing an individual's ability to better solve the tasks of love, work, and friendship. For the reader, although we hope you learn practical "how to" access lifestyles, we also challenge you to use the interventions in this book to enhance the quality of life of your clients. In addition, we hope some of your own psychological fingerprints will become clearer for yourself.

Exploring one's psychological fingerprints through what we refer to as lifestyle is an accumulation of the expertise of many. We would like to acknowledge all those significant individuals who have spent years refining the lifestyle concept and its use. If you, the reader, find these ideas useful, the authors have also placed a membership for the NASAP (North American Society for Adlerian Psychology) in Appendix One.

A client's "psychological fingerprints" are always there. It is our goal as clinicians to make the covert into the overt so that we can see the psychological fingerprints for assisting the client. In this book, we are synthesizing a variety of tools created by many different individuals. For example, Richard Kopp has made significant contributions to the therapeutic process by his utilization of metaphors in therapy. He stresses that language is not the only form in which lifestyle is expressed.

Indeed, current research by co-author Roy Kern indicates that the traditional "talk-therapy" utilized by therapists is only successful with about 40% of clients.

Obviously, a child experiences many impressions prior to the development of language skills. Many therapists contend that tactical, sensory, and auditory images are in fact "closer" to the unconscious than verbal words. Co-author Daniel Eckstein was fortunate to spend a year studying cross-cultural appreciation with Jean Houston. In a visit to Egypt she noted that Egyptian hieroglyphics contained the literal nature of a word. For example, the Egyptian equivalent of our English word "wood" actually contained an image of a tree. Conversely, the English language is merely a symbolic representation of what one learns to associate with the word "wood."

It is for that reason that the authors have introduced the metaphor of psychological fingerprints into our book title. In this book we will be presenting both verbal and objective non-verbal creative approaches to accessing lifestyle. Because psychological fingerprints are always present, this book helps the clinician, like the famous detective Sherlock Homes, to better understand the ever present, and yet often overlooked, invaluable clues to understanding a person's personality.

As a child grows, both psychological fingerprints and one's personal physical fingerprints become clearer and clearer. Our psychological fingerprints can be used for better or worse. The same style that carries us to our heights of success is the same style which leads to our depths of despair. To use a baseball metaphor, the goal of the counselor is to help clients keep their eye on the ball, to "improve their batting average." The person still has the same bat, the same stance but the coaching is better, being to better discern balls and strikes. The similarity between both the psychological and physical fingerprints is that they are consistent, recognizable, re-occurring, and unique. The task of the counselor is to work with individuals so they can discover the psychological fingerprints of consistency, uniqueness, and predictability.

Lifestyle is one clue for learning about one's psychological fingerprints. We would hope that as you next read the authors' brief biographies, you will begin to comprehend lifestyle and psychological fingerprints more clearly. As you begin your journey in relation to understanding the lifestyle concept, you hopefully also will see why we have chosen the terms "psychological fingerprints" to describe the lifestyle.

Endnote

[1] Fiedler, F.E. "A Comparison of Psychoanalyic, Non-Directive, and Adlerian Therapeutic Relationships." *Journal of Cousulting Psychology, 14.* (1950): 436–445.

Introduction to the Authors

Daniel Eckstein, Ph.D.

It was during my doctoral program at the University of South Carolina in 1971 that Frank Walton, then president of the North American Society of Adlerian Society, introduced me to Adlerian psychology in general and life style assessment in particular. Over the next several years I attended many life style workshops presented by such eminent Adlerians as Harold Mosak, Bernie Shulman, and Bob Powers. While I was impressed by their incredible clinical skills, I was concerned by how often I heard students and workshop participants say "Wasn't —— just wonderful in his lifestyle summary? How does he do it?" That last question led me to wonder that myself—did the master's "sprinkle magic fairy dust" on the data like the "great Oz"? I was also concerned that I did not hear others saying they too would go out and do lifestyle assessments.

Toward the end of my doctoral program I met a new faculty member named Lee Baruth. He was a doctoral graduate of another prestigious Adlerian family therapist, Oscar Christenson of the University of Arizona. When I told him of my idea to write a practical "how-to" book containing concrete suggestions for both the interview and the interpretation of lifestyles, he asked if he could join me in the project. We later added another University of Arizona colleague, David Mahrer. Our first version was printed in 1973 by the *Mother Earth News*. In 1976 we began what has now been a 21-year history with Kendall/Hunt publishers.

Both Lee and David have given me the ability to write the material in this new book independently of them. I am pleased to have Roy Kern, my 25-year friend and colleague, join with me in this latest version of the creative process of lifestyle assessment. He and his colleagues have made major empirical contributions to the conceptualization of lifestyle theory and research through several versions of an instrument now called the BASIS-A.

I consider the present work to be a good "first step" in lifestyle assessment. Significant additional clinical examples are found in the contemporary writings of Harold Mosak, Bernie Schulman, Bob Powers, Jane Griffin, Michael Maniacci, Donald Lombardi, Frank Walton, Robert Willhite, and Richard Kopp just to name a few of the more significant contributors to the extension of the original contributions of Alfred Adler and Rudolf Driekurs to lifestyle assessment. Their work and the ideas of many others will be cited throughout this workbook.

Let me take a moment to say "thank-you" to several people. I begin with appreciation to my own parents, the late Oscar Gotlieb Eckstein and my mother, Frances White Eckstein. They truly have "walked the talk." I appreciate the generosity of both Lee Baruth and David Mahrer in letting me go forward with our original ideas. Frank Walton has been my mentor, friend, and cherished colleague—he and his wife Kathy have also both lived and written about Adlerian concepts for three decades. I would also like to thank Amy Zimmerman who has played a major role in the production of the book itself.

I trust that you the reader will feel encouraged and empowered as you develop your own creative life style assessment skills. The authors welcome any creative applications to the process by others for future editions.

Daniel Eckstein

E-mail—deckstein333@aol.com

Website—www.encouragingleadership.com

Roy Kern, Ed.D.

I often ask myself why have I invested much of my professional career in expounding the viewpoints embedded in the Individual Psychology of Alfred Adler.

I guess my only conclusion is because it fits my lifestyle. Robert Powers, a highly respected Adlerian, may have said it best when he stated to me that if you believe in a theory and it seems to fit, then there was a high likelihood that it included many of the ideas, philosophies, and knowledge that you had already decided were important to you. Whatever the reason, I believe I can briefly and pragmatically describe why the approach has affected me.

As I was growing up in a family of two brothers, a sister, and two parents I can honestly state that at some level I was always aware of the dynamics of people. I questioned why my older brother had difficulty connecting with my father, the challenge of understanding a sister who was one year younger than myself, and the absolute comfort level I experienced with my youngest brother. I was sensitized as to how best to handle a very strong willed father and covertly strong mother. As I was growing up in a rural location in western Pennsylvania, I continued to assess why people do what they do. Thus, after attending college, getting married, and working for several years with challenging youth in an inner-city school experience and entering an advanced degree program at West Virginia University the stage was set for me to be influenced by some form of psychology.

During that time I, as all graduate students, was required to take courses in abnormal psychology, human growth and development, counseling theory, and of course, practicum and internship experiences. As this was occurring, the department at West Virginia University became one of the academic centers for the teachings of Individual Psychology. With this came a department chairperson, Edward Stormer, who had studied with Rudolph Dreikurs, regular summer institutes with Dreikurs, Mosak, etc., and our own died-in-the-wool resident Adlerian by the name of one Manford Sonstegard. Now I had to make a decision to accept this position or find another that was compatible with my personal ideas of understanding human behavior. If you had the opportunity to be in the presence of these individuals and in particular the Manford Sonstegard one would venture that the odds would be that you would accept the Adlerian position.

From that point of being schooled, mentored, and influenced by the forgoing experts I began my own journey. Again the theoretical approach not only prepared me to understand one's lifestyles, raising children, and therapeutic interventions, but it also afforded me the opportunity to acquire my first position in higher education in the Department of Counseling and Psychological Services at Georgia State University. In summary, the department at that time was looking for a person who could work with families, children, and schools. What better approach than Individual Psychology to fulfill this job description. Since that time I have been blessed with being associated with a majority of the experts in the field of Individual Psychology. I have nurtured close friendships with the Bettners, Christensens, Dinkmeyers, McKays, Waltons, Ansbacher, Balla, Bitter, Carlson, Evans, Ferguson, Griffith, Hawes, Kopp, Linden, Manaster, Mosak, Mozdzierz, Nash, Nelson, Powers, Shulman, Sperry, Sulliman, Watts and the now deceased Kurt Adler, Don Dinknieyer Sr. and Bronia Grunwald. I presented at the North American Society of Adlerian Psychology (NASAP), served as a delegate and executive board member for the society, elected to the faculty and board of the International Congress of Adlerian Summer Schools Institutes (ICASSI), co-founded the Regional III Adlerian Conferences in the Southeast and the Atlanta Adlerian Society, co-authored two books on Adlerian Psychology, fifty articles, created three objective instruments to measure the lifestyle construct, and I am presently the co-editor of the *Journal of Individual Psychology* with my close friend Dr. William Curlette. However, of all the forgoing activities, the one that stands out most for me is that I have been instrumental in establishing another Mecca for higher education, which to date includes more trained Adlerian clinicians and educators within a department of higher education than any research institution in North America or Europe.

AN OVERVIEW: THE MAN AND HIS THEORY

Although psychology is a modern twentieth-century phenomenon, the study of human behavior dates to the very origins of civilization. Philosophers, poets, spiritual teachers, political leaders, educators, and others have spoken of their personal theories relative to the motivations, wants, and needs of human beings.

Sigmund Freud, Carl Jung, and Alfred Adler are generally acknowledged as the three major Western formative personality theorists. They formed the cornerstones for the early development of psychological explanations of human behavior. Despite theoretical differences between them, they shared a common belief in the importance of early childhood experiences in the formation of an individual's later personality. The purpose of this book is to provide the reader with a practical introduction and application of some of Alfred Adler's major contributions to the art and science of human behavior, most specifically focused on lifestyle assessment, interpretation, and change. The sequencing of the book begins with a brief autobiographical sketch of Adler, an integrative overview of his theory, a comprehensive examination of lifestyle theory, application, and research findings.

Because one's personality influences one's psychological theory, a brief description of Adler's life begins the journey.

Alfred Adler: The Man

Alfred Adler was born outside of Vienna, Austria, in 1870. His father, Leopold, was a grain merchant. Adler grew up in a comfortable physical environment, enjoying nature, music, and the cultural opportunities of Vienna.

Despite physical comfort, Adler described his childhood as challenging at times. He felt he was undersized and ugly when compared to his peers. He was the second of seven children, and he had a rivalry with his more athletic and "model child" older brother. He felt his mother preferred the older brother to him.

Adler experienced many physical challenges as a child. He suffered from rickets and consequently did not engage in much physical activity. At age five, he caught pneumonia and almost died. This experience, coupled with the death of a younger brother in the bed next to his when he was three and his being run over twice, created an intense fear of death for him. He resolved to become a physician, believing that doing so would be a way of conquering death.

Adler found school to be challenging, particularly mathematics. In fact, one of his teachers urged his parents to train him as a shoemaker. Nonetheless, Adler later became a gifted student, and he received his medical degree from the University of Vienna in 1895. He first specialized in diseases of the eye, but then he changed to general practice and finally psychiatry. Two years after graduating from medical school, he married Raissa Epstein, a powerful militant socialist. Because Marxism stressed hard working conditions and the need for socialized medicine it influenced Adler's first publications. From Marx, Adler learned the important role that one's social context plays in personality formation.

The Adlers had four children. One of their daughters, Alexandria, and their only son, Kurt, both became psychiatrists who later carried on their father's work.

After writing a defense of Freud's book, *The Interpretation of Dreams*, Adler was invited and accepted an invitation to become one of Freud's colleagues in 1902 as a member of the Vienna Psychoanalytic Society. He became president of that group in 1910, a year before his official break with Freud. The two men never met again after 1911.

Adler then founded the Society of Free Psychoanalytic Research, demonstrating the break from what he felt was the oppression of Freud's methods. However, he soon changed the name to the Society of Individual Psychology to avoid being labeled as just rebels against psychoanalysis. He chose that term to imply that although individuals are unique, inner harmony and a striving to cooperate with others also distinguish them.

Adler was a physician in the Austrian army during World War I. He was later asked by the government to open several child-guidance clinics in Vienna.

In 1926, Adler visited the United States, where he was warmly received. After being a lecturer at Columbia University in 1927, he became a professor of medical psychology at Long Island College of Medicine in 1932. Partly because of the Nazi takeover in Austria, Adler made the United States his permanent home in 1935. He died in 1937 of a heart attack in Aberdeen, Scotland, while on a lecture tour.[1]

Rudolph Dreikus was a psychiatrist who brought many of Alder's ideas to the United States. He further defined and advanced Adler's theories in many ways that will be described later in this book. Here are some of his selected quotes.

The lifestyle is based on the need to have a guiding line through the complexities of life.

We have harmony only among equals.

We all have biased apperception. We have no direct access to facts.

We have the courage to be imperfect.

We constantly encourage or discourage those around us and, thereby,
contribute materially to their greater or lesser ability to function well.

Core Adlerian Principles: A "SUPER" Theory

Fundamental Adlerian principles of human behavior can be illustrated by a "SUPER" acronym as developed by co-author Eckstein. Each respective letter represents a major theoretical Adlerian belief.

Social Interest
    U
        P
            E
               R

Social Interest

Gemeinschaftsgefühl is the most distinctive concept in Adler's individual psychology; conversely, it is also the most difficult and the one that has the least recognition in general psychological literature. It is generally translated from German into English as "social interest" (SI) or "social feeling." There actually is no accurate English word that seems to communicate the German sense of community.[2] O'Connell prefers the term "humanistic identification."[3] "The center theme is that Gemeinschaftsgefühl, as community feeling, is ultimately experiential and may be a characteristic of the nature and structure of human consciousness itself. . . . Community feeling can be understood to be as experientially real as phenomena such as anger, grief, or the sense of one's own existence."[4]

Adler proposed *Gemeinschaftsgefühl* as the measure of psychological well-being. The term implies belongingness, cooperation, and responsibility toward society—good adjustment depends upon and varies with the amount of social interest. For example, psychosis presents a picture of minimal social interest.[5] SI is a "barometer" of effective mental health; conversely, mental illness is characterized as the absence of social interest. By nature human beings are social beings, and it is social feeling that has to be cultivated. [6]

> Do all the good you can,
> By all the means you can,
> In all the ways you can,
> In all the places you can,
> At all the times you can,
> To all the people you can,
> As long as you can.
> —Shakthi, December 1997, p. 38

Existentialist philosophers have used the term *anomie* (lawlessness) to indicate the antipathy of SI. Anomie is a condition in which an individual's sense of social cohesion is broken or weakened. Such a detachment from a feeling of "embeddedness" or a "connectedness" to others results in various antisocial behavior. It is as if some people have lost their "existential anchors" and thus drift aimlessly with no direction and are lost and tumbled by the "sea" of life. Having no existential anchor often results in "drowning" (death) or severe damage (neurosis/psychosis) to such individuals. American Indians have referred to the concept as Mother Earth. Leak, Gardner, and Pounds[7] present a creative comparison of Western Christianity and of Eastern Buddhism with the Adler's concept of SI. Adler believed that the best in human nature as exemplified by SI was congruent with the ideals of religion.

Social interest and some contemporary Christian perspectives include such issues as:

1. **Ecological Spirituality.** The essence of religious maturity can be found in people who find God in their relationships with all life. Such a theology stresses that we have an obligation to care for, or at least desire the well-being of, all sentient beings. Such care must be inclusive, just, and intimate for all life. This goal of world care is based on the idea that one's "neighbors" are all the earth's creatures, and its achievement requires "imaginative ego-transcendence" or the expansion of one's ego boundary to allow a person to identify with all life.

2. **Creation Spirituality.** Creation spirituality shares a great deal of overlap with the major Eastern religions in its emphasis on order and balance as primary universal principles. The universe reveals the divine, and thus the universe is spiritual and sacred. It is governed by moral and affectionate forces. Here compassion is a supreme, cosmic power (*jen* or *Karuna*), and thus the very essence of the universe has an intimate and compassionate quality. Humans are intimately interconnected with the multitude of life communities. In such a context, people are more than just a human community; they are also intimately related to all

living beings. The concepts of "world loyalty" and of an existence in an expanded world where all creatures are neighbors ("brothers and sisters") are in agreement with the Adlerian view that social interest has relevance beyond a strictly human level of care and obligation.

3. **Liberation Theology.** This theology is based on the life and ministry of Jesus by focusing on attaining the kingdom of God on earth, especially for those suffering from injustice and poverty. The normative standard of moral behaviors concerns how actions serve to foster the coming of this kingdom of justice and peace. Both liberation theology and social-interest theory emphasize personally and socially meaningful goals, such as personal growth, equality among people, and justice for all individuals.

Buddhism and social interest share such constructs as:

1. **Transpersonal Orientation.** All major Eastern religions encourage a transpersonal orientation beyond the boundaries of the self. Eastern religions, like Adlerian theory, deal with the relationships of the individual to a larger frame of value and concern.

2. **Innerconnectedness and the Principle of Compassion.** Buddhism states that all objects in the cosmos are part of one "Whole" (in science, this is known as Bell's theorem). From this, it follows that all people are related, and further, they are related to all life forms. *Mahayana* Buddhism emphasizes the importance of compassion and service to others. It rests on the "twin pillars" of wisdom and compassion.

3. **The Four Noble Truths and Ideal Development.** "Two of the first three of Buddhism's Four Noble Truths (i.e., essential characteristics of human nature) are similar to notions inherent in Adlerian social interest. These three trusts are: (a) suffering is intrinsic to human existence (*duhkha*); (b) the cause of this suffering is the unworthy cravings of the ego (*tanha*); and (c) to find release from suffering we must remove our desires by egotranscendence (ultimately to the negation of the ego and the attainment of nirvana)."[8] The most mature and evolved people do not seek enlightenment for self alone, but instead devote themselves to helping others end their suffering before entering into nirvana.

4. **Compassion in the World.** Buddhist teachings stress that compassion, the ideal emotional state, must not remain an intellectual abstraction. Enlightenment means active participation in everyday affairs to serve others and to perfect our original nature; that is, to become what we already are. Thus, Buddhist teachings must be acted on in the world, especially in one's social relationships. In Buddhism, salvation is both a personal and social concern.[9]

5. **The Noble Eightfold Path.** Frager and Fadiman have divided the eight aspects for the Path or Middle Way into three categories: *ethical conduct, mental discipline,* and *wisdom.* They stress that "Ethical conduct is built on the fundamental Buddhist teachings of universal love and compassion for all living beings."[10] Ethical conduct is the most relevant of the three categories to Adlerian theory as it includes the parts of right speech, right action, and right livelihood. Such Buddhist principles agree with Adlerian theory's position that well-being comes from service in life tasks of friendship, love, and work. For example, one should work at an occupation that benefits others.[11]

One of Adler's early associates, the physician Lydia Sicher, describes the relationship of SI to empathy as follows:

> Empathy could not exist if we did not have any social interest. Empathy is only possible if we can place ourselves in the situation of the other person. . . . Empathy is looking at the world from the standpoint of another person. It is an inner understanding of the other person, not just knowing something about the problem. Empathy is a large part of social interest.[12]

Adler believed that one of the tasks of the counselor or therapist is to supplement the unfinished work of the parents, to develop the clients' heightened sense of SI. Through such an identification with humanity Adler links SI and moral behavior.[13] Adlerians are optimistic in their belief that human beings are born with the potential for cooperative, constructive behavior. Thus, they have the potential to develop into cooperative members of society.

"Rebellious" Social Interest

The notion of social interest is not to be confused with adaptation out of blind obedience or of conformity to authority. Nationalism, racism, and sexism are too often prevalent societal norms. The rebellion or confrontation of such systems and individuals characterizes aspirations of a better world for all people. For example, social interest paradoxically may take the form of civil disobedience to preserve the environment.

Rebellion may paradoxically have much social interest. Again, the goals of such rebellion hopefully are motivated by a sense of social interest, a concern for the highest good of all life. That should be the yardstick by which an individual embarks on what Buddhists call the path of "right action."

Such legendary individuals as Mahatma Gandhi and Martin Luther King, Jr., have been imprisoned and/or assassinated for their "insurrections" and "traitorous" behavior. Yet a higher commitment to such universal principles as nonviolence and basic civil liberties are contemporary examples of "rebellious" social interest.

Abraham Maslow credited Adler's belief in SI as a primary description of self actualized individuals. Maslow defined it as follows:

> This word (*Gemeinschaftsgefühl*—social interest) . . . is the only one available that described well the flavor of the feeling for mankind by self actualizing subjects. They have, for human beings in general, a deep feeling of identification, sympathy, and affection in spite of occasional anger, impatience or disgust. . . . It is as if they were all members of a single family.[14]

Kaplan has described in concrete ways behaviors, feelings, and cognition (thoughts) associated with social interest.

Behaviors associated with social interest include helping, sharing, participating, compromising, encouraging, reforming, being respectful, compromising, encouraging, and reforming. It also involves being cooperative and empathic.

Feelings associated with social interest include belonging, feeling at home, commonality, faith in others, the courage to be imperfect, being human, and being optimistic. Kaplan believes the cognitions affirmatives associated with social interest are:

1. "As a human being, my rights and obligations are equal to the rights and obligations of others."

2. "My personal goals can be attained in ways consistent with the welfare of the community."

3. "The survival of society is dependent on the willingness and the ability of its citizens to learn to live together in harmony."

4. "I believe in responding to others as I want them to respond to me."

5. "The ultimate measure of my character will be to what extent I promoted the welfare of the community."[15]

Psychological Tolerance (PT) and Social Interest

Slavik and Croake suggest social interest is actually more understandable by Adler's concept of psychological tolerance (PT).

Adler writes that psychological tolerance is "the amount of threat a person can bear without losing courage. Psychological tolerance depends on the strength of social ties."[16] Psychological tolerance is the amount of threat a person can face without choosing anger and leaving a situation, "caving in" to despair or fear, renouncing one's ability to handle a situation or simply by withdrawing.

Psychological tolerance is a direct measure of one's willingness to stay with changes in life tasks as they present themselves, particularly difficult changes. Individuals with lower psychological tolerance may have lifestyle convictions that encourage them to withdraw from situations. Beliefs that they are helpless, unable, and cannot cope, plus a perception that the world or others within it have more power than they do and perhaps that they are malicious, often causes such people to withdraw from others.[17]

Consider the example of psychological tolerance as a type of "emotional thermostat." For example, if one's comfort range if 65°–75°, the basic "fight or flight" response would only be activated with the emotional temperature below 65° or above 75°. However, someone else with a much narrower "comfort zone" of 73°–75° would be much more frequently "plugged in" with coping mechanisms. High social interest helps to expand one's psychological tolerance comfort range that prejudiced issues such as racism, sexism, homophobia, antisemitism, and ageism keep one constricted rather than expansive with the larger community.

Mosak presented the biblical mandate to love one's neighbor as oneself (Leviticus 19:18; Matthew 22:39; Mark 12:31; Luke 10:27) as a succinct illustration of SI. The word for love in the Biblical mandate from the language in which the New Testament was originally written (Koine Greek) is *agape*. *Agape* is the highest form of love and is primarily volitional and self-giving rather than emotional and self-centered.[18]

Watts postulates a strong parallel appears to exist between biblical *agape* and social interest. *Agape*, much like Adler's description of social interest, exists as a possibility in every person and, being strongly attitudinal, must be consciously developed in individuals.[19]

The following descriptors of *agape* are consistent with Adler's model of high social interest—"patient, kind, not jealous, does not brag, not arrogant, does not act unbecomingly, does not seek its own, not easily provoked, does not take into account a wrong suffered, rejoices with the truth, bears all things, believes all things, hopes for things, and endures all things" (Adapted by the *New American Standard Bible*, 1997).

It is certainly not necessary to be a Christian to appreciate the following attitudinal-behavioral characteristics illustrating high social interest.

1. Persevering—patient and forbearing, courageously encounters and transcends difficult life circumstances.

2. Benevolently useful—gracious, kind, and helpful.

3. Trustworthy—honest and happy when justice prevails, not jealous or covetous of another person's station in life.

4. Humble—genuine and not consumed with inflated ideas of self-importance, not "grudge bearers" and does not seek to humiliate others for their mistakes.

5. Altruistic—treat others with dignity and respect.

6. Unselfish—interested in others—"altruism."

7. Optimistic—believes the best about other people and their intentions, and generally views life in terms of hope and potential for growth.[20]

The philosopher Nietzsche wrote that:

A man who has a "why" for his life can withstand almost any "how." For Adlerians, social interest is that "why." As such, it is the cornerstone (*eckstein* in German) of Adler's theory.

Social Interest
Unity
P
E
R

Unity

In contrast to Freudian theory, which described separate "parts" of the personality as "id," "ego," and "superego" or the transactional analysis "parent," "adult," and "child" ego states, Adler stressed the unity or wholeness of an individual. Manaster and Corsini stressed that "individual psychology firmly takes the position that we are indivisible units. Like the flower which came from a single fertilized cell, we are a unity; we are not an assemblage of parts like a machine. The word individual in individual psychology does not mean the opposite of 'social' or 'group.' The term individual in German has the connotation and denotation of unity, an indivisible whole. It refers to the unique individuality of individuals."[21]

The unity of personality was what Adler called one's **style of life**. The concept of style includes the characteristic of cutting across ordinary boundaries and uniting what might otherwise be quite separate entities. Thus, in the case of Bach, Beethoven, and Mozart, if one knows their music at all, one can easily match the musical manuscripts with the composer. Adler used the metaphor of the musical "notes" versus the total "melody" in the following way:

The style of life commands all forms of expression; the whole commands the parts. In real life we always find a confirmation of the melody of the total self, of the personality, with its thousand fold ramifications. . . . The foremost task of individual psychology is to prove this unity in each individual . . . we are not satisfied with the Gestalt alone, or, as we prefer to say, with the whole, once all the notes are brought into reference with the melody. We are satisfied only when we have recognized in the melody the author and his attitudes as well, for example: Bach and Bach's style of life.[22]

Holistic health and holistic medicine is based on the mind/body/spirit interrelationships and is becoming extremely popular. An emerging discipline known as *psychoneuroimmunology* (*PNI*) explores such topics as the breakdown of the immune system as the total interrelated emotional and physical united self. For example, many researchers believe that self-hatred is correlated with the breakdown of the immune system in AIDS patients while unresolved anger often accompanies the onset of cancer. (More on the body/mind connection will be presented in Chapter 4.) Thus, the unified self is the focus of Adlerian psychology.

Social Interest
    Unity
        Private Logic
           E
               R

Private Logic

We don't see things as they are, we see things as we are.
—Anais Nin

Out of the countless events occurring in one's life, each individual decides what conclusions are to be drawn about life in general, others, and one's self. Such a "private" or "personal" decision relates to the philosophical field known as phenomenology. Although Adler did not use the term, he spoke of the need for the counselor to understand the personal views of individuals by saying "we must be able to see with his eyes and listen with his ears."[23] Phenomenology means that one does not experience reality directly or objectively; instead, it is subjectively "filtered" through personal "prescriptive" lenses, or "glasses" that uniquely focus the world.

External events are "filtered through" one's internal subjective frame of reference and thereby "distort" or "shape" objective reality to confirm to our own internal attitudes. Myers and Myers describe private logic in the following metaphor:

> Imagine you are given the task to find out the size of the fish in Lake Michigan. So you get yourself a net and go to the lake to gather a sample of the fish. Maybe your net has a 4-inch mesh. After you gather some fish you write a report in which you say, the fish in Lake Michigan are 4 inches in diameter or bigger. Let's say a friend of yours is given the same assignment, but his net has 2-inch mesh. His report reads, the fish in Lake Michigan are 2 inches in diameter or bigger. Now, which report is right? Both? What are you and your friend reporting on? The size of fish? No. Each of you is reporting on the size of the net you used. The size of the net you use determines the size of the fish you can collect. [24]

Myers and Myers then conclude their "net" analogy in a manner that provides and excellent illustration of a private logic:

> We have nets in our heads. These nets are not made of threads, but of past learning, past experiences, motives, fears, desires, and interests: these nets act as a filter so the stimuli from our environment go through that filter to be perceived. Of course, each one of us has his own little net, his own little personal, individual filter. Even though we may be placed in the same environment we will not see it in the same way since we will filter different aspects. Most of us are not even aware that this filtering process is happening. Many of us have defective filters. Filters that are so clogged up that we see very little of what's going on. Some of us have filters that distort the stimuli that come to us from the environment. The important thing to remember, though, is that whenever we make a comment about something we are not describing the something but rather our net, our filter. When I say that the painting is beautiful, I am not commenting on the painting as much as I am commenting on myself, my taste, my value system. [25]

The ability to understand the private inner world of another person is a core component of empathy, the ability to "walk a mile in another person's moccasins." So, the "P" in the SUPER acronym refers to one's "private logic." The term *was* originally used to connote a "private" versus most "public" accepted standard of behavior. More typical now is the idea that each of us indeed has a personal filter. To illustrate these filters one might draw the following analogy of three baseball umpires. The first said, "I call them as I see them", the second replied, "I call them as they are." The third umpire wisely noted, "It ain't nothing till I call it." Private logic, similar to George Kelly's concept of *personal constructs,* is the creative way each of us "calls" the "balls and strikes" of life.

Social Interest
    Unity
        Private Logic
            Equality
              R

Equality

Equal political, economic, and social rights are considered to be the essence of democratic ideology. Equality is also a pivotal principle of Adlerian psychology by replacing the authoritarian stance with a dialogue between equals in an atmosphere of mutual respect, candor, and acceptance.[26]

Adler's term "masculine protest" was formulated as a precursor to the sexism upon which the woman's movement was founded. In a culture that inherently values traits defined as "masculine" over what it defines as "feminine," both men and women suffer negative consequences. Equality may be contrasted by describing the "vertical" versus the "horizontal" means of approaching people. The "horizontal" approach to life views all people as being equally worthy of respect and consideration, although people are obviously unequal in some other respects. Such equality does not mean sameness but rather a "no more or less than one" whole human being whose basic birthright is unconditional mutual respect and dignity. By contrast the "vertical" approach measures people in a "one up" or "one down" perspective. "Mirror, mirror, on the wall, who is the fairest one of all?" the queen in *Snow White* implores. "Better than/less than" characterizes the vertical approach, whereas "different than" is the horizontal perspective.

"Inferiority" and "superiority" were two sides of the same coin for Adler. Both result in a feeling of separateness or disconnection from others. Alder discussed the horizontal view as leading to contentment and happiness, while the vertical view means one is "on a ladder" viewing others "up" and "down."[27] Social interest is related to mental health based on equality and democratic living in contrast to striving for a personal superiority that is "above" others. Dreikurs wrote that:

> The vertical movement of self-elevation, regardless of the height it leads to, both in status and accomplishments, can never bring lasting satisfaction and inner peace. There is a constant danger of falling and failing; the gnawing feeling of real or possible inferiority is never eradicated, regardless of success. There is no sense of security possible on the vertical plane; one remains highly vulnerable. The competitive individual can stand competition only when he wins.[28]

Dreikurs contrasts the vertical and the horizontal planes in the following manner:

> Quite different is the function of horizontal movement. The desire to be useful can never be frustrated. Self-fulfillment no longer depends on what others think or do, but on what one can contribute.

This basic distinction between self-elevation and usefulness has far-reaching consequences for the evaluation of other social values. Once the assumption that everybody is good enough as (s)he is can be accepted without the fear of disastrous results, both for the individual and society, a new orientation in social living is possible and mandatory.[29]

> From the wall of the middle room, fresh pure water drips constantly. It is as if the walls are weeping; it is as if the soul of contentment is weeping. Why does it weep? It weeps for the decline of poets; it weeps for the bone of the buffalo; it weeps for the black people that think like white people; it weeps for the Indians who think like settlers; it weeps for children who think like adults; it weeps for magic that has been forgotten; it weeps for the free who think like prisoners, but most of all, it weeps for cowgirls who think like cowboys.
>
> —Tom Robbins, *Even Cowgirls Get the Blues*

Personal superiority issues have a national correlate. Sociologists use the term **ethnocentricism** to refer to the personal preferences of one's own particular group or cultural norm. For example, an American was in Japan attending a Shinto funeral. When he observed food being placed on the casket, he said to his host "Why do you put food on the casket—the person surely can't eat it?" His Japanese host replied, "Why do you Americans put flowers on your caskets—the person surely can't smell them?"

Ethnocentricism relates to regional, cultural, and national feelings of superiority or inferiority; it is a major cause of strife between races. Collectivistic and egalitarian values promoting social cohesion, human solidarity, and community life are superior to individualism and competition, which foster economic domination and class exploitation.[30] But globalization is also too often marked by a spirit of free enterprise tending to exert economic and political power over poor nations, exploiting their labor force, supporting political repression, and treating people as commodities.[31]

Members of individualistic cultures emphasize self-reliance, independence, and mobility; conversely, interpersonal relationships are based on the exchange of benefits. Other characteristics include emotional detachment, competitiveness, and an emphasis on personal well-being and individual survival.[32] The members of individualistic cultures are often ranked from superior to inferior, a process that creates strained relationships because of the value given to independence, competition, winning, and domination. Individualistic cultures are relatively indifferent toward communal justice, and they favor the interests of those with relative wealth and power over the rest of the population. In addition, they are potentially destructive to the environment.[33] North American and European countries generally represent individualistic cultures.

The contrast is in collective cultures where individuals subordinate private goals and emphasize cooperation and mutual obligations. They tend to share resources and to be concerned about the effects their actions may have on others. Failing to perform the culturally prescribed roles of obligation to others and service to the community is considered deviant behavior.[34] Members of collective cultures are linked on the basis of equality, mutual support, cooperation, respect, and caring. They strongly endorse social justice, commitment to the common good, and the preservation of the environment.[35] Asian, African, and Latin American cultures are generally collectivistic. "The nail that sticks up is the nail that gets hammered down" is frequently spoken in Asian countries. Perhaps surprising to Westerners, about 70 percent of the world's population belong to non-Western cultures.[36]

Nikelly believes that therapists will usually face resistance if they attempt to transpose collective values in clients who are expected to function in an individualistic economic environment. "Individual psychology goes beyond self-interest and advocates cooperation, community feeling, interpersonal connectedness, and social equality; it promotes ethical relationships between individuals, groups, and nations. Education would then stress a sociocentric view, one that sees that interpersonal relatedness (social feeling) and self-development (individualism) are interrelated and that individual endeavors become meaningful through reciprocity, mutuality, and embeddedness in the society at large." [37]

Consider the following three strategies for shifting from an individualistic to a more collective view of the community. The first is to integrate historical and experiential information from cultures demonstrating the positive aspects of collectivism in daily living over individualism. The second tactic is to show empirically that cooperation is more rewarding and less stressful than competition, just as competitive sports produce winners, and analogous belief holds that competitive free market capitalism promotes prosperity. In contrast to competition, cooperation facilitates learning, encourages amiable interpersonal relationships, and fosters mental health. The third strategy is to address broad economic policies through political action by challenging the uncontrolled spread of globalization that is a frequent U.S. activity.[38]

A viable society is based on a moral economic system that ensures that resources are distributed fairly to all citizens.[39] According to Adler, poverty accentuates inequality and limits the ability to cooperate and to act in the best interests of society.[40] In addition to improving lifestyles, therapists should encourage their clients to alter the adverse social environment that shapes lifestyles. Adler maintained that people are affected by broader social and economic factors and that illness is often the outcome of adverse social circumstances that can be prevented. His observation of low-income persons struggling against those striving for power led him to make the association between a poor standard of living and a marginalization from mainstream society that weakens social feeling.[41] For this reason, he addressed the social dimension of medical practice and advocated that the helping professions align themselves with the economic, political, and social demands of the working class. Adler disliked political activities based on power and competition and generally was politically neutral. Instead, he stressed community feeling and social usefulness in individuals and families and in civic groups. He felt those values could be instilled through the public schools with teachers and parents serving as role models.[42]

Consider that possibly the real enemy of world peace is the perception of differences between oneself and others. The illusion of difference creates separation of judgment, both in an inferior or in a superior belief. Remember, red blood is the common denominator for all human beings and DNA is the "building blocks" common to all life forms on earth.

Equality is a fundamental Adlerian principle. Just as kings and monarchies are giving way to democratic forms of government, interpersonal relationships are shifting from an inferior or superior vertical comparison to a more encouraging/connected "all life shares the same basic DNA molecules and God don't make no junk" orientation.

Social Interest
   Unity
      Private Logic
      Equality
         Reasons

Reasons

Reasons or motivators can be reframed as purposeful or goal-directed behavior; everyone is striving for some type of significance or perfection. Adler disagreed with Freud's emphasis that people are driven by instincts or molded by heredity, experience, or environment. Rather it was goals or a "guiding self-ideal" that energized individuals in a chosen direction.

He stressed that:

Individual psychology . . . developed out of the effort to understand that mysterious creative power of life. This power is teleological—it expresses itself in the striving after a goal.[43]

Dreikurs identified four classic "misguided goals" of behavior which are formulated in early childhood as being undue **attention**, **power**, **revenge**, and **inadequacy**. Dreikurs' four misguided goals are shorthand explanations/descriptions of consistent patterns of misbehavior in children. Dreikurs declared that all misbehavior in children could be understood from the perspective of one of these four goals. [44] These goals were largely unconscious in children because a lack of awareness facilitates fluidity of action and safeguards the child from having to consciously confront the uselessness of certain behaviors.[45]

Such goals are discouraged methods of striving for significance. Striving for significance is in essence a movement toward fulfillment of the goal to achieve unique identity as well as to belong. This movement toward a unique identity is the motivating force behind all human activity, which can be called a type of "master motive." "Adlerians see this process too, from a teleological rather than casual perspective—as a pull by the goal rather than a push by the drive. . . . A question counselors always ask themselves is: 'How is the person seeking to be known?' Most ways of behaving that are eventually accepted by the person reflect the current concept of the self."[46]

Teleology (from the Greek *telos*—goal) means "purposive, moving toward goals." Adler claimed: "Only when we know the effective direction-giving goal of a person may we try to understand his movements." [47] Basic life goals, while generally unknown to the person, give direction to all behavior. To the extent that goals are aligned with social interest, the direction of the person's life is useful, positive, and healthy. Conversely, if goals lack social interest and are simply an expression for overcoming perceived inferiorities by achieving personal superiority, the direction of the person's life tends to be useless, negative, and unhealthy.[48]

Carl Rogers similarly described the "upwardly light" seeking tendency toward growth when he observed that "the organism has one basic tendency and striving—to actualize, maintain, and enhance the experiencing organism."[49]

There is a useful distinction between two different kinds of striving. *Striving for perfection* means to move in line with the common sense of communal living, while *striving for superiority* means to move in a vertical direction, toward personal superiority over others. "Movement in striving for perfection and movement in striving for superiority are both efforts to overcome the individual's feelings of inferiority. To the degree that one strives for perfection we can expect positive mental health, a greater sense of well-being, sense of connectedness with others and humanity. To the degree that one is striving for superiority we can expect disease, a sense of separateness."[50]

Summary

This chapter presents an overview to the theory of Adlerian psychology. In Chapter 2, the specific theory of lifestyle assessment will be addressed

Endnotes

1 Hergenhahn, B., and Olson, M. *An Introduction to Theories of Personality* (5th ed.). Upper Saddle River, NJ: Prentice-Hall 1999.
2 Ansbacher, H. "The Concept of Social Interest." *Individual Psychologist 47*, no.1 (1991): 30–44.
3 O'Connell, W. "Humanistic Identification: A New Translations from Gemeinschaftsgefühl." *Individual Psychology 47*, no 1 (1991): 26–27.
4 Hanna, F. J. "Community Feeling, Empathy, and Intersubjectivity: A Phenomenological Framework." *Individual Psychology 52*, no. 1 (1996): 22

[5] Adler, A. *The Individual Psychology of Alfred Adler.* H. L. Ansbacher and R. Ansbacher, eds. New York: Harper and Row, 1956, 80–81.

[6] Nikelly, A., ed. *Techniques for Behavior Change.* Springfield, IL: Charles C Thomas, 1971.

[7] Leak, C. K., Gardner L.E., and Pounds, B. "A Comparison of Eastern Religion, Christianity, and Social Interest." *Individual Psychology 48,* no. 1 (1993): 58

[8] *Ibid.*

[9] Frager, R., and Fadiman, J. *Personality and Personal Growth.* New York: Harper & Row.

[10] *Ibid,* p. 445.

[11] Leak, G. et al., 53–64.

[12] Davidson, A. *The Collected Works of Lydia Sicher: An Adlerian Perspective.* Ft. Bragg, CA: Q & D Press, 1991 p. 22.

[13] Edgar, T. "The Creative Self in Adlerian Psychology." *Individual Psychologist 41,* no. 3 (1985): 336–41.

[14] Ansbacher, H. "The Concept of Social Interest." *Individual Psychologist 47,* no.1 (1991): 5.

[15] Kaplan, H. "A Guide for Explaining Social Interest Laypersons." *Individual Psychology 47,* no. 1 (1991): 82–85.

[16] Adler, A. *The Individual Psychology of Alfred Adler.* H. L. Ansbacher and R. Ansbacher, eds. New York: Harper and Row, 1956: 243.

[17] Slavik, S., and Croake, J. *Psychological Tolerance and Mood Disorders.* Port Coquitlam, B.C.: Canadian Counseling Institute, 1995.

[18] Mosak, H. H. "Adlerian psychotherapy." In R. J. Corsini & D. Wedding (Eds.), *Current Psychotherapies* (4th ed.). Itasca, IL: Peacock 1989: 65–116.

[19] Watts, R.E. "Biblical Agape as a Model of Social Interest" *Individual Psychology 48,* no. 1 (1992): 35–40.

[20] *Ibid,* p. 38

[21] Manaster, G., and Corsini, R. *Individual Psychology: Theory and Practice.* New York: F. E. Peacock, 1982, 2–3.

[22] Ansbacher, H., and Ansbacher, R., ed. *The Individual Psychology of Alfred Adler.* New York: Harper & Row, 1964, 1967, 175.

[23] *Ibid.* p. 14.

[24] Myers, G., and Myers, M. *The Dynamics of Human Communication.* New York: McGraw-Hill, 1973: 14

[25] *Ibid* p. 19.

[26] Dreikurs, R. *Social Equality: The Challenge of Today.* Chicago: Regnery, 1971.

[27] Alfred, G. *On the Level with Self, Family, Society.* Provo, UT: Brigham Young University, 1974.

[28] Dreikurs, R. *Psychodynamics, Psychotherapy and Counseling* (rev. ed.). Chicago: Alfred Adler Institute, 1973,116.

[29] *Ibid,* p. 117

[30] Nikelly, A.G. "Globalization and Community Feeling: Are They Compatible?" *The Journal of Individual Psychology,56.* no. 4 (2000):435.

[31] Navarro, V. "Health and equity in the world in the era of globalization." *International Journal of Health Services 29* (1999):215–226.

[32] Triandis, H. C. *"Individualism and Collectivism"* Boulder, CO: Westview Press, 1995.

[33] Eisler, R. *"The Chalice and The Blade"* San Francisco: Harper & Row, 1987.

[34] Landrine, H. "Clinical Implications of Cultural Difference: The Referential Versus the Indexical Self." *Clinical Psychology Review 12* (1992):401–415.

[35] *Loc. cit.*

[36] *Loc. cit.*

[37] Nikelly, *op. cit,* 440.

[38] Ibid.

[39] Elshstain, J.B. *"A Call to Civil Society."* Society 36. (1999):11–19.

[40] Ansbacher, H. L. & Ansbacher, R. R. *"The Individual Psychology of Alfred Adler."* San Francisco: Harper & Row, 1956.

[41] Hoffman, E. *"The Drive for Self: Alfred Adler and the Founding of Individual Psychology."* Reading, MA: Addison-Wesley 1994.

[42] Nikelly, A. G. "Globalization and Community Feeling: Are They Compatible?" *The Journal of Individual Psychology 56* no. 4 (2000): 435–448.

[43] Dreikurs, R. *Fundamentals of Adlerian Psychology.* Chicago: Alfred Adler Institute, 1953.

[44] *Ibid.*

[45] Bitter, J.R. "Conscious Motivations: An Enhancement to Dreikurs' Goals of Children's Misbehavior" *Individual Psychology 47* no. 2 (1991).

[46] Dinkmeyer, D., Dinkmeyer, D., and Sperry, L. *Adlerian Counseling and Psychotherapy.* Columbus, OH: Merrill Publishing, 1987, 17.

[47] Adler, A. *The Individual Psychology of Alfred Adler.* H. L. Ansbacher and R. Ansbacher, eds. New York: Harper and Row, 1956, 19.

[48] Manaster, G., and Corsini, R. *Individual Psychology: Theory and Practice.* New York: F. E. Peacock, 1982.

[49] Rogers, C. R. *Client-Centered Therapy.* Boston, MA: Houghton Mifflin, 1951, 487.

[50] Manaster, G., and Corsini, R. *Individual Psychology: Theory and Practice.* New York: F. E. Peacock, 1982, 75.

Lifestyle Theory

In this chapter, Adlerian theory will be applied to the specific techniques of lifestyle assessment. The ability to understand as well as to predict human behavior are two of the major goals of psychology. Adler was one of the first to recognize this process in human development. He called the arrangement of our experiences into a technological narrative our "lifestyle," our unique way of being, of coping, and of moving through (and approaching) the tasks of life.[1] Disque and Bitter richly describe Adlerian lifestyle theory this way:

> We live 'storied' lives. As humans, we not only experience life directly through our senses, but we also transform it in an effort to make meaning out of what we experience. We live constantly with other human beings, and as such, we frame all that we do in the context of social relationships. The ordering of the meaning we experience in our lives with others most often takes the form of a story or narrative about who we are; who others are; what we are worth to ourselves, others, and the world; and what conclusions, convictions, and ethical codes will guide us. In a sense, lifestyle is what psychologists have called personality, but it is not so much about traits we possess (or have) as it is about our characteristic way of handling life (doing). Indeed, the explanations for why we do what we do are often the foundation of our lifestyle narratives or stories.[2]

Early in life children enter into a larger community, often by using parents and family as an anchor.[3] They move into new parts of experience, to what is unknown and unfamiliar, and return home, to what is known and secure. This movement out into the world and then back home again, this testing of experience and return to safety, builds over time into a pattern of living, a style of coping, a unique way of being in the world with others. It becomes our lifestyle.[4]

Disque and Bitter note that "what we remember of our past is selected to provide a foundation for the present and our projection of the present into some anticipated future. This ordering of life with a beginning, a middle, and a projected end creates the story of who we are and what we are all about. It is a story (one story of many that may be possible, . . .), but we act constantly as if this story is real life and is, furthermore, the only life we will ever have."[5]

Adler used the following analogy in presenting his definition of lifestyle:

> If we look at a pine tree growing in a valley we will notice that it grows differently from one on top of a mountain. It is the same kind of a tree, pine, but there are two distinct styles of life. Its style on top of the mountain is different from its style when growing in the valley. The style of life of a tree is the individuality of a tree expressing itself and molding itself in an environment.[6]

He then relates the pine tree analogy to the human experience as well as introducing the term lifestyle:

> We see the style of life under certain conditions of environment. As long as a person is in a favorable situation, we cannot see his style of life clearly. In new situations, however, where he is confronted with difficulties, the style of life appears clearly and distinctly. A trained psychologist could perhaps understand a style of life of a human being even in a favorable situation, but it becomes apparent to everybody when the human subject is put into unfavorable or difficult situation. Individual psychology has long called the consistent movement toward the goal a plan of life. But because this name has sometimes led to mistakes among students, it is now called a style of life.[7]

Every individual from earliest childhood develops his or her own unique law of movement. The direction of this movement aims always at overcoming the difficulties of one's life.[8] The individual's consistent movement toward a personal goal of security and significance is his or her lifestyle. Adler summarized lifestyle as a "general concept comprising, in addition to the goal, the individual's opinion of himself and the world and his unique way of striving for this goal in his particular situation." One's unique lifestyle is a bridge toward achieving a personal goal.[9]

There are a number of questions related to Adler's concept of life style. For example, how can one's choices at an early age influence the rest of one's life? How can a child have the cognitive ability to make such a decision? How is it that no one remembers making such a decision? Furthermore, what is the ontological status of this choice of a lifestyle? What is it? How does it exist? How does it develop?[10]

Adler recognized the cognitive limitations of a child making core decisions about oneself at an early age:

[The] 'style of life' is constructed by the child at a time when he has neither adequate language nor adequate concepts. As the child grows further in terms of the lifestyle, it grows in a movement which was never formulated in words and therefore unassailable by criticism, and is also withdrawn from the criticism of experience.[11]

Adler believed that a segment of the individual's style of life developed at a preconscious level due to the fact that the child lacked cognitive skills to conceptualize the environment. It is a matter of concepts hiding away in some unconscious or subconscious recesses of our minds, but of parts of our consciousness the significance of which we have not fully understood.[12]

By utilizing Vaihinger's philosophy of the "as if," Adler claimed that the child is not making an actual deliberate conscious choice; rather it is "as if" the child has made a choice of a lifestyle. For Adler the unconscious meant simply the "not understood." The lifestyle is unconscious in that what is "not understood" is the person's core presuppositions about themselves, others, and about life. Adler suggests that these stabilities are the result of a choice the child makes—it is "as if" the child has chosen a particular lifestyle.

According to Christopher and Bickhard:

Adler posits that we do not really know why and how such persistencies in personality develop. However, it is useful from a clinical and therapeutic perspective to consider such persistencies as the result of a choice. In other words, the supposed choice of a lifestyle is an acknowledged fiction—it is a falsehood but one that provides the psychologist with a useful heuristic for making sense of personality development. Functionally, the choice provides conceptual navigating tools for mapping the lives of individuals.[13]

Complete understanding of a person can only occur through a clear grasp of his or her lifestyle. The genetics or environment of an individual fail to explain his or her behavior; it is the person's unique interpretation or response that is of primary importance. Lifestyle permeates throughout all aspects of the unified self. Outward manifestations of lifestyle are evident in personality traits, which direct our consistent patterns of acting toward others. We also express lifestyle through defensive reactions, our psychic defenses. Lifestyle is the strategy people use to achieve a sense of significance, or a place in this world.[14] According to Lombardi and colleagues, "It is an organized and consistent manner of viewing oneself, others, and adapting to life in one's own personal manner. Lifestyle can also be distinguished from personality. One's personality is a compilation of all that an individual possesses and is a descriptive term. Lifestyle, on the other hand, is the expression of what one has. It is an active term. Lifestyle is personality in action."[15]

Abnormal behavior patterns such as personality styles, neurotic styles, personality disorders, and academic styles are nothing more than expressions of faulty lifestyles. Berne's transactional analysis concept of scripts, cognitive maps, premorbid personality, and transference and countertransference is also related to Adlerian lifestyle theory.[16]

Personality Styles

This refers to "a repertoire of states of mind, self-concepts and patterns of relationships, and ways of coping with stress and defending against threat. This includes characteristic patterns of regulating perceptions, thoughts, feelings, decisions, plans and actions." It has been offered as a replacement for Diagnostic and Statistical Manual (DSM-IV) Axis II personality disorders. [17] Lifestyle transcends DSM-IV axis classification. Lifestyle is evident in Axis I and II disorders, and must be understood for effective treatment.

Neurotic Styles

Neurotic style indicates that a personal mode of functioning is idiosyncratic of neurotic conditions, particularly subjective experiences and modes of thinking and experiencing emotions.[18] Neurosis is the general way a person lives his or her life, not a specific deficit in an otherwise healthy personality.

Lifestyle encompasses all aspects of one's unique life, including personality. Neurosis, as a materialization of a faulty personality organization, is also a materialization of lifestyle. The neurotic style is a direct derivative of the formulation of one's lifestyle that is faulty in its expression or movement toward a goal.

The concept of neurosis is no longer included as a diagnostic category in the DSM-IV classification system.[19] This absence suggests it is less of a discrete disorder, and more a general pattern of behavior. Neurotic styles can be viewed as tendencies toward maladjustment, but not evidenced by concrete, observable symptoms.[20]

Personality Disorders

Allport defines personality as "the dynamic organization within the individual of those psychophysical systems that determine his characteristic behavior and thought."[21] According to the DSM-IV, "a personality disorder is an enduring pattern of inner experience and behavior."[22] These disorders are divided into three clusters: Cluster A includes paranoid, schizoid, and schizotypal disorders; Cluster B is comprised of antisocial, borderline, histrionic, and narcissistic disorders; and Cluster C contains the avoidant, dependent, and obsessive-compulsive disorders. Personality disorders are primarily revealed through behavioral deviations.[23,24]

Understanding lifestyle as the forerunner to distorted personality development is important in understanding personality disorders and other clinical disorders. Lifestyle is formed in early childhood and is manifested in all aspects of one's life. Personality disorders are not usually evidenced until adolescence as they stem from the established lifestyle. Personality disorders can be viewed as the diagnostic classifications of those lifestyles that tend toward a particular pattern of maladjustment. [25]

Transactional Analysis and the Concept of Scripts

Berne, the originator of transactional analysis, speaks of "script" and "script analysis." He states that one decides early in childhood how he or she will live and die. All important behaviors and life decisions are dictated by one's script or life plan. Periods of one's life, or even an entire lifetime, are organized to accommodate one's unique script. Every person is the personal architect of his or her script and, with the appropriate freedom, has the power to carry out that unique script.

Script analysis is a focal point of transactional analysis. An understanding of a client's script is expected to shed light on current behaviors, behavioral antecedents, as well as future goals.[26]

The concept of script is remarkably similar to Adler's lifestyle concept. Berne credits Adler with coming the closest to "speaking like a script analyst."[27] Lombardi and colleagues observe that "Like lifestyles, scripts are personal life plans which shape all attitudes, beliefs and behaviors. They are formed early in life with parental influence, yet also contain an element of conscious choice. Both scripts and lifestyles involve the striving for a particular goal. The primary difference is that scripts involve specific and even short-term goals. Lifestyle entails a more general striving for personal significance."[28]

Premorbid Personality

Premorbid personality is defined as the personality as it was before the onset of psychopathology. It is the personality prior to the traumatic event that precipitated the abnormal symptoms and behavior. Thus, when an accident, illness, natural disaster, or some other severe stressor is experienced, the response of the individual depends on previous experience and enduring lifestyle.[29]

Premorbid personality is a variant of the lifestyle. Not only is lifestyle consistent throughout the entire personality, but there is also a temporal consistency. Premorbid personality determines one's interpretation and reaction to a stressor, as well as subsequent responses, including relapse and recovery. While people with healthy lifestyles are better able to cope with traumatic experiences, people with unhealthy lifestyles are likely to experience continuing problems.

Transference and Countertransference

Transference is a person's reacting to people in the present on the basis of similar encounters he or she has had with others at an earlier time. Ingrained learning patterns continue to exist with different people and in different places. Transference in the counselor, a reaction to the patient or client, is referred to as countertransference. Adler described transference as merely nothing more than social interest; in this case, the social situation is the therapeutic relationship. One way of viewing these reactions is to know and to explain them as the result of two interacting lifestyles. One's lifestyle dictates the manner in which he or she perceives and interacts with others.[30]

Lombardi and colleagues observe that "understanding lifestyle is like deciphering a code that unlocks the mystery of one's personality and behaviors. Lifestyle is a blueprint for the way in which we live our lives. It determines how one perceives and interprets information, as well as one's reaction to that information. Lifestyle is a pervasive and encompassing concept whose theme is found in all a person is or does, and is consistent over time. It affects the way one lives, bears old age, and dies. Nothing is foreign to, or divorced from, lifestyle. Its echo is found everywhere."[31]

Inferiority in Lifestyle Development

Another aspect of lifestyle theory central to individual psychology is the sense of inferiority. Adler stated that children are born with the sense of being inferior because they are physically small and dependent on adults. Such characteristics "bring about the impression that we are hardly equal to life."[32] This sense of inferiority represents the feeling of not being capable and, as such, not belonging in one's family, in a group, or in society as a whole. Adler stressed that the degree to which a person feels inferior is dependent on individual perceptions of self and surroundings. He also stated that striving for perfection was a natural way to overcome feelings of inferiority and that, as long as this striving was approached in a socially useful manner, it was a positive trait.[33]

Despite the vast diversity concerning different meanings for the term "lifestyle" itself, and despite related concepts by other psychologists employing slightly different terminology, the Ansbachers summarize the common "lifestyle" properties by systematizing the following similarities.

UNIFYING ASPECT

The word "style" includes the characteristic of cutting across ordinary boundaries and uniting what might otherwise be quite separate entities. Thus, in the case of Bach, Beethoven, and Mozart, if one knows their music at all, one can easily match the musical manuscripts with the composer.

UNIQUE AND CREATIVE ASPECTS

One style is always different from others, although there are similarities between styles. For example, children learn to write following a standard cultural model; nevertheless, each person varies the model in a unique, idiomatic manner. Of course, spontaneous and unique behavior implies choices on the part of individuals. And such choices are based on a forward-oriented, purposive, value psychology rather than on a causalistic, reductionistic psychology.

OPERATIONAL, FUNCTIONAL, AND CONSTANCY ASPECTS

In the book *A Manual for Life Style Assessment*, two of the foremost post-Dreikurs clinicians, Bernard Shulman and Harold Mosak, proposed that although Adler often used the term in a collective sense (the lifestyle of a pampered child), he stressed that "the life style of any individual was a singular pattern of thinking, feeling, and acting that was unique to that individual and represented the context . . . in which all specific manifestations had to be considered."[34] The development of lifestyle begins at an early age when an infant uses elementary "trial and error" means to organize the world. Such early efforts are formed into beginning "rules" or patterns serving as an integrator for the rules. Early patterns are continually reinforced as the child grows until what Shulman and Mosak call "the rule of thumb" is elevated to the status of a law, the unique law of movement. "Because it is a unique personal law, it receives all of the person's loyalties . . . Because it seems to permit better coping, it becomes as a private religion or personal myth."[35] Mosak further writes that: "If it is recalled that the Life Style is a subjective bias which the individual embraces as if it were true, then the Life Style can be conceived as a personal mythology. This individual will behave as if the myths were true because for him, they are true." It becomes a type of "self-fulfilling prophecy."

Although individuals develop such a habitual pattern to organizing the world, Adlerian theory maintains that one can always change, modify, or "break" such patterns. Thus, insight and awareness of one's general "rules" of life is essential to the counseling process.[36]

Dinkmeyer, Dinkmeyer and Sperry present an apt metaphor of the "theater of an ongoing drama" relative to the child's development of his or her personal lifestyle:

> The style of living is created in the course of an ongoing drama that takes place in the theater of the family, with parents and siblings all playing a part—a drama in which the child functions as his own director and whose last act he has already sketched out in broad outlines. The nuclear family is society to the small child, and the child's efforts to find a place in this society influence how he creates his life style. In elucidating an individual's life style, the counselor tries to get some idea of what it was like to be in that childhood drama, what roles were played by the different actors, and how the "director" interpreted the drama—that is, what role he played and what conclusions he drew about himself and life.[37]

A lifestyle investigation begins in the present and then shifts to the person's first social group—the family (or its equivalent). Implications for the present and future are the goal of a lifestyle assessment. An investigation of this type focuses on such familial concerns as birth order, interpersonal relationships between family members, the siblings' main competitors, family values, and the individual's early recollections of formative experiences. Adlerian theory is based on the assumption that one's phenomenological personal decisions and conclusions ("private logic") are the crucial determinants of behavior.[38] The optimistic belief that an individual's past decisions and patterns can be continually reviewed, modified, and/or changed is essential to lifestyle theory.

A child's formative decisions later become formulated into basic *convictions* about "'what is'—that is about the nature of our individual selves and the 'reality' we face; and those about the values and behaviors we will pursue in our efforts to master 'what is.'"[39]

Convictions of life are further developed into what they call "I am . . . , Life is . . . , therefore . . ." *conclusions* about behavior. For example, Adler's observation of two vastly different *therefores* or conclusions) given a similar "fear of death" major lifestyle theme:

A physician: "*I am* concerned about the disease, decay and ultimate death I see around me. *Life* is filled with much suffering but also contains the possibility of discovering cures for such discomfort; *therefore*, I will dedicate my life to conquering disease and extending life."

A gravedigger: "*I am* afraid of death. *Life* is simply an inevitable progression toward death; *therefore*, I will celebrate my own superiority each time I bury another person who was conquered by death."

Note the similar motivating convictions but drastically differing *decisions* reflecting social interest or the lack thereof.

Mosak and Shulman call long-continued patterns of behavior the *methods* of obtaining a goal. The method for the physician involved enrolling in medical school, while the gravedigger symbolically triumphed in each burial. They summarize the major elements of an overall lifestyle as being:

1. **Convictions about "what is,"** including (a) Self-image (What am I?); (b) world-image—life in general (How does it work?); and (c) "Weltbild"—the social world (What is the relationship between myself and others?).

2. **Convictions about "what should be,"** including ethical value of (a) the ideal world (How should life be?); and (b) moral judgments (What is good and proper behavior?).

3. **Instructions for behavior,** including (a) dominant goal/self ideal (What shall I pursue? and What must I become?), and (b) methods (How shall I do it?) [40]

Lifestyle: "The Story of Our Life"

A paradox of lifestyle is that, although it is often constant and stable, each of us are continually growing and shaping our beliefs about ourselves, others, and the world. There are early formulative patterns that form what Shulman called a "pre-formed working hypothesis" through which our later experiences are filtered. Jim Bitter calls a lifestyle the "story of our life." He also believes that the purpose of therapy is to help enlarge the client's story to make it fuller and richer.

In many ways, such a story of our life may contain more core fiction than actual core truth. For example, some of our remembrances of previous stories are indeed made up, and many of us can't remember what is true and not true. For example, Adler relates an early formative childhood experience of being deathly afraid of having to cross a graveyard, which he felt was between himself and his elementary school grounds. It was only many years later that he discovered that there was no actual graveyard that existed between those two places; however, the reality of such a graveyard in his own mind was as real to him as was the physical existence of that feared place. One's lifestyle is a narrative in story form and is not necessarily "accurate" to the "objective" facts as we leave out certain incidences and re-emphasize others.

However, we "act as if" such conclusions are true, for we are living more in our own interpretations of our experiences than the actual events themselves. The process of understanding one's lifestyle consists of helping to find meaning of what is being told to the counselor. As each of us journeys through life certain stories become what Bitter calls "dominant knowledge" with two primary functions of such events:

1. to reinforce itself and its own importance upon the self; and

2. to eliminate alternative ideas or stories which may be inconsistent with one's own self-perceived dominant knowledge.[41]

Thus, the lifestyle assessment is a creative way to help learn about "one's own personal story."

The American Indians often say, "if you want to understand my world, walk a mile in my moccasins." A lifestyle assessment is one way to learn about one's own inner world. Becoming aware of one's own inner world including potential fictional parts of that story can then help a person "rewrite," "recreate," or "expand" such a story to include new possibilities and new options.

Summary

In this chapter, Adlerian lifestyle theory has been explored within the context of a developmental Adlerian counseling approach. Chapter 3 will contain eight actual assessment interview forms as a suggested guideline for obtaining formative information.

Endnotes

[1] Adler, A. *What Life Should Mean to You*. A. Porter, ed. New York: Capricorn Books, 1958.

[2] Disque, G., and Bitter, J. R. "Integrating Narrative Therapy with Adlerian Lifestyle Assessment: A Case Study." *The Journal of Individual Psychology 54* no. 4 (1998):431.

[3] Powers, R. L. & Griffith, J. *Understanding Lifestyle: The Psycho-clarity Process*. Chicago: The Americas Institute of Adlerian Studies. (1987)

[4] Shulman, B., and Mosak, H. *Manual for Lifestyle Assessment*. Muncie, IN: Accelerated Development, Inc., 1988.

[5] Loc. cit.

[6] Adler, A. *The Science of Living*. New York: Greenberg Publishers, Inc., 1929, 98.

[7] Ibid.

[8] Ansbacher, H. L., and Ansbacher, R. R. (eds.). *The Individual Psychology of Alfred Adler*. New York: Harper & Row. 1964,1967.

[9] Ansbacher, H. L., and Ansbacher, R. R. (eds.). *The Individual Psychology of Alfred Adler: A Systematic Presentation from His Writings*. New York: Basic. (1956):172.

[10] Christopher, J. C. and Bickhard, M. H. "Remodeling the 'As If' in Adler's Concept of the Lifestyle" *Individual Psychology 48*, no. 1 (1992): 77.

[11] Adler, A. *The Individual Psychology of Alfred Adler*. (H. L. Ansbacher, and R. R. Ansbacher, Eds.) New York; Harper & Row. (1956): p. 191.

[12] Ibid., pp. 232, 233.

[13] Christopher and Bickhard, op. cit., p. 78

[14] Lombardi, D. N. *Search for Significance*. Chicago: Nelson Hall, 1975.

[15] Lombardi, D. N., Melchior, E.J., Murphy, J. G. & Brinkerhoff, A. L. "The Ubiquity of Lifestyle." *Individual Psychology 52*, no. 1 (1996): 32.

[16] Berne, E. "*What do You Say After You Say Hello?*" New York: Grove (1972)

[17] Horowitz, M., Marmor, C., Krupnick, J. Wilner, N., and Katreider, N. *Personality Styles and Brief Psychotherapy*. New York: Basic, 1984.

[18] Shapiro, D. *Neurotic Styles*. New York: Basic, 1965.

[19] American Psychiatric Association. *Diagnostic and Statistic Manual of Mental Disorders*. (4th ed.) Washington, DC: Author.

[20] Carson, R. C. and Butcher, J. N. *Abnormal Psychology and Modern Life* (9th ed.). New York: HarperCollins, 1992.

[21] Allport, G. W. *Pattern and Growth in Personality*. New York: Holt, Rinehart, and Winston, 1937, 28.

[22] APA, op. cit., p. 629.

[23] Ibid.

[24] Carson and Butcher, op. cit.

[25] Lombardi et al., op. cit., p. 35

[26] Berne, op. cit.

[27] Ibid., p. 58

[28] Lombardi et al., p. 36.

29 Zax, M., and Cowen, E. L. *Abnormal Psychology-Changing Conceptions* (2nd ed.). New York: Holt, Rinehart, and Winston, 1976.

30 Ansbacher and Ansbacher, op. cit., p. 115.

31 Lombardi et al., pp. 38-39.

32 Ansbacher and Ansbacher, op. cit.

33 Dinter, L. D. "The Relationship Between Self-Efficacy and Lifestyle Patterns." *The Journal of Individual Psychology 56*, no. 4 (2000): 469–473.

34 Shulman, B., and Mosak, H. *Manual for Lifestyle Assessment*. Muncie, IN: Accelerated Development, Inc., 1988, 1.

35 Ibid., p. 3.

36 Ansbacher and Ansbacher, op. cit.

37 Dinkmeyer, D., Jr., and Sperry, L. *Counseling and Psychotherapy: An Integrated, Individual Psychology Approach*. Columbus, OH: Prentice Hall, 1999.

38 Loc. cit.

39 Shulman and Mosak, op cit., p. 5

40 Ibid., p. 12.

41 Bitter, J. "The Narrative Study of Lives: Lifestyle Assessment as Qualitative Research." Program presented at NASAP Annual Conference, Minneapolis, MN. May 27, 1995.

LIFESTYLE INTERVIEW GUIDES AND USE

In this chapter, seven representative lifestyle interview guides will be presented. They will include the following:

1. a "Now & Then" questionnaire that helps introduce the concept of lifestyle;

2. the "Eckstein Lifestyle Interview" (ELSI) for use with adolescents and adults;

3. a modified version for children under the age of 10;

4. a sample group lifestyle interview;

5. a mini-lifestyle interview;

6. a "most memorable adolescent observation"; and

7. an empirical-based description of lifestyle assessment by Kern and associates.

Because Adler so often used musical metaphors, perhaps one might consider the following structured formats as important introductory musical "scales" that serve as a useful guideline for beginning the skill of learning lifestyle interviewing skills. However, as one masters those scales, creative and artistic "improvisations" are appropriate.

Historical Overview to the Development of Lifestyle Formats

Despite encouraging a creative approach to lifestyle assessment, Powers and Griffith state that "Structure reduces uncertainty; it strengthens the possibility of a useful process and beneficial results."[1] The Ansbachers reference Adler's early children's and adolescent lifestyle forms[2]. Even then, he recommended the forms as an "informal act," not to be adhered to rigidly. His childhood assessment featured fifteen basic questions, using the following subheadings: "Disorders, social relationships, interests, recollections and dreams, discouraged behavior, and positive assets." His adult form featured eighteen questions to which he noted that "by adhering to it the experienced therapist will gain an extensive insight into the style of life of the individual already within about half an hour."

Dreikurs created a longer questionnaire from which many of the questions in the present authors recommended format originated.[3] Harold Mosak and Bernard Shulman revised their format into a Lifestyle Inventory (LSI), published and copyrighted by Accelerated Development, Inc., Muncie, Indiana.[4]

Similar forms can be found in Manaster and Corsini,[5] Sweeney,[6] and Eckstein, Baruth, and Mahrer.[7] Raymond and Betty Lowe (appendices H & I, in Baruth and Eckstein, 1981), created two separate forms, an "Interview Guide for Establishing the Lifestyle," and "Lifestyle Interpretation." Dinkmeyer, Dinkmeyer, and Sperry[8] report on Roy Kern's "The Lifestyle Scale" (available from CMTI Press in Coral Springs, Florida), as well as their format. Powers and Griffith describe their own "initial interview inquiry" [9] as well as a "Lifestyle Assessment Inquiry" [10] as part of what they describe the "psycho-clarity" process.

Because a lifestyle assessment is usually done in an interview format, here are some general considerations in tabular form for the basics of interviewing. That is then followed with specific questions and answers relative to the lifestyle interview process.

The Approach to a Lifestyle Interview

The checklist on the following page was designed for use in general interviewing skills training workshops in counseling, and for use in business settings. Such preparatory contemplations help determine in advance the purpose and focus of the interview, whether it is to learn about an organization or an individual. Listed are fifteen interview considerations; they are then summarized in a series of questions that can serve as both an initial and a "final" checklist for conducting an interview. The fifteen considerations are then applied to the lifestyle theory.

Basic Interviewing Considerations

Although some basic lifestyle information can be obtained by having a person fill out a basic questionnaire, a complete lifestyle assessment is best conducted in an interview format. Effective interviewing is one of the most important skills for human counselors. The following fifteen questions are meant to serve as a pre-interview checklist. Responses to the questions can also serve as a mid-session guide and/or a debriefing evaluation at the conclusion of an interview. General considerations are shown in the following checklist.

INTERVIEW ISSUES AND CONSIDERATIONS

A CHECKLIST SUMMARY
DANIEL ECKSTEIN

The following chart provides a summary checklist of questions for designing, conducting, and critiquing interviews.

Issue	Considerations
1. Purpose	What do I hope to accomplish in this session?
2. Focus	Is my primary mission to highlight individual, group, team, or content-related issues?
3. Levels of confidentiality and/or anonymity	Who has access to the information? What are my ethical parameters?
4. Session content	What specific topics and behaviors are desirable? Acceptable? Unacceptable?
5. What is the context of this interview?	For example, what system(s) have a "vested interest" in this interview (i.e., family, school, agency, church, or synagogue)?
6. Initiating the interview	How will my verbal and nonverbal behavior help establish an atmosphere of trust and respect?
7. Pacing and leading skills	What is the appropriate balance of responsiveness and directiveness?
8. Sharing versus dumping	How will I deal with inappropriate anger, cynicism, sarcasm, scapegoating, gossip, and so on?
9. The alone/together paradox	How can I be connected with the client while concurrently maintaining my own separateness?
10. Integrating left and right brain hemispheres	How can I be both an intuitive artist and a rational scientist in my listening and intervention skills?
11. First and second order change[11]	Is behavioral change (first order) and/or client attitude (second order change) part of my consultant role? If so, what strategies will facilitate such movement?
12. Interviewer reactions	How am I feeling in this interview and/or in this organization? How can I use my personal awareness as another assessment technique?
13. Encouragement and confrontation skills	How can I help the client identify strengths as well as appropriately confronting discrepancies?
14. Closing the interview	What needs to be done to have a sense of closure to the meeting?
15. Follow-up and evaluation	How can I assist in the proper individual/family/organizational feedback and implementation?

Considerations Prior to Use of Following Instruments

Although each particular lifestyle assessment interview has its own unique aspects, the following questions may be important when using the instruments on the following pages.

1. *What is the purpose of a lifestyle interview?*
    A lifestyle interview is a systematic exploration of early formative childhood experiences. Although the focus is both on the present as well as backward in time, current and future decisions become the purpose of exploring one's initial social experiences. Themes of life, hopes, dreams, and fears emerge from such a systematic examination.

2. *Who or what is my focus?*
    One's first family or equivalent, including brothers and sisters, mother and father as relevant, is the focus. Although there is a structured interview available, the actual session may be spent on one or two key formative experiences. Family atmosphere and early recollections will be highlighted.

3. *When is it appropriate to use the lifestyle assessment?*
    In general a lifestyle assessment is most valuable when the interviewee appears to be extremely confused about certain ways of acting, reacting, or experiencing emotions. The lifestyle assessment process is also of highest benefit when the standard active listening model of helping does not seem to be effective. Finally, the lifestyle assessment tools are warranted when teaching the theory of Individual Psychology or as an educational tool in workshops or seminars.

4. *Who gets the data?*
    Unless prior agreements are made with the interviewee relative to releasing the data to a particular agency, family member, or significant other, ethical consideration of respecting the privacy and confidentiality of the individual needs to be followed.

5. *What types of data are "admissible"?*
    In keeping with the projective nature of a lifestyle interview, individual creativity and spontaneous sharing is encouraged. When early recollections are explored, one specific memory is wanted in contrast to something someone else told the person. Basic respect dictates that the person may elect to "pass" on any question asked.

6. *What is the context of the interview?*
    Interviews are often conducted as part of a couple and/or family conseling session. Others present can provide "here and now" behavioral examples as well—to gain insight into the person's behavior. The user of the clinical tool must plan how the nonparticipating members are to participate within the interview.

7. *What interviewing skills could enhance the interview process?*
    The SOFEL acronym can be used to describe attending preparatory interview guidelines:

    S = sitting square
    O = open body posture
    F = leaning forward
    E = eye contact
    L = active listening skills[12]

    Allen Ivey describes other interview encouragers consisting of such phrases as: "could you tell me about . . . ?"; "oh?"; "so?"; "then?"; "and?"; "tell me more"; "and how did you feel about that?"; "can you give me a specific example?"; "what does that mean to you?"; "umm-humm"; or the repetition of one or two key words.[13]

8. *How can the interviewer acquire the most from the lifestyle assessment process?*
    Open yourself up to allow your own creative intuitive problem solver to cooperate with your own scientific exploration. Dreikurs called it "digging gold mines," that is, respecting and paying attention to a key word or phrase that impacts you. The more centered you can be, the more open to your own creative process you will be.

9. *How can I gain additional information from the interview?*
    Allow yourself to experience your feelings related to the person you are interviewing. Many times it is the interviewer's own reaction to the person that enhances the identification of the lifestyle dynamics.

10. *What about closing the interview?*
    After the initial data-gathering, set a follow-up appointment. Encourage the person to keep a journal for other thoughts that may emerge. Stress that the interpretation will be done collaboratively. A traditional approach to a lifestyle assessment process would require a follow-up appointment to discuss the results of the interview. However, this is dependent upon the psychological well-being of the individual, overall good rapport of interviewer/consultant, and/or the systemic context.

11. *What about the growth process for the user of the technique?*
    We would suggest that the interviewer request the interviewee to assess what they learned from the process as well as the interviewer enlisting information from the client on his/her interviewing skills.

LIFESTYLE: A SELF-ASSESSMENT

As a way of exploring the concept of style and your psychological fingerprints, complete, score, and give your own interpretation to the following questionnaire.

In order to introduce the idea of personality differences as reflected in style, the following self-scoring questionnaire has been developed.

A.   The first step is for you to consider the following five animals:

Tiger

Chameleon

Salmon

Eagle

Turtle

B.   Now, answer the following questions:
   1.   Which one of these animals is most like you?

      a. _____

   2.   Why or how is it like you?

   3.   How are the other four animals like or unlike you?

      a. _____

      b. _____

      c. _____

      d. _____

C.   Now take the "Now & Then" Lifestyle Questionnaire (interpretation and scoring instructions will follow).

The "Now & Then" Lifestyle Questionnaire

Daniel Eckstein

Instructions—Read each of the following statements and assign points according to these guidelines:

always	5 points
usually	4 points
sometimes	3 points
seldom	2 points
almost never	1 point

A. Answer questions 1–30 based on your *current* life:

_____ 1. I persist at a task until it is finished.

_____ 2. In a new job or class, I find out what is expected of me and then do it without a lot of fanfare.

_____ 3. I am the kind of person who "sticks my neck out" to take a lot of chances.

_____ 4. I am constantly seeking a better way of doing things.

_____ 5. I have been fired or have resigned from a job or failed a class because my boss or teacher thought I had a poor attitude.

_____ 6. I am often recognized by others as an expert or an authority in one or more areas.

_____ 7. Others can count on me to keep my agreements.

_____ 8. I prefer to be alone or with just one or two friends than in a large group.

_____ 9. I can anticipate problems before they arise.

_____ 10. I protest causes of injustice, unfairness, or hypocrisy.

_____ 11. I am interested in time management, planning the most efficient use of my day.

_____ 12. I follow the rules.

_____ 13. I think before I act.

_____ 14. I like being my own boss.

_____ 15. I mistrust authority.

_____ 16. I set goals for myself and work hard to attain them.

_____ 17. I blend my feelings with those of others just to keep things harmonious.

_____ 18. I am "set" in my ways, my habits, and my opinions.

_____ 19. In a conflict, I am confident that I have the ability to "rise above it" and thereby gain a better perspective.

_____ 20. I believe most people compromise their true feelings just to conform to the status quo.

_____ 21. When I'm riding in a car, I'd prefer to be the driver.

_____ 22. I am seldom absent from school or work.

_____ 23. Compared with others, I feel I am more private and sensitive than them.

_____ 24. I will stick to my own opinion or beliefs even if others disagree with me.

_____ 25. Creating a better world will require destroying old habits, thoughts, and systems.

_____ 26. I go after what I want.

_____ 27. I focus so much on the feelings of others that expressing my own emotions makes me uncomfortable.

_____ 28. I am successful when people see that my way of doing things contributes to others.

_____ 29. I am confident as long as I am free to follow my dreams.

_____ 30. The truth is more important to me than social graces or what people think of me.

B. Answer questions 31–60 based on your **childhood** (up to age seven):

_____ 1. I would have been considered as a leader by my friends.

_____ 2. I went along with what was expected of me.

_____ 3. I spent a lot of time alone.

_____ 4. I was willing to speak my opinion.

_____ 5. I disagreed with my parents or teachers and I often got in trouble because of my strong beliefs.

_____ 6. I was competitive.

_____ 7. I was good at figuring out what was wanted or needed in a situation and then doing it.

_____ 8. If someone yelled at me, I would withdraw into myself.

_____ 9. I wanted to have things go my way.

_____ 10. I was aware of the amount of injustice and unfairness in the world.

_____ 11. I could persuade my other friends to follow my ideas or wishes.

_____ 12. I enjoyed helping around the house or at school.

_____ 13. I had a private place in my house or neighborhood that was just mine.

_____ 14. I sought new adventures.

_____ 15. I didn't go along with the rules others made for me.

_____ 16. I was very energetic, always on the go.

_____ 17. I was interested in hearing opinions of other people.

_____ 18. I often knew things were going to happen before they actually happened.

_____ 19. I considered myself to be intelligent.

_____ 20. I never understood why people didn't speak their own opinions.

_____ 21. I was confident that ultimately I would succeed

_____ 22. It was okay for others to have different opinions than me.

_____ 23. I desired quietness, order, and safety.

_____ 24. I considered myself to be a free spirit.

_____ 25. I began to realize there were significant injustices in the world.

_____ 26. I set high standards for myself.

_____ 27. If the whole group was happy, then I was happy.

_____ 28. To deal with my hurt, I developed a hard shell.

_____ 29. I liked deciding things for myself.

_____ 30. I stood up for the smaller kids or the outsiders if someone bullied them.

THEORY INPUT

After reading the theory behind the "Now & Then" Lifestyle Questionnaire, you are invited to predict your results prior to actually scoring it. After scoring, you will be asked to reflect and compare these results to your own initial assessment of your personality or lifestyle.

According to Adler our characteristic reactions to life ("lifestyle") are formulated before the age of five.[14] Once such a framework (or template) has been selected, all new experiences tend to be subjectively interpreted or "filtered" through that original framework. Although each of us has our own unique and creative style, early formative experiences help establish a "pre-formed working hypothesis" through which later preferences, values, and beliefs are evaluated and formulated.[15]

Through the use of factor-analysis research, Thorne identified the following five trait descriptive categories: **aggressive, conforming, defensive, individualistic,** or **resistive.**[16] In order to identify possible negative stereotyping plus to identify the strengths of these more clinically oriented personality descriptions, the five lifestyle categories are given five representative animal labels: tiger, chameleon, turtle, eagle, and salmon.

Here are the descriptions of the five typologies:

Tigers are generally considered to be *aggressive*. They enjoy exercising authority, like to be the center of attention, and may insist on having their own way. Tigers usually were childhood leaders and continue in this role as adults. They are also enterprising, vigorous, and ambitious.

Chameleons are generally seen as *conforming*. They are flexible, and more likely to face problems directly. Chameleons frequently move up rapidly in business as they are dependable, hard-working, and honest. They are cooperative, sociable, warm, helpful, and practical and may be aesthetic.

Turtles are generally thought to be *defensive*. They are earnest and resourceful and lead self-controlled, stable lives. Turtles are frequently "loners" with one or two close relationships. They are intuitive and sensitive and have some trouble admitting fallibility. Others may consider turtles to be stubborn because they have no interest in changing the status quo.

Eagles tend to be seen as *individualistic*. They are not concerned with public opinion and may be egotistic and infringe on the rights of others to get their own way. Eagles are capable, industrious, assertive, and adventurous—idealizing "progress." They are found in any field that values independence and are frequently entrepreneurial.

Salmon usually are considered *resistive*. They prefer to "swim against the current" rather than support "establishment" values. Salmon may take up causes against oppression and demand that they be heard. They are vigorous, progressive, and rebellious and dislike what they consider to be false social niceties.

TYPOLOGY CONSIDERATIONS

Adler was careful to caution against reifying typologies and was clear about their usefulness. "We do not consider human beings as types, because every person has an individual style of life. If we speak of types, therefore, it is only as an intellectual device to make more understandable the similarities of individuals."[17]

Boldt and Mosak stress that "Each person has a unique story of my life that a personality typology cannot portray. In addition, no one is pure type. . . . Indeed, as one gets closer to another's story one finds more, not less, complexity. As therapists, we must remain humble in our interpretations as we stand in awe of the complexity of another person's story. People get larger as we get closer, not smaller as implied by the misuse of typologies."[18]

They also note that therapists who use typologies "know full well that many adjustments will have to be made to fit a client's unique shape. As we become more and more skilled, we rely less and less on ready-made patterns, and we can begin with patterns more and more highly specific to individuals. But we still go through the process of fitting the garment to the unique shape, and we also know that shape can change. So we remain flexible and never use type theory to pigeonhole a human being."[19]

Barzon further states:

I personally abhor the kind of reductionist thinking that some mental health professionals practice when thinking and talking about the individuals who come to them for help. To believe that one can capture so mysterious an entity as a complex human being in a diagnostic [word] or phrase is self-deluding and invalidates the assertion that psychological investigation is a quest for the truth: all too often, it is a gathering of evidence to reaffirm what someone already believes about a particular set of behaviors.[20]

PREDICTING YOUR SCORE

First, circle the adjectives you feel are most characteristic of you now.

Tiger	Chameleon	Turtle	Eagle	Salmon
aggressive	cooperative	stable	capable	persuasive
confident	sociable	self-controlled	industrious	independent
persistent	warm	placid	strong	vigorous
persuasive	helpful	earnest	forceful	demanding
self-reliant	diligent	defensive	foresighted	rebellious
independent	persistent	stubborn	clear thinking	protecting
initiator	gentle	apologetic	independent	forceful
potential leader	sincere	resourceful	spontaneous	progressive
ambitious	honest	insecure	intelligent	competitive

Now, based on the adjectives you have circled and your answers in the questionnaire, prioritize which of the above animals you feel represents you:

1. _____

2. _____

3. _____

4. _____

5. _____

Do you predict any significant difference between your "now" versus "then" ratings?

_____

_____

Now proceed to the next page, and find out how you scored. You will note that all five animal types are presented sequentially throughout the questionnaire. Simply transfer your scores horizontally across the answer sheet, and then add the total column vertically for each animal type.

Instructions

- Transfer the points you assigned each item on the questionnaire into the appropriate box.
- Add the number of points in each column. This is your raw score for the column
- Record the total in the large box at the bottom of the column.

Column I	Column II	Column III	Column IV	Column V
Item 1 ☐	Item 2 ☐	Item 3 ☐	Item 4 ☐	Item 5 ☐
6 ☐	7 ☐	8 ☐	9 ☐	10 ☐
11 ☐	12 ☐	13 ☐	14 ☐	15 ☐
16 ☐	17 ☐	18 ☐	19 ☐	20 ☐
21 ☐	22 ☐	23 ☐	24 ☐	25 ☐
26 ☐	27 ☐	28 ☐	29 ☐	30 ☐
31 ☐	32 ☐	33 ☐	34 ☐	35 ☐
36 ☐	37 ☐	38 ☐	39 ☐	40 ☐
41 ☐	42 ☐	43 ☐	44 ☐	45 ☐
46 ☐	47 ☐	48 ☐	49 ☐	50 ☐

Raw
Score   ☐   ☐   ☐   ☐   ☐
Totals

Instructions for completing this score sheet.

- This graph provides a convenient transformation of each of your total raw scores and converts it into a standard score. (Standard Scores are raw scores transformed with a mean of 50 and a standard deviation of 10.)
- Connect each of your standard scores to provide a profile.

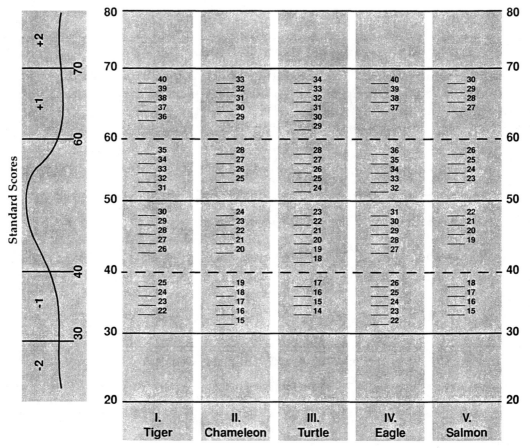

Design of the scoring sheets © Copyright Phyliss Cooke, Ph.D.—Used by the permission of the author

As a final summary, now respond to the following questions:
How did your predictions compare with your final scores, as well as with your original animal selection?

_____

_____

_____

Were there any surprises? If so, what were they? Do you agree with your scores?

_____

_____

_____

_____

One key ingredient that is lacking in the above five clinical scales is social interest, or what O'Connell has termed "humanistic identification." Altruism, nurturing, compassion, and empathy need to be healthy additions to each typology. One of Adler's frequent prescriptions to his clients was to "go out and help *someone else*—you are too preoccupied with yourself!"

_____

_____

_____

Now apply the results of this questionnaire to your own understanding of your personal style. Write one or two paragraphs summarizing your self-assessment of the strengths and weaknesses of your style.

_____

_____

_____

_____

_____

_____

_____

Use this self-assessment as your personal guide to add meaning to your reading.

Classroom Application of Lifestyle Assessment

Henry Dunkerson is a fourth-grade teacher at Lafe Nelson Elementary School in Safford, Arizona. After completing a graduate course in Adlerian psychology, he utilized the "Now and Then Questionnaire" (see p. 29) in the following creative way with his elementary students. Here is his first-person account—a very creative adaptation that he utilizes with his students.[21]

In *The Mixed-Up Chameleon*[22] by Eric Carle, there was a chameleon who found that his life was not very exciting. He ate flies and changed colors, like all chameleons, but he wished to be different. Upon arriving at the zoo, the chameleon began wishing to be like other animals. His wishes were granted and before long he was part flamingo, fox, fish, deer, giraffe, turtle, elephant, seal, and human. With each change he made, a new chameleon was drawn, forming a unique looking creature. At the end of the story, the chameleon was feeling hungry but was unable to catch a fly because he was so mixed up about who he was. He decided the best thing to do was to wish to be back to his original self. Of course, his wish was granted and he turned back into a chameleon. This story has great possibilities when working with children on being whom they are. When they attempt to be someone they're not, they become mixed up and are unsure about whom they truly are and how they fit in. With this book, children can identify with the animals and relate it to themselves, making it easier to make the choice of being whom they are inside.

Henry goes on to suggest ways to incorporate his ideas into the Lifestyle Assessment:

Here is an idea for a self-esteem building activity for the classroom. After reading *The Mixed-Up Chameleon*, generate a discussion with your class about why the chameleon may have wanted to change and be different from what he was.

Introduce the five animals from the Lifestyle Assessment. Lead your class in a discussion about describing these animals using human characteristics. For instance, the turtle might be described as shy and would prefer to be alone, while the tiger might be strong and prefer to be the leader. Try to avoid descriptions like "it has legs, feet, eyes" but work for human behavior characteristics "shy, brave, clever, and so on."

For this next activity, you may want to have a class set of coloring pictures of each of the five animals. Then have each student choose one of the five animals that most closely resembles his/her own characteristics. Lead the class in a discussion on what features of the other four animals they would like to add to the animal they chose. Let them cut and paste these features to their animal. Have them write a descriptive paragraph about this new animal. Have them name their new animals and color them.

Following this activity generate and lead discussion in how each person is unique. Help them conclude that everyone has many different characteristics that make each of us unique individuals. End the discussion by having a writing activity where each student fully describes him/herself. They may include a drawing of themselves and include what makes them different from other people.

Expanding Your Social Interest

One of our goals in writing this book is obviously for readers to learn greater self awareness. Then hopefully that will translate to helping others through the utilization of personal gifts for the betterment of humanity. Although this book is meant to be a self guided experiential process, it is suggested that you to use a partner if possible. Let Person A interview Person B and then later switch roles. Then let Person B share a summary of Person A and Person A share the summary for Person B. Because everyone has personal blind spots, it makes it difficult but not impossible, to conduct one's own life-assessment. Sheldon Kopp observes that:

Along the way, on his pilgrimage, each man must have the chance to tell his tale.
And, as each man tells his tale, there must be another there to listen.
But the other need not be a guru. He need only rise to the needs of the moment.
There is an old saying that whenever two Jews meet,
if one has a problem, the other automatically becomes a rabbi.[23]

The forms in this book can (and hopefully will) be used as a dyadic partner in a college or university class, a family education center, and so on. Having gained more experience during the beginning skill development, the counselor is then ready to use the forms with actual clients.

The Eckstein Lifestyle Interview (ELSI)

INTRODUCTION

There are three subsections to the following interview.

Part I explores the person's current "Way of Being' in the World" by utilizing what Dreikurs[24] calls the "subjective situation" in which all the client's concerns, complaints, illnesses, stressors, and so on, are identified. The "objective situation" then focuses on one's own self-assessment of the five life tasks. Both sets of information are linked by what Dreikurs called "The Question"—"What would be different if you had all of these problems or concerns solved?" The answer to such a question helps explain the client's complaints and emotional stresses. It also indicates in what area the person is experiencing difficulty and where or on whom the problem is centered.

Part II consists of sibling descriptions, including sibling ratings. A description of one's parent(s) completes the family atmosphere. Because not all children grew up in a single family, one's first social group or family equivalent should be used. Also, if one has no brothers or sisters, early childhood friends and/or cousins should be used as the basis for comparison. Cultural and ethnic heritage are also examined.

Part III consists of the early recollections (ERs) and recurring dreams. The following nine guidelines are recommended for obtaining and for recording early recollections:

1. Introduce early recollection as follows: "Think back as far as you can and tell me the first thing you remember."

2. Distinguish between an early recollection and a report. An early recollection should be a specific event beginning with "one day I remember . . ."; conversely, a report is more global typified by: "I (or we) used to . . ." or "Many times I . . ."

3. Also make sure the incident is personally remembered by the person as opposed to having been seen in a photograph or in home movies or having been reported to the individual by someone else (i.e., a parent, sibling, or other significant person). While it is valuable to note what others said to and about the interviewee, his or her own personal experience is the focus of early recollections ("immaculate perception").

4. Be certain to write down all the events exactly as stated word by word in the person's own memory, although some abbreviation may be necessary in an extremely long language. The goal is to obtain first-person narratives using the client's own exact language.

5. After the person finishes speaking of the incident, encourage additional information by asking "and then what happened?" The memory itself is complete when the interviewee responds with "that's all I can remember."

6. After the report itself is recorded, ask (a) "what was most vivid about the incident?" and (b) "what were your feelings during this event?"

7. A good guideline is getting three to five early recollections and one or two reoccurring or formulative dreams.

8. If a person says he or she can't remember any specific events, encourage the individual to "make one up." Projective theory will be just as valid for such a "fantasized" memory as a "real" one.

9. Obtain any similar reoccurring or formative dreams in a similar format as the early recollections.

(Additional interpretative guidelines will be presented in Chapter 4.)

THE ECKSTEIN LIFESTYLE INTERVIEW (ELSI)

DANIEL ECKSTEIN

Adapted from previous lifestyle instruments developed by Mosak, Schulman, Powers, Griffin, and Walton. Solution-focused questions by O-Harlon and InSoo Kim Berg have also been added as well as the Life Tasks suggested by Myers, Sweeney, and Witmer.

Counselors are requested to respect the client's right to "pass" on any of the questions.

I. The interviewee's current "way of being in the world" (present tense).
   A. The subjective situation:
      1. What are some of the things that bring you joy and happiness in your life now?

      _____

      2. What are your specific concerns physically and emotionally? _____

      _____

      3. What are your major stressors? Any major illness or sickness? _____

      _____

      4. What (if anything) do you do primarily with or for yourself alone that brings you happiness? _____

      5. What was the highlight of the last year for you personally? _____

      _____

      6. Can you remember a time recently when you pleasantly surprised yourself or did something out of character that pleased you? _____

      _____

      7. How do you think your friends would describe you? _____

      _____

      8. What do you consider to be some of your own reoccurring challenges? _____

      _____

      9. How might exploring your past, positively impact your present and future life?

      _____

B. Rating of life-tasks
   1. Rate yourself on a 1–10 scale, 1 being very low and 10 being very high, relative to your satisfaction with the following five tasks of living. List the numbers for each task. Ask for specific reasons why the person gave each numerical rating and fill in the response beneath the chart on the provided lines.

	Work (or School)	Friendship	Love	Self-Esteem	Spiritual/ Existential
10	□	□	□	□	□
9	□	□	□	□	□
8	□	□	□	□	□
7	□	□	□	□	□
6	□	□	□	□	□
5	□	□	□	□	□
4	□	□	□	□	□
3	□	□	□	□	□
2	□	□	□	□	□
1	□	□	□	□	□

   2. Explanation of ratings

     a. Work (or School)—Explanation of Rating _____

_____

_____

     b. Friendship—Explanation of Rating _____

_____

_____

     c. Love—Explanation of Rating _____

_____

_____

     d. Self-esteem—Explanation of Rating _____

_____

_____

     e. Spiritual/Existential—Explanation of Rating _____

_____

_____

C. Additional wellness self-direction assessments
Assess your own level of satisfaction (1 = low; 10 = high) on these dimensions. Provide a brief explanation of each rating.

1 - 10 Rating

1. ____   Self worth

Explanation of Rating _____

_____

_____

2. ____   Sense of control

Explanation of Rating _____

_____

_____

3. ____   Realistic beliefs

Explanation of Rating _____

_____

_____

4. ____   Emotional assessment and coping

Explanation of Rating _____

_____

_____

5. ____   Problem solving and creativity

Explanation of Rating _____

_____

_____

6. ____   Sense of humor

Explanation of Rating _____

_____

_____

7. ____   Nutrition

Explanation of Rating _____

_____

_____

8. ____ Exercise

Explanation of Rating _____

_____

_____

9. ____ Stress management

Explanation of Rating _____

_____

_____

10. ____ Gender identity

Explanation of Rating _____

_____

_____

11. ____ Cultural identity

Explanation of Rating _____

_____

_____

D. Reflective questions
   1. If you had all of the stresses, challenges, and concerns in your life resolved, how would your life be different?

   _____

   _____

   2. If you were to wake up tomorrow and a miracle has occurred in your life and all the challenges had been resolved, how would your life be different?

   _____

   _____

   3. Assume that the "miracle" occurred during the night when you were asleep, what small differences would you be able to identify the next morning that would indicate that indeed a miracle had occurred?

   _____

   _____

   4. What needs to be different in life to make your life more happy now?

   _____

   _____

5. How would others around you be able to know your life has changed in a posi-
    tive manner?

    _____

    _____

II. Family atmosphere

Now we are going to explore some significant events from your past. Answer these questions as you remember your experience as a child (past tense up to age seven).

A. The "naming" process
    1. Who decided your name?

    _____

    _____

    2. Were you named for someone or something special?

    _____

    _____

    3. How do you feel about your name?

    _____

    _____

    4. What nicknames have you had? What are your personal reactions to them?

    _____

    _____

    5. Have you ever wanted to (or actually) changed your name (e.g., last name
        through marriage)? If not, what name do you wish to have and why? If you have
        actually changed your name, how do you feel about your new name(s)?

    _____

    _____

B. Sibling descriptions

Write the name and age of each sibling (including yourself) in descending order beginning with the oldest. Include any deceased siblings, siblings separated from the family,
or siblings living elsewhere. Also note any other known pregnancies terminated by
abortion, miscarriage, or still-birth, entering the appropriate in the ordinal positions.
Include any step-siblings and note when they entered the family. Using your age as a
baseline, note the differences in years of age, plus or minus, between each other sibling
and yourself.

When you have listed all the siblings, describe each sibling again including yourself.
(Circle the appropriate sex, male or female, for each sibling. Attach another sheet if
needed for more siblings.)

	Sibling 1			Sibling 2			Sibling 3	
Name:		M F	Name:		M F	Name:		M F
Age:	+/-:		Age:	+/-:		Age:	+/-:	
Description:			Description:			Description:		

	Sibling 4			Sibling 5			Sibling 6	
Name:		M F	Name:		M F	Name:		M F
Age:	+/-:		Age:	+/-:		Age:	+/-:	
Description:			Description:			Description:		

C. Further sibling descriptions

The following questions are to be answered as you would have responded when you were a young child of three to eight years of age. If there were only two of you, answer each question in relation to your sibling. If you are a single child, answer the questions from the perspective of "children in general."

1. Who was most different from you? How? If you are an only child, in your peer group who was the most different from you? How?

_____

_____

_____

2. Who was most like you? How?

_____

_____

_____

3. Who fought and argued?

_____

_____

_____

4. Who played together?

_____

_____

_____

5. Who took care of whom?

_____

_____

_____

6. Who had a handicap or prolonged illness?

_____

_____

_____

D. Sibling ratings

Look over the following descriptive adjectives. Note three to five of the *most characteristic* descriptors for you as a child by circling the specific adjectives. Also note three to five descriptors that were *least characteristic* of you as a child by putting a box around them.

If you are an only child, rate yourself in comparison to the peer group you associated with as a child or with "children in general." Focus your ratings on your personal opinion of your family situation during the first seven years of your life as much as possible.

Now respond to each of the following characteristics by circling the adjectives that are most like you and boxing in the adjectives that are least like your characteristics.

Characteristic:

1. Intelligent	6. Rebellious	11. Getting one's way	16. Materialistic	21. Attractive
2. Hardest worker	7. A pleaser	12. Sensitive, easily hurt	17. Standards of accomplishment	22. Spoiled
3. Best grades in school	8. Critical of others	13. Temper tantrums	18. Athletic	23. Punished
4. Helped around the house	9. Considerate	14. Sense of humor	19. Physically strong	24. Spontaneous
5. Conforming	10. Selfishness	15. Idealistic	20. Emotionally strong	25. Any other descriptive objectives

E. Additional childhood and adolescent developmental considerations
   1. What were your favorite TV stories, movies, books, video games, or fairy tales that you remember as a child? What was it about them that you liked?

_____

_____

_____

   2. What were some of your major childhood fears or traumas?

_____

_____

_____

3. What were your major hopes and dreams as a child?

_____

_____

_____

4. Were you ever physically or sexually abused? If so, by whom?

_____

_____

_____

5. Were there any incidents of alcohol and/or drug abuse in your family? If so, describe its impact on you.

_____

_____

_____

6. Describe your bodily development (height, weight, speed, strength, etc.) as an adolescent in relationship to your peers. Were you more mature, average with others, or a "late bloomer"? Did you have any specific difficulties (e.g., bedwetting, rocking back and forth) as a child and/or adolescent?

_____

_____

_____

7. a. Describe a memorable or formulative adolescent experience:

_____

_____

_____

b. What were your feelings about the incident?

_____

_____

_____

c. What conclusion(s) do you feel you made about that incident?

_____

_____

_____

F.   Description of parents (select either parent to describe first)
   1.   Father

   Current Age: _____ Occupation: _____

   Description of Father

   _____

   _____

   _____

   Father's favorite child? Why?

   _____

   _____

   _____

   Ambitions for his children?

   _____

   _____

   _____

   Emotional relationship to children?

   _____

   _____

   _____

   Which sibling was most like the father? In what way(s)?

   _____

   _____

   _____

   2.   Mother

   Current Age: _____ Occupation:

   Description of Mother:

   _____

   _____

   _____

   Mother's favorite child? Why?

   _____

   _____

   _____

Ambitions for her children?

_____

_____

_____

Emotional relationship to children?

_____

_____

_____

Which sibling was most like the mother? In what way(s)?

_____

_____

_____

3. If you were very honest, which of your parents (if any) was your personal favorite? Why?

_____

_____

_____

4. Describe the nature of your parents' relationship.

_____

_____

_____

5. What do you feel were some of the primary values that your parent(s) (or parent equivalents) had for the children?

_____

_____

_____

6. To what extent did you accept, reject, or modify the family motto and other family values?

_____

_____

_____

7. What was the "family motto" your parents had for their children?

_____

_____

_____

8. Stepfather or stepmother (if appropriate)

Current Age _____ Occupation: _____

Description:

_____

_____

_____

His or her favorite child? Why?

_____

_____

_____

His or her ambitions for the children?

_____

_____

_____

Emotional relationship to children?

_____

_____

_____

Which sibling was most like him/her? In what way(s)?

_____

_____

_____

9. If a stepfather or stepmother has been in your life, how has that affected you?

_____

_____

_____

10. If there were other parental figures in your family, describe the effect they have had on your personality.

_____

_____

_____

11. Were there any other significant people in your life in childhood (aunts, uncles, cousins, teachers, priest, rabbi, minister, friend, etc.)? If so, describe their effect on your life:

_____

_____

_____

12. Describe your opinion of the impact of your own spiritual and cultural heritage (for example, what special holidays do you observe? How?)

_____

_____

_____

13. Growing up did you consider yourself to be the majority or the minority culture in your community? What were the implications of being in the majority or the minority of your community?

_____

_____

_____

III. Early Recollections

Think back as far as you can and describe the first specific incident that you remember. Describe what feeling you had at that time. Make sure it is a specific situation and not a generalization. If you had a memorable or recurring dream when you were a child, describe the dream and discuss how you felt.

INTERVIEWER NOTE: Write the ER word for word in the person's own language. Keep asking "and then what happened?" until the memory fades from conscious awareness.

A. First incident

Description:

_____

_____

_____

_____

_____

_____

_____

_____

_____

_____

Most vivid moment:

_____

_____

_____

Your feeling(s):

_____

_____

B.   Second incident
     Description:

_____

_____

_____

_____

_____

_____

_____

_____

_____

_____

Most vivid moment:

_____

_____

_____

Your feeling(s):

_____

_____

C. Third incident
    Description:

    _____
    _____
    _____
    _____
    _____
    _____
    _____
    _____
    _____

    Most vivid moment:

    _____
    _____
    _____

    Your feeling(s):

    _____
    _____

D. Memorable or recurring dream
    Description:

    _____
    _____
    _____
    _____
    _____
    _____
    _____
    _____

    Most vivid moment:

    _____
    _____
    _____

Your feeling:

_____

_____

E. Global reflections on all memories and dreams:
    1. If you could change anything or anyone in these incidents, how would it or they
        be different?

        _____

        _____

        _____

        _____

        _____

        _____

    2. Can you think of any connections these past events may have to your present life?

        _____

        _____

        _____

        _____

        _____

        _____

    3. What do you think some future indications, trends, or patterns might be indicated
        from these formulative experiences?

        _____

        _____

        _____

        _____

        _____

        _____

4. Is there anything else you would like to add regarding events/experiences/people in your life?

_____

_____

_____

_____

_____

_____

5. Please conclude by sharing a "peak experience," an extra special moment in your life when you felt especially happy.

_____

_____

_____

_____

_____

_____

_____

Thank you !

CHILDREN'S LIFESTYLE GUIDE (CLG)

Don Dinkmeyer, Sr., and Don Dinkmeyer, Jr.,[25] developed a children's lifestyle guide (CLG). The CLG has eight major sections, six of which are completed with information from the child, and two are summaries by the counselor.

I. Family Constellation
    A. List all members of the family from oldest to youngest.

    _____

    _____

    _____

    B. Answer the following questions:
        1. Who is most different from you? How?

        _____

        _____

        _____

        2. Who is most like you? How?

        _____

        _____

        _____

        3. What was life like before you went to school?

        _____

        _____

        _____

II. Functioning at Life Tasks
    A. Socially: How do you get along with adults? Children?

    _____

    _____

    _____

(Adapted from Dinkmeyer and Dinkmeyer, "Concise Counseling Assessment: The Children's Lifestyle Guide." *Elementary School Guidance & Guidance & Counseling* 12, no. 2 (1977): 117-124. Reproduced in Eckstein, Baruth, and Mahrer. *An Introduction to Lifestyle Assessment.* Dubuque, IA: Kendall/Hunt Publishing Company, 1992. Used by permission of the authors.)

B.   Work: How do things go for you in school?

_____

_____

_____

C.   What subject do you like best? Like least? Why?

_____

_____

_____

D.   What would you like to be when you grow up?

_____

_____

_____

E.   What do you fear the most?

_____

_____

_____

III.   Family Atmosphere
A.   What kind of a person is your father?

_____

_____

_____

B.   What kind of a person is your mother?

_____

_____

_____

C.   Which of the children is most like your father? In what ways?

_____

_____

_____

D.   Which of the children is most like your mother? In what ways?

_____

_____

_____

IV.   Sibling Characteristics

A series of questions (such as "Who is most intelligent?") are asked until a child makes a response to each item with respect to other siblings or other children in general.

A.   Smartest _____

B.   Hardest worker _____

C.   Best grades in school _____

D.   Does what others expect _____

E.   Gets in trouble _____

F.   Helps around the house _____

G.   Critical/not nice to others _____

H.   Nice _____

I.   Thinks mostly of oneself _____

J.   Tries to please others _____

K.   Gets feelings easily hurt _____

L.   Temper _____

M.   Likes to get nice things _____

N.   Most friends _____

O.   Most spoiled _____

P.   Wants to do a lot _____

Q.   Athletic _____

R.   Strongest _____

S.   Attractive/prettiest _____

T.   Most punished _____

V.   Early Recollections

What can you remember that is a specific event (like a picture of one certain time) from when you were younger? What were you feeling at the time?

A.   Memory One

_____

_____

_____

Feeling

_____

_____

B.   Memory Two

_____

_____

_____

Feeling

_____

_____

C.   Memory Three

_____

_____

_____

Feeling

_____

_____

VI. Three Wishes and Fantasy
     A.   If you could have three wishes, what would they be?

     1. _____
     2. _____

     3. _____

     B.   If you were going to pretend to be an animal, which would you choose? Why?

VII. Summary

Utilizing the information in Chapter 4 on interpretation skills, write a summary of the family constellation, including birth order and sibling ratings. Summarize general lifestyle themes, the "Number-one Priority," and early recollections.

_____

_____

_____

_____

_____

_____

_____

_____

_____

_____

_____

_____

_____

_____

_____

_____

_____

_____

_____

_____

_____

_____

_____

_____

_____

_____

Frank Walton[26] adapted the following format originally developed by Robert Powers for use in adolescent and adult groups.

Part I: A Guide for Presenting Yourself to the Seminar

    A.   You have ten minutes, uninterrupted, in which to tell us who you are.

    B.   Stay, as much as possible, in the present tense. Later on you will have an opportunity to tell us about your childhood.

    C.   Life challenges each of us, and each person is now approaching challenges in a way unique to him/herself. Tell us about your responses to these challenges.

        1.   What kind of friends have you made? What kind of friend are you? How do you get along with strangers in chance meetings? How do people treat you generally? How do you feel about other people most of the time?

        2.   What kind of work do you do? What kind of worker are you? Do you enjoy what you are doing? Do those with whom or for whom you work appreciate your contributions?

        3.   Whom do you love? What kinds of problems have you had over loving and being loved? Do sex, closeness, and intimacy have a comfortable place in your life or not? What does masculinity mean to you? What does femininity mean to you? How do you measure up to whatever you expect of yourself as a man or a woman?

Part II: A Guide for Sharing in Responses

    A.   Someone has just spent ten minutes presenting himself or herself. How did you receive what he/she has presented?

    B.   Did you recognize things in yourself that were mentioned? Was it easy or difficult to understand him or her? Did he/she sound strange or familiar?

    C.   How do you feel toward one another? Did your feelings toward anyone change as a result of the sharing? How?

    D.   Do you feel invited to act in any particular way toward another? Did you welcome that invitation or resent it? What would you like to do for this person? What would you like to do with this person? What would you like to do to this person?

Part III: A Guide for Drawing Your Family Constellation

In childhood each of us learned how to define the place he/she had amongst others. Help the members of the seminar to see the kind of place you had as a pre-adolescent child in your family.

A. How many children were there in your family and where did you fit in among them? How were you different from the others, and how were you like them? Which of the others was most nearly like you, and which was most different? What were you good at? What was hard for you?

B. What was your father like? Who was his favorite?

C. What did he expect from you?

D. How did you feel about his expectations?

E. What was your mother like? Who was her favorite? What did she expect from you?

F. How did you feel about her expectations?

G. How did your parents get along with each other? What were their differences/arguments/fights about? To which parent did you feel closer? Why?

H. Were grandparents or other relatives important to you? How?

I. Did anything change at adolescence? How? What did puberty, physical development, and dating mean to you?

    1. Males: What did "being a man" mean to you? Did you think you would have been happier, luckier, better off if you had been born a girl?

    2. Females: What did "being a woman" mean to you? Did you think you would have been happier, luckier, better off if you had been born a boy?

Part IV: A Guide for Discussing a Family Constellation

A. Can you share any feelings about yourself in your family with the person who just told you about his or her childhood?

B. Can you understand this person better? How?

C. Can you see something as a result of the sharing that initially didn't make sense to you?

D. What more do you want to know about this person?

E. Can you see a relationship between the role played as a child, in the family and among other children, and the way in which he or she has tried to find a place in this seminar?

F. Each of us has the private goal of playing a certain kind of social role.

Parts I and II are repeated for each member of the group before the group moves on to Parts III and IV, which are also repeated for each member of the group. A fifth and sixth part can be added at the option of the leader. Part V would consist of obtaining two or three early memories, while Part VI would be devoted to the interpretation of the memories by the leader and participants. These additional segments are limited to ten minutes each in the fashion of Parts I through IV.

A group may terminate at the conclusion of Part IV or Part VI, or it may continue to meet periodically in order to help group members work at relating the increased awareness of the purposes and patterns of their behavior to the challenges of social living.

Frank Walton has also developed the following five "Brief Lifestyle Clues." These can be used as part of a general counseling session or part of a family or couples session, or in a group setting. It provides a "snapshot" or a "one-minute manager's lifestyle" from which the therapist can formulate some tentative hypotheses.

Brief Lifestyle Clues

Introduction

My effort to be encouraging to clients (by being helpful to them quickly) stimulated me to be parsimonious in my questioning when gathering lifestyle clues. Clients can make substantial progress in understanding their approach to life (and its relationship to presenting problems) in the initial session. The practitioner can also offer a holistic interpretation of the answers to five questions. Additional data can be gathered in subsequent sessions when desired.

1. I was the kid who always . . .

    _____

    _____

2. Which brother or sister was most different from you? How?

    _____

    _____

3. a. What was most positive about your mother?

        _____

        _____

    . . . about your father?

        _____

        _____

    b. What did you reject or wish was different about your mother?

        _____

        _____

    about your father?

        _____

        _____

4. Do you remember making some conclusion or observation about life when you were a child or teenager that seemed very important? Perhaps a conclusion about how you wanted life to be different for you when you became an adult, or perhaps something you wanted to be exactly the same when you became an adult?

_____

_____

_____

_____

_____

_____

_____

_____

5. Describe two early memories (recollections).

_____

_____

_____

_____

_____

_____

_____

_____

_____

_____

_____

_____

_____

_____

_____

_____

_____

The Most Memorable Adolescent Observation

Francis Walton has also developed what he calls "the most memorable observations, an Adlerian technique, by utilizing an autobiographical memory for understanding the belief system of parenting style." Counselors can use the following instructions in helping to identify such a memorable observation.

He notes that "Sometime in our early teenage years, or even in late preteen years, it seems very common for each of us to look around our family life and draw a conclusion about some aspect of life that appears to be important. Sometimes it is positive, 'I really like this aspect of life in our family. When I get to be an adult I'd like it to be just this way in my own family.' Often it is negative, 'I don't like this at all. This is really distasteful. When I get to be an adult I am going to do everything I can to keep this from occurring to my family.' What was it for you? As you think of life in your family about age 11, 12, 13 or so, what conclusion do you think you drew? It may have been positive, it may have been negative, or it may have been both.[27]

Your most memorable adolescent observation

_____

_____

_____

_____

_____

_____

_____

_____

_____

_____

_____

_____

_____

_____

_____

_____

_____

_____

Case Study #1

The parents had expressed concern about their six-year-old daughter who was causing disruptions at school and had been diagnosed with attention deficit hyperactivity disorder. When asked to relate a memorable adolescent observation, the father replied:

"Sure, I remember. You see, I came from a large family. My parents seemed to have time for everybody in the family except me. I promised myself when I got to be a father, I would never let that happen to a child of mine."

Walton interpreted the experience by observing that the father's basic belief: "Neglect is painful to a child. I would be remiss as a parent if I did not provide attention to my child."

The influence of overcompensation regarding this case might include ideas like: The amount of attention lavished on Sally made attention-getting behavior useful and greatly reduced opportunities for her to learn skills necessary for cooperative social interaction.[28]

Case Study #2

A second case study involved an eight-year-old daughter who according to the parents "will not do her work and can't follow directions. She always is moving and tries to get her way. She wants me to sit with her and help her do her homework."

Here is the mother's memorable adolescent observations: "I remember the role my mother played. She was a maid to everyone." (She breaks into tears.) Walton then offers the following interpretation for her consideration: "A good woman lays down her life for her family, but the thought of weakness of such a role is more than I can take at times. The mother's belief system has influenced her to be a servant to her family, even a martyr, but she resents the role she has accepted. She provides service in an effort to be good enough, but she hates it and frequently erupts into anger, yelling and screaming."

Walton makes additional comments regarding both positive and negative memorable observations. "Negative observations reveal situations or a particular kind of problem that the client attempts to guard against the life of the present family. The positive observations indicate what the client is striving to accomplish, while also alerting the counselor to what would constitute a position of inferiority in the mind of the client, that being defined as the absence of the positive quality or circumstances the client guards against."[29]

In interpreting the most memorable adolescent observation, counselors are encouraged to point out the reasonableness of the client's parenting style and technique, given the situation the client so strongly wishes to avoid. Often the parent's desire is either to help the family avoid what they have experienced so negatively, or to help the family avoid missing out on a situation that the parent has concluded is extremely valuable.

Walton believes that memorable adolescent observations indicate the following three types of parental compensations for which the situation has been protected.

1. The parent(s) overemphasize(s) the likelihood of occurrence of the situation guarded against.
2. The parent(s) overemphasize(s) the negative influence of such a situation if it should occur.
3. The parent(s) underestimate(s) his or her ability to deal with the situation in an effective problem-solving way if it should occur.

Here are some counselor suggestions in talking with adults about their most memorable experiences.

1. It is the same style that takes us to our successes that also leads us to our difficulties.

2. The therapist can find specific examples of the client's overemphasizing the likelihood of occurrence of the situation guarded against, and/or overemphasizing how bad it will be if that situation does occur.

3. They can be helped to develop a repertoire of techniques to deal with challenging situations. Walton notes "By showing the client how the use of the techniques can help bring about the desired scenario, the therapist can stimulate the client to be encouraged and to be motivated in implementing the newly learned techniques. For example, by setting limits for a child instead of giving in, the parent can help the child learn to respect the concerns of fellow humans, thus resulting in more instances of the cooperative, kind behavior which the parent had previously sought in mistaken ways. The therapist might show the parent who guards against loss of control how much less likely it is for her to feel she has no positive influence upon loved ones when she discards dominating, coercive behavior and substitutes techniques that have established their value for winning the cooperation of children and adolescents."[30]

Making the Lifestyle Concept Measurable

Roy Kern, EdD, Jason Snow, PhD, and Kelli Ritter, EdS

For many years the clinical assessment tools described so far in this chapter have provided clinicians with systematic procedures to conduct the lifestyle assessment. However, through this period from the inception of the inventories and guides there have constantly been questions raised by scholars that there was little if any research based studies to show the existence of this construct coined by Adler. In some ways, this inhibited the expansion of this valuable construct to the broader community. Some would say that with the limited recognition that the only believers in this construct were those who adhered to the principles of Individual Psychology. From a scholarly or academic perspective, Adlerians would rebuke these critics with the argument that there is little need to research a construct that has shown its existence and usefulness through the test of time in clinical practice. Yet, the constant move toward accountability, managed care, and empiricism in our clinical practices behooves the users of the construct to answer the question of, "does this construct really exist?" and if so "can it be measured from a quantitative perspective?"

The purpose of this section will be to provide the reader with a 25-year research journey related to the development of objective lifestyle instruments that were employed for research and as clinical and educational instruments for professionals and organizational consultants. The journey will begin with a developmental history that will include the empirical, clinical, and educational findings related to the process. The first portion of the chapter will trace and explain the rationale for need to objectify the lifestyle construct. This will be followed with an overview of the Lifestyle Questionnaire Inventory (LQI), the Kern Lifestyle Scale (KLS), and the Lifestyle Personality Inventory (LPI). The final segment of the chapter will be devoted to the most used lifestyle objective instrument in North America and Europe, the Basic Adlerian Scales for Interpersonal Success -Adult Form (BASIS-A). The explanation of the instrument will include a description of the BASIS-A, the psychometric properties, a variety of ways in which the instrument is used, and conclude with a comprehensive review of research related to the instrument.

IN THE BEGINNING

Alfred Adler created the lifestyle concept in the early 1900s. This construct can be viewed as a cluster of personality attributes that an individual subjectively arranges into a systematic schema at a very early age. The young child, within the social context of the family, creates this schema or lifestyle. Adler believed the individual developed his/her lifestyle along a line that was most helpful for him/her to solve problems related to three life tasks: social interactions with peers, work (or productivity), and intimacy. Adler talked about lifestyle as a construct and proposed four broad ways of categorizing the lifestyles of individuals. These four types of lifestyle themes or priorities were named *useful*, *getting*, *ruling* and *avoiding* as cited in Ansbacher & Ansbacher.[31] Adler was a strong proponent of education and the application of theory. The chapter content to this point has clearly highlighted the impact of Adler's ideas on lifestyle with the extensive descriptions of questionnaires, guides, and inventories developed by his followers.

In fact, the questionnaire or interview guides described herein are the standard interviewing tools used to teach students and professionals to conduct lifestyle interviews in most university or clinical settings. The Lifestyle questionnaire or guide is an instrument with open-ended questions designed to help the clinician collect family dynamics information, ordinal position (or birth order) characteristics, and early recollections (a projective technique asking the client to recall early memories). To acquire a knowledge and skill level base for using the guide, the potential user could attend universities/professional schools and study with the masters of the use of the instrument. Other educational opportunities that developed later were workshops where the master lifestyle interviewers presented at conferences like North American Society of Adlerian Psychology (NASAP) and the International Congress of Adlerian Summer Schools Institutes (ICASSI).

The first author (Kern) had the opportunity to observe the masters interviewing clients. Rudolph Dreikurs, Harold Mosak, Bob Powers, and Manford Sontegard mesmerized him, as each spun their own unique way of collecting information related to the use of the lifestyle interview process. For example, one of the masters might follow a very cognitive systematic data collection process, whereas another would skip from one question to another. One would formulate the majority of his ideas on the individual's lifestyle by simply asking questions about the client's family constellation; however, another would go directly to the collection of early recollections. The observer watching the process, whether a novice or experienced clinician, might get the impression that the masters were practicing some form of astrology versus psychology. Each with their own unique interviewing style was effective in helping the client understand lifestyle dynamics and problem areas. Yet, there were inherent problems voiced by many professionals related to this procedure. This problem was that a great deal of time and clinical knowledge was necessary to identify what information was most important. Furthermore, a high level of skill, time, and experience was required to decide what information was relevant as it related to making a clinical judgment on a client's lifestyle.

THE LIFESTYLE QUESTIONNAIRE INVENTORY (LQI)

Over the years, as Kern was teaching students and clinicians about the use of the lifestyle interview and its importance, he and his colleagues began to discuss and to conceptualize the possibilities of investigating the lifestyle construct from a more quantifiable research base perspective. Through dialogues with colleagues and with encouragement by students, the Lifestyle Questionnaire Inventory (LQI) was developed in 1973. The inventory was based on the original questions used by Adler in his clinical interview guide but with the added dimension of a Likert scale that allowed assessment of the many personality characteristics or attributes related to ordinal position and parental attributes. The instrument is a paper and pencil research tool or it can be used as a structured interview inventory for the clinician. The LQI was the first attempt to develop an instrument based on the total lifestyle questionnaire interview.

From the development of this instrument the quantification of the lifestyle construct was implemented at Georgia State University in Atlanta, Georgia. The research on this inventory was conducted over a five-year period. The empirical studies focused on topics related to career choice,[32] the association of lifestyles to particular clinical codes on the Diagnostic Statistical Manual Third Edition (DSM III),[33] and findings that novice counselors could recognize lifestyle themes from written information on the LQI.[34] The most consistent finding of this body of research was that Adlerian experts were able to agree upon specific lifestyle themes based exclusively on written protocols completed by subjects in the studies. The second consistent finding was that the experts, regardless of sample, were only identifying a limited number of lifestyle themes. Despite these encouraging findings, the instrument did have limitations. Research on the LQI required extensive effort and time to identify qualified Adlerians to rate and assess the protocols for each of the studies. It was from this research effort that a second lifestyle instrument was created.

KERN LIFESTYLE SCALE (KLS)

As Kern continued to employ the LQI to teach the lifestyle concept to his students at the university, he continued to receive comments from students and others that a more objective measure of lifestyle was needed. Students and clinicians desired an instrument that was paper and pencil in nature, but that did not require expert raters, or the extensive time needed to conduct the clinical interview. Utilizing his experiences and knowledge obtained from research on the LQI coupled with clinical observations of some ten years, he developed the first objective paper-and-pencil instrument to measure lifestyle in 1975.

The Kern Lifestyle Scale (KLS) is a 35-item instrument possessing five scales: *Control*, *Perfection*, *Need to Please*, *Self-esteem*, and *Expectations*. One of the benefits of the KLS is that the instrument takes less than ten minutes to complete. The client is requested to assign a rating on a five-point rating system of how close any given item is similar to their beliefs about themselves. Once the individual completes the instrument, the clinician is able to provide immediate feedback to the client based on the information provided in the interpretative manual created for the KLS. Though there are several research studies on this instrument,[35,36] its major contribution to the objective lifestyle process is that in a short period of time the clinician can acquire lifestyle information in approximately ten minutes on the client or individual under review. In addition, the instrument is easy to administer in workshop settings. The instrument can be used with teachers, parents, high school students and professionals. To follow are brief descriptions of each scale.

The *Control* Scale assesses a person's need to direct others, control emotions, and to approach problems in a rational logical fashion. The *Perfection* Scale identifies a person's need to work hard at organizing his/her life and to avoid mistakes. The *Need to Please* Scale focuses on how important it is for the individual to go along with others, not cause interpersonal problems, and work hard at being liked by all. The *Self esteem* Scale addresses an individual's belief that he/she can handle most of life's problems and that one can encourage others and oneself. Finally, the *Expectation* Scale is designed to assess how realistic an individual is in setting goals and in setting expectations on self and others. More extensive scale descriptions are available in the interpretative manual and Chapter 4 in this text. As alluded to earlier, the instrument is unique in that it takes less than fifteen minutes to complete and can be used in clinical and non-clinical settings. An additional advantage is it requires no clinical interview. It also set the stage for research designed to create additional objective lifestyle instruments as well as the four priorities instrument developed by Steven Langenfeld. To date, the instrument has been translated into Chinese, Greek, Korean, Latvian, Lithuanian, and Estonian languages. (To obtain further information on the instrument the reader can access the publishers by e-mail CMTI Press@ earthlink.com or the Website cmtipress.com.)

THE LIFESTYLE PERSONALITY INVENTORY (LPI)

During the time the KLS was in use by students and professionals another instrument called the Lifestyle Personality Inventory (LPI) was being developed by the research team of Wheeler, Kern, and Curlette. Between 1978 and 1993 the LPI, the predecessor of the Basic Adlerian Scales for Interpersonal Success—Adult Form (BASIS-A), was employed in numerous empirical studies. The LPI studies included research with couples,[37,38] clinical populations,[39,40] employees in organizational settings,[41,42] parents,[43] substance abusers,[44,45] normative studies,[46–48] and a unique study designed to assess leadership, team, and personality attributes in a outdoor ropes experiences.[49] The findings and applications of these studies were presented at conferences and workshops in North America and abroad.

Again, a consistent finding from the combined research on the Lifestyle Questionnaire Inventory (LQI) and the Lifestyle Personality Inventory (LPI) was the limited number of lifestyle themes or typologies that were identified by Adlerian experts and factor analytic studies. Another major finding was that the choice of the actual words for describing several of the scales or themes tended to be confusing and discouraging to individuals using the instruments. The authors listened to the feedback and came to a similar conclusion. For example, in retrospect, it is easy to see how lifestyle themes or scale labels such as "victim, martyr, exploitive, or discouragement" might be difficult to use in therapy with clients who are discouraged or vulnerable.

BASIC ADLERIAN SCALES FOR INTERPERSONAL SUCCESS— ADULT FORM (BASIS-A)

By 1993, and 20 years of research on three instruments (the LQI, KLS, and LPI), a new instrument was introduced that combined the strengths as well as the corrective feedback from professionals and consumers. This new pencil and paper instrument, with more client-friendly scale names, is the *Basic Adlerian Scales for Interpersonal Success—Adult Form (BASIS-A)*. The procedures for instrument development, reliability, validity, and empirical studies plus the meaning of the scales and how to present the information to individuals is currently available in the technical and interpretative manuals that accompany the instrument. The instrument is widely researched, listed in *Test in Print*, and reviewed in the *Burros Mental Measurement Yearbook*. One of the reviewers for *Burros Mental Measurement Yearbook* reported that the BASIS-A was the instrument of choice for individuals wishing to apply an empirical approach to the lifestyle construct.[50]

The BASIS-A is a 65-item standardized objective inventory that can be used for research or as a clinical or educational tool for clinicians, educators, and organizational personnel. The BASIS-A yields a profile of five major scales and five supporting scales. Internal consistency estimates on the five major scales yield alpha coefficients ranging from .82 to .87. Test-retest coefficients based on a one to four week interval yielded coefficients of .81 to .90.[51] Numerous studies related to reliability and validity issues on BASIS-A support the structure of the scales and the overall psychometric properties of the instrument.[52]

The five major scales are named *Belonging-Social Interest, Going Along, Taking Charge, Wanting Recognition*, and *Being Cautious*. The *Belonging-Social Interest* scale measures a person's sense of community involvement. People who score high on this scale tend to be extroverted and prefer group interactions, whereas people low on this scale tend to be introverted and prefer one-on-one interactions with others. The *Going Along* scale measures how rule-focused a person tends to be in the three life task of social, work and intimacy areas. People who score high on this scale tend to prefer rules and organization, whereas people low on this scale tend to disregard rules or rebel against them. The *Taking Charge* scale measures how comfortable one is with directing others. People who score high on this scale tend to be more dominant in social groups and tend to direct others, whereas those who score low on this scale prefer to have others take on the responsibility of leadership in social situations. The *Wanting Recognition* scale measures how much importance one places on opinions from others. People who score high on this scale tend to desire reassurance or feedback from others on a job well done, whereas people who score low on this scale tend to place little value on feedback from others so long as they feel good about their own accomplishments. The *Being Cautious* scale measures how trusting an individual is in interpersonal situations. People who score high on this scale tend to be highly suspicious or skeptical of the motivations of others, whereas people who score low on this scale tend to be more trusting and accepting of others at face value.

The supporting scales on the BASIS-A are referred to by their acronym (HELPS) and are *Harshness, Entitlement, Liked by All, Striving for Perfection*, and *Softness* scales. The *Harshness* scale measures whether a person tends to have a negative self-view. The *Entitlement* scale measures whether a person tends to prefer being treated as special or unique in social settings. The *Liked by All* scale measures whether one places an importance on the approval from others. The *Striving for Perfection* scale measures a person's level of organization, problem-solving, and stress coping skills. The *Softness* scale tends to measure the level of optimism one has about self and the world. Because the HELPS scales are interpreted in terms of cut scores, reliability of the scales is assessed based on the coefficient of agreement for two administrations. A coefficient of agreement is described as the probability of classifying a person consistently into a category upon two administrations of an assessment instrument.[53] The coefficient of agreement on the HELPS scales ranges from .92 to 1.00.[54]

BASIS-A RESEARCH

Since its introduction in 1993, there have been numerous research-based articles, a large number of dissertations, as well as narrative publications that have employed the BASIS-A. The publications have addressed a wide variety of research populations and topics.

Research and publications using the BASIS-A include assessment in supervision,[55] teacher's lifestyles,[56,57] profiles of incarcerated individuals[58,59] and parolees,[60] coping resources and stress in relation to lifestyle,[61] the relationship between self-efficacy and lifestyle,[62] lifestyle and participant attrition in parenting education groups,[63] predictive aspects of substance abusers,[64] profiles of ADHD young adults,[65] sexually abused adolescents,[66] aggressive adolescents,[67] emotional behavioral disordered adolescents,[68] insulin dependent diabetic patients,[69] seminary couples,[70] and articles related to interpretative uses and interpretations of the instrument.[71,72] To follow is a brief summary of some of the studies.

The survey begins with two studies assessing teachers' lifestyles relative to their perceptions of classroom climate and to children's behavior in school settings. The first study was completed with 115 graduate students enrolled in a college of education in southeastern United States.[73] The study revealed that teachers scoring high on the Taking Charge scale also scored high on Pupil Control Ideology. Pupil Control Ideology (PCI) is defined as a concept, separating democratic style classrooms from the traditional style classrooms. How a teacher uses discipline versus punishment to control student behavior in the classroom defines their Pupil Control Ideology. Lower scores on the PCI scale indicates a more humanistic attitude toward behavior control in the classroom. Teachers who score high on the PCI scale employ a custodial or authoritarian attitude toward managing children in the classroom. There were also significant findings reported in the study of the positive association of the Striving for Perfection supportive scale on the BASIS-A and Pupil Control Ideology scale. One of several interesting findings by the researchers in this study is that high school teachers when compared to elementary school teachers are more likely to endorse a more authoritarian or traditional style as it relates to disciplining students in the classroom setting. A second study assessed the impact of a teacher's level of social interest on their perceptions of children's behavior in the classroom.[74] Results from 62 teachers and 1,366 students participating in this study indicate that the greater a teacher's level of social interest, as measured by the Belonging-Social Interest scale, the less disruptive behaviors the teachers perceived in the classroom. Along the educational theme, but with a parent sample, the BASIS-A was employed to assess its potential discriminate function as it related to the prediction of parents who would complete a series of ten week Systematic Training for Effective Parenting courses.[75] The Entitlement Scale was the only scale on the instrument that was found to identify parents who were most likely not to complete the ten-week experience. The value of this study is that it identified for the first time in the extended period of time that Adlerian parent education courses have been conducted for specific information and reasons for attrition. The authors provide specific recommendations for maintaining attendance in these groups.

Moving from single scale score results, another group of studies were conducted using a profiling approach to describe research results. Kutchins, Curlette and Kern[76] discovered a new way to use BASIS-A scores. They decided that more information was attainable by viewing combinations of high and low scores related to the sample population under review. This study examined lifestyle by comparing the BASIS-A results with the Langenfeld Inventory of Personality Priorities. The sample of the study included 210 undergraduate students.

Specifically the data analysis approach focused upon what combinations of high and low scores are representative of certain clinical or non-clinical populations. Thus began a change in research focus with the BASIS-A towards the assessment and use of the trend of combinations of scores and profiling. Additional research with clinical populations begins with Bauman,[77] who studied the use of the BASIS-A with substance abusers. He found four scales that significantly differentiated participants (160) with a substance abuse diagnosis from those with a psychiatric diagnosis. The four scales were Going Along (negatively), Taking Charge (positively), Wanting Recognition (negatively), and Liked by All (negatively). The importance of this study is that clinicians now have a tool from an Individual Psychology perspective to assess potential substance abusers within a clinical setting.

Other clinical population included inmates, adjudicated youth, and parolees. Two studies to date using the BASIS-A with inmates found three criminal profiles.[78,79] Of interest to the researchers is that these two studies identified similar profiles related to these populations. In general, the profiles that surfaced in both studies are three different groups of prisoners related to lifestyle dynamics. One group appears to be similar to the normal population; another resembles the classical criminal profile in the literature while a third group consists of the psychologically impaired. Another study conducted by a team of researchers revealed similar profiles in a group of adjudicated youth.[80] Adding to the research on antisocial behavior are the two studies completed by Kemp and Center.[81] Their first study focused on the socialization of young adult parolees. They administered the BASIS-A, the Eysenck Personality Questionnaire, and the National Youth Survey. The BASIS-A findings of interest were that the parolee sample when compared to a norming group has lower scores on the Going Along and the Wanting Recognition scales. A second study investigated the socialization variable in a sample of matched pairs of 75 emotionally and behaviorally disordered youth between the ages of eleven and eighteen. Findings with this group support the contention that the behaviorally disordered youth score significantly lower on the GA and WR. In addition, these youth score higher on the H, TC, and BC scales. The conclusions related to these findings are that the scores on the BASIS-A Scales reflect weak socialization skills in the targeted sample. The importance of these studies is that again the profiles of former studies are being further supported.[82]

In continuing with the clinical population research, Attention Deficit Hyperactivity Disorder in college age and adult populations has been investigated from a lifestyle perspective.[83,84] In a study whereby the screening of ADHD clients is optimal as it relates to paper pencil, clinical, and physiological assessment procedures, Dinter[85] found that the high and low scores on the Going Along scale were able to be used to correctly predict membership in the ADHD diagnosed group as well as participants in the Quasi-ADHD group who exhibited ADHD symptoms but who were not diagnosed as ADHD clients. The prediction or placement in to the correct groups was achieved at a rate of 69%. The Going Along and the Taking Charge scales were found to be significantly elevated in the college age sample researched by Kern et al.[86] These two studies are important in that the findings provide a holistic perspective of people with ADHD. These studies also highlight the potential interrelatedness of lifestyle personality attributes and ADHD symptoms in young and older adults.

Consistent results were obtained related to social interest and cooperation with abused adolescents. This study assessed the impact of sexual abuse on development of lifestyle.[87] Sixteen girls living in a residential treatment facility for sexually abused adolescents completed the BASIS-A and MMPI-A. The results, although not surprising, are very discouraging in terms of the apparent lasting damage sexual abuse has on an individual's personality. These girls show a general lack of social interest and cooperation with low Going Along and Wanting Recognition scores, and elevated scores on the Being Cautious Scale. This profile paints a picture of someone who has little concern for rules, does not cooperate, and is generally untrusting of others. These results are consistent with the earlier mentioned results of individuals lacking positive early socialization experiences.[88–91] Thus, it appears clear that Adler[92] was correct in saying that development of cooperation and social interest is key in development of a healthy lifestyle.

Moving from clinical to non-clinical groups, the instrument also shows promise in the areas of health, wellness, self-esteem, and the acculturation process. A study using the BASIS-A and the Coping Resources Inventory for Stress (CRIS) revealed that six of the ten scales correlate with the measure of overall Coping Resource Effectiveness (CRE). Specifically, these correlations with the CRE are Belonging-Social Interest, Softness, Striving for Perfection, Being Cautious, Harshness, and Going Along. Research in this area provides the researcher and consumer with an objective instrument to quickly assess stress coping styles. A recent study conducted on the relationship of self-efficacy and lifestyle patterns found that higher Belonging-Social Interest and Striving for Perfection scores had higher general self-efficacy scores.[93] Another study was conducted related to the area of acculturation with a population of Latino adults.[94] Results indicated that bicultural Latinos had a higher mean score for Belonging Social Interest and Taking Charge scales than did participants with either low or high acculturation. These findings are of high value for educators and clinicians because each of these studies demonstrates the relationship of one's lifestyle to potential physical illness and/or perceived competence in dealing with the task of life.

In summary, the BASIS-A has been used with a variety of individual populations and in a number of different settings. The value of the BASIS-A appears to be an instrument that can be employed in a variety of studies to further the understanding of lifestyle and human behavior. One would hope that the empirical findings will now squelch the critics who question the importance of the lifestyle construct. Finally the research should provide a solid base of documentation on how best to create treatment strategies and prevention programs for professionals.

THE BASIS-A IN PRACTICE

The BASIS-A is useful in a variety of settings due to its easy application, self scoring aspect, and non-pathological interpretation. The authors use the BASIS-A within the therapeutic context with individuals, couples, and groups. For example, a use of the instrument in an individual therapy setting could be to use the *Being Cautious* scale to assist clients to gain a deeper understanding and appreciation of family of origin issues. This information can then lead to further understanding of why a particular person may be more suspicious, skeptical, or mistrusting of others. In a couple's counseling scenarios, the *Wanting Recognition* Scale is useful for couples to identify one of their most challenging obstacles: giving or receiving positive or negative feedback from their spouses. The Wanting Recognition Scale helps not only in the understanding of how one spouse may need more reassurance in the relationship, but it also illustrates to the spouse's mate how this feedback may be fundamental to the overall feeling of stability within the relationship. Likewise, in group settings, understanding which group members are likely to follow group rules can efficiently be determined by simply reviewing the group members' score on the *Going Along* Scale which measures rule focused versus non rule focused tendencies.

Another effective use of the BASIS-A deals with treatment planning and choice of interventions. Because the BASIS-A is an instrument that can be administered and interpreted rapidly, the clinician is able to quickly identify the lifestyle themes of the client. This aids in not only establishing a course for treatment but also assists in building rapport quickly as well. Clients are frequently fascinated at a clinician's ability to quickly isolate problem areas as well as validating feelings and thoughts they struggle with on a daily basis. The BASIS-A allows the clinician to deal more effectively with the client because the therapy sessions can focus on the lifestyle themes and how they periodically create conflict for the client rather than merely focusing on individualized manifestations of their interpersonal struggles. Specifically, the user of the BASIS-A can quickly assess a client's tendency to sometimes be too rigid in having to always be in charge (indicated by a very high Taking Charge Scale) which could lead to resistance between the clinician and client and/or the phenomenon known as the constant repeating of the problem in the counseling session. Armed with BASIS-A information the clinician can quickly and more effectively tailor the therapy with this particular client to address this rigid lifestyle theme instead of wasting valuable sessions stumbling around attempting to identify the underlying problem based on incomplete data.

In parenting groups, the BASIS-A is useful to tailor the programmatic information in the parenting classes to fit the individual participants. In programmatic parenting groups like Systematic Training for Effective Parenting (STEP), the information is taught to groups of individuals in a very systematic approach. Some participants may need more work at learning to encourage whereas other parents may need more concentration in learning to disengage from power struggles. In current parent group formats, the parent educator is never quite sure as to how and to whom the specific information needs to be focused. By incorporating the BASIS-A, certain lifestyle themes that may cause obstacles for the participants can be identified and the material can be tailored to address these needs. For example, a person very high on the Taking Charge Scale would have a difficult time with the basic concepts of democratic parenting when his/her stress level is high. Thus, by identifying this characteristic in the parenting class, the instructor can help the parent identify this potential barrier and learn effective coping strategies.

In conducting workshops or seminars, the BASIS-A is useful in providing structure for experiential learning activities. Participants in workshops can be given the BASIS-A and then divided into groups based on their scores for each of the five major scales. The groups can then engage in dialogue about their perceived strengths and limitations; they can also write these attributes on either a flip chart or dry-erase board for others to see. Not only does such an activity promote a sense of belonging and connection within the workshop but also the activity makes the concept of lifestyle themes more real to the participants.

There have been other applications identified by various clinicians, educators, and consultants using the BASIS-A. Some of these uses include: informing organizational personnel of leadership and management styles, identification of teacher-student interactions in the classroom, informing owners of businesses on how their lifestyles impact employees, as a supportive tool for hiring practices, and finally as a coaching tool with management personnel and supervisors in graduate training programs.

Thus, the BASIS-A has not only succeeded where earlier attempts have failed with regard to objectively measuring the lifestyle construct, but it also has surpassed its predecessors in providing information that is easy to incorporate into a variety of research, clinical, teaching, and consulting activities. Adlerian researchers, teachers, and clinicians can confidently use the notion of lifestyle knowing that there is an objective way to measure the construct. Consistent with the current managed care market, clinicians now have a tool allowing for rapid assessment and effective treatment planning in a variety of settings (e.g., individual, group, and couples counseling). Likewise, consultants have a reliable tool assisting in workshop development and delivery, and in identifying useful information for participants concerning interpersonal attributes. Adler stressed that individual psychology was a psychology of use, not possession. The BASIS-A is a culmination of years of research and clinical experience that brings this notion of use into practice as it concerns the concept of lifestyle.

(Information on cost and how to purchase the instrument can be accessed at the website www.minspring.com/~trtbasis or e-mail at trtbasis@hotmail.com or telephone consultation at 404-406-8781.)

Summary

In this chapter we presented lifestyle assessment tools for adolescents, adults, and children. A method for using lifestyle assessment in group settings was reported. The first section of the chapter focused on the qualitative side of assessment. The final section focused on the quantitative side of reporting lifestyle information. Chapter 4 will address how to interpret the interview process and content generated from the guides.

Endnotes

[1] Powers, R.L. and Griffith, J. *Understanding Lifestyle: The Psycho-clarity Process*. Chicago, The Americas Institute of Adlerian Studies. 1987: 18.

[2] Ansbacher, H., and Ansbacher, R., ed. *The Individual Psychology of Alfred Adler*. New York: Harper & Row, 1964, 1967. (1929a, pp. 110-14; 1930a, pp. 251–258; 1933a, pp. 200–203; 1933b, pp. 299–304)

[3] Dreikurs, R. *Psychodynamics, Psychotherapy and Counseling*, (rev. ed.). Chicago: Alfred Adler Institute, 1973:88–90.

[4] Shulman, B., and Mosak, H. *Manual for Lifestyle Assessment*. Muncie, IN: Accelerated Development, Inc., 1988.

[5] Manaster, G., and Corsini, R. *Individual Psychology: Theory and Practice*. New York: F. E. Peacock, 1982.

[6] Sweeney, T.J. *Adlerian Counseling* (3rd ed.). Muncie, IN: Accelerated Development, 1979, 1989.

[7] Eckstein, D., Baruth, L., and Mahrer, D. *Lifestyle: What It Is and How To Do It*. Dubuque, IA: Kendall/Hunt Publishing Company 1981.

[8] Dinkmeyer, D., Dinkmeyer, D., and Sperry, L. *Adlerian Counseling and Psychotherapy*. Columbus, OH: Merrill Publishing, 1987.

[9] Powers, R.L. and Griffith, J. *Understanding Lifestyle: The Psycho-Clarity Process*, Chicago: The Americas Institute of Adlerian Studies. 1987, 32–66.

[10] Ibid., pp. 67–97.

[11] Watzlawick, P., Weakland, J., and Fisch, R. *Change*. New York: W.W. Norton & Company, 1974.

[12] Carkhuff, R. *The Art of Helping*. (6th ed.). Amherst, MA: Human Resource Development Press, 1987.

[13] Ivey, A. *Microcounseling: Innovations in Interviewing Techniques*. Springfield, IL: Charles C Thomas, 1971.

[14] Adler, A. "Nochmals-die Einheit der Neurosen." *International Journal of Individual Psychology* 8(1930): 201–216.

[15] Shulman, B. *A Comparison of Allport's and the Adlerian Concept of Lifestyle*. Chicago: Alfred Adler Institute, 1973.

[16] Thorne, F. "The Lifestyle Analysis." *Journal of Clinical Psychology* 31, (1975): 236–240.

[17] Adler, A. *The Science of Living*. New York: Greenberg, 1929, 102.

[18] Boldt, R.M., and Mosak, H.H. "Understanding the Storyteller's Story: Implications for Therapy." *The Journal of Individual Psychology* 64, no. 4 (1998): 496.

[19] Ibid.

[20] Barzon, B. *Permanent Partners*. New York: Penguin, 1990: 6–7.

[21] Eckstein, D., and Baruth, L. *The Theory and Practice of Lifestyle Assessment*. Dubuque, IA: Kendall/Hunt, 1996.

[22] Carle, Eric. *The Mixed-Up Chameleon*. New York: Harper Trophy, 1984.

[23] Kopp, R., and Kivel, C. "Traps and Escapes." *Journal of Individual Psychology* 46, no. 2 (1990): 21–22.

[24] Loc. cit.

[25] Dinkmeyer, D., and Dinkmeyer, D. "Concise Counseling Assessment: The Children's Life Style." *Elementary School Guidance & Counseling* 12, no. 2 (1977): 117–124.

[26] Walton, F. "Group Workshop with Adolescents." *Individual Psychologist* 12, no. 1 (1975): 26–28.

[27] Walton, Francis X. Use of the most memorable observation as a technique for understanding choice of parenting style. *The Journal of Individual Psychology* 54, no. 4 (1998): 488.

[28] Ibid., p. 489.

[29] Ibid., p. 491.

[30] Ibid., p. 493.

[31] Ansbacher, L.H., and Ansbacher, R.R. (eds.). *The Individual Psychology of Alfred Adler: A Systematic Presentation in Selections from His Writings*. New York: Harper & Row, 1956.

[32] Riodan, R., and Kern, R. "Lifestyle Analysis and Vocational Choice" *Lifestyle: Theory Practice and Research*. Idaho: Cole Publishing, 1981.

[33] Kyser, L. L. "A Study of the Adlerian Life Style in Relation to Psychiatric Diagnosis" (Unpublished Dissertation, Georgia State University). Digital Dissertations, AAT 7908495 (1978).

[34] Davis, J.B., Jr. "Personality and Validity Issues of Adlerian Lifestyle Analysis. (Unpublished Dissertation, Georgia State University). Digital Dissertations, AAT 7908489 (1978).

[35] Allers, C., and Snow, M. "Use of Adlerian Assessment Techniques in the Treatment of Dissociative Identity Disorder: A Case Study. *The Journal of Individual Psychology* 55, no. 2 (1999):162–175.

[36] White, J. and Campbell, I. "Associations of Scores on the White-Campbell Psychological Birth Order Inventory and the Kern Life Style Scale." *Psychological Reports* 77, no. 3 (1995):1187–1197.

[37] Logan, E., Kern, R., Curlette, W., and Trad, A. "Couples Adjustment, Lifestyle Similarity, and Social Interest." *Individual Psychology* 49. (1993):456–467.

[38] Harrison, M.G. "The Relationships among Adlerian Life Style Themes, Gender Roles, Cooperative Negotiation, and Marital Satisfaction" (Unpublished Dissertation, George State University). Digital Dissertations, AAT 9335061 (1993).

[39] Johnston, T. B. "Validation of the Life Style Personality Inventory and the Prediction of Success in Treating Pain." *Dissertational Abstracts International*, 49, 2406B (1988).

[40] Bertelson, S. K. "Clinical Correlations of Lifestyle Patterns Found in Psychiatric Inpatients." *Dissertational Abstracts International*, 52, 3332B (1991).

[41] Sauls, M.B. "A Manager Matching Strategies Model for Buyers: A Discriminant Analysis Based on Adlerian and Jungian Theory." *Dissertational Abstracts International*, 49, 906B (1987).

[42] Ranft, V.A. "The Effects of Cooperative Reorganization on Job Satisfaction." *Dissertational Abstracts International*, 53, 1405A (1992).

[43] Earles, T.D. "Adlerian Lifestyles and Clinical Depression in Mothers of Disturbed Children." *Dissertational Abstracts International*, 43, 1834A (1982).

[44] Boynton, R. "Drug Addiction, Lifestyle Personality Factors and Psychotherapy." *Dissertational Abstracts International*, 50, 647 (1989).

[45] Keene, K.K. Jr., and Wheeler, M.S. "Substance Use in College Freshman and Adlerian Lifestyle Themes" *Individual Psychology* 50, no 1 (1994): 97–109.

[46] Wheeler, M.S. "Factor Analysis of An Instrument Developed to Measure Adlerian Lifestyle." *Dissertational Abstracts International*, 40, 5032B (1980).

[47] Mullis, F.Y. "Factor Analysis of the Wheeler-Kern-Curlette Lifestyle Personality Inventory." (Unpublished Dissertation, Georgia State University) Digital Dissertations, AAT 8412518 (1984).

[48] Mullins, F.Y., Kern, R.M., and Curlette, W. L. "Lifestyle Themes and Social Interest: A Further Factor Analytic Study." *Individual Psychology* 43 (1987): 339–352.

49 Overrocker, J.M. "Development of a Scale to Measure the Team Player: Relationships Between Items of the Life Style Personality Inventory and An Observation of Behavior During an Outdoor Ropes Experience." *Dissertational Abstracts International, 53,* 106A (1992).

50 Choca, J.P. "Review of the BASIS-A Inventory" In J.C. Impara and B.S. Plake (eds.), *The Thirteenth Mental Measurements Yearbook.* Lincoln, NE: Buros Institute of Mental Measurements, 1998.

51 Curlette, W.L., Wheeler, M.S. and Kern, R.M. "The BASIS-A Inventory Technical Manual." Highland, NC: TRT Associates, 1997.

52 Ibid.

53 Ibid.

54 Ibid

55 Kern, R. M. and Riordan, R. J. "Assessing Family-of-origin Issues in Supervision" Family Journal 3, no. 4. (1995): 350–355.

56 Appleton, B.A. and Stanwyck. D. "Teacher Personality, Pupil Control Ideology, and Leadership Style." *Individual Psychology 52.* no. 2 (1996): 119–129.

57 Kern, R., Edwards, D., Flowers, C., Lambert, R., and Belangee, S. "Teachers' Lifestyles and Their Perceptions of Students' Behaviors." *The Journal of Individual Psychology 55,* no. 4. (1999): 422–436.

58 McGreevy, N.H., Newbauer, J.F., and Carich, M.S. "Comparison of Lifestyle Profiles of Incarcerated Sexual Offenders with Those of Persons Incarcerated for Other Crimes." *The Journal of Individual Psychology 47,* no. 1 (2001): 67–77.

59 Slaton, B.J., Kern, R.M., and Curlette, W.L. "Personality Profiles of Inmates." *The Journal of Individual Psychology 56,* no. 1 (2000): 88–109.

60 Demp, D.E., and Center, D.B. "Troubled Children Grown-up: Antisocial Behavior in Young Adult Criminals." *Education and Treatment of Children 23,* no. 3 (2000): 223–238.

61 Kern, R., Gfroerer, K., Summers, Y., Curlette, W., and Matheny, K. "Lifestyle, Personality, and Stress Coping." I*ndividual Psychology 52,* no. 1 (1996): 42–53.

62 Dinter, L. D. The Relationship Between Self-efficacy and Lifestyle Patterns." *The Journal of Individual Psychology 56,* no. 4 (2000): 462–473.

63 Snow, J. N., Kern, R. M., and Curlette, W.L. "Identifying Personality Traits Associated with Attrition in Systematic Training for Effective Parenting Groups." *The Family Journal 9,* no. 2 (2001): 102–108.

64 Bauman, G. S. "Clinical Usefulness of the BASIS-A Inventory with Substance Abusers." (Unpublished Dissertation, Georgia State University) (2000).

65 Dinter, L. D. "An Adlerian Conceptualization of Attention Deficit Hyperactivity Disorder: Personality Traits and Lifestyle." (Unpublished Dissertation, Georgia State University) (2000).

66 Rassmussen, P. R., Martin, M. F., and Sorrow, D. L. "BASIS-A Lifestyle Themes, MMPI-A, and Childhood Sexual Abuse: Conclusions From a Residential Sample." *The Journal of Individual Psychology 57,* no. 1. (2001): 78–80.

67 Smith, S., Kern, F., Curlette, W., and Mullis, F. "Personality Profiles Using Adlerian Lifestyle Themes among Adjudicated Adolescents." *The Journal of Individual Psychology 57,* no. 3. (2001) (in press).

68 Kemp, D. and Center, D. "Personality, Socialization, and Behavior in Adolescents." (Unpublished Dissertation, Georgia State University) (2001).

69 Kern, R., Penick, J. and Hambry, R. "Personality, Stress and Prediction of Diabetic Regimen Compliance and BASIS-A Personality Indicators." *The Diabetes Educator 22,* no. 4 (1996): 367–373.

70 McMahan, O. "Programmed Distance Writing as an Intervention for Seminary Couples." (Unpublished Dissertation, Georgia State University) Digital Dissertations, AAT 9911561 (1998).

71 Curlette, W. L., Kern, R. M. & Wheeler, M. S. "Uses and Interpretation of Scores on the BASIS-A Inventory." *Individual Psychology 52,* no. 2 (1996):95–103.

72 Wheeler, M.S. "Using the BASIS-A Inventory: Examples From a Clinical Setting." *Individual Psychology 52,* no. 2. (1996): 104–118.

73 Appleton and Stanwyck, op. cit.

74 Kern et al., op. cit.

75 Snow et al., op. cit.

76 Kutchins, K., Curlette, W. L. and Kern, R. M. "To What Extent Is There a Relationship Between Personality Priorities and Lifestyle Themes." *Journal of Individual Psychology 52,* 2 (1997): 373–387.

77 Bauman, op. cit.

78 McGreevy et. al., op. cit.

79 Slaton et. al., op. cit.

80 Smith et. al., op. cit.

81 Kemp and Center, op. cit. (2000, 2001).

82 Ibid

83 Dinter, op. cit.

84 Kern et al., op. cit.

85 Dinter, op. cit.

86 Kern et al., op. cit.

[87] Rassmussen et al., op. cit.

[88] Kemp and Center, op. cit. (2000, 2001).

[89] McGreevy et al., op. cit.

[90] Slaton et al., op. cit.

[91] Smith et al., op. cit.

[92] Adler, A. *What Life Could Mean to You*. Center City, MN: Hazelden, 1931–1998.

[93] Dinter, op. cit.

[94] Miranda, A., Frevert, V., and Kern, R. "Lifestyle Differences Between Bicultural and Low-and-High Acculturation-Level Latino Adults." *The Journal of Individual Psychology 54*, no. 1 (1998): 119–134.

Lifestyle Interpretive Skills

In Chapter 3, various formats for obtaining lifestyle information were presented. The purpose of this chapter is to provide a deeper understanding of the stages of the lifestyle interview and to the meaning of the content that is acquired during the interview. This chapter will include discussion of life tasks, family atmosphere, sibling ratings, birth order, and early recollections. Additional lifestyle features to consider in the interpretation phase will include the "#1 Priority," general lifestyle themes, and a recommended systematic summary.

Consistent with the Adlerian concept of equality, interpretation is not "given" to the client by an "all-knowing, wise, and superior" counselor. Consider an analogy of Carl Rogers relative to traditional learning, by what he called a "mug and jug" approach to learning. A client comes to the counselor with an empty "mug." The wise counselor pours forth from his or her "jug" of knowledge. The client passively holds out his or her mug, hoping it will be filled from the vast insights of the therapist.[1]

Consistent with the equalitarian nature of Adlerian theory, interpretation should be viewed as a joint venture between a counselor and a client. "Psychological ownership" of one's style of life will usually be higher if the client is actively involved in the interpretative process. The goal of interpretation is an "ah-ha" insight, greater insight, and greater awareness of the past issues relative to present and future implications for the client. The theory is that one cannot change something until one is aware of the attitude, concept, or behavior. Interpretation helps provide the insight. Chapter 5 will then address the change process Adlerians call "reorientation."

The usual lifestyle developmental therapeutic process generally involves explaining the purpose of the interview and gathering data in the initial one or two sessions. At times the interpretation occurs spontaneously in the moment—simply focusing one's awareness back to core childhood issues sometimes results in spontaneous "a-ha's," thus flexibility and the ability to be 'in the moment' with the client should always be a counselor's response.[2]

Most often the counselor collects the basic information and then spends some time alone organizing the data. This chapter presents some guidelines to assist that organization. Remember to trust your own intuitive guesses or hunches. Perhaps for no apparent (linear) reason a word or a phrase may suddenly "pop" into your head. The authors have had some dramatic results by having the courage to trust that spontaneous inner creative wisdom. For example, Eckstein was completing an initial interview. The name "Shirley" just kept "flashing" in his mind. But nowhere did her name appear in the siblings, ERs, and so on. So, toward the end of the session, he simply acknowledged the name "Shirley" was haunting him and asked the client if the name had significance.

Her immediate "recognition reflex" was a look of shock and disbelief. "How did you know about her?" she exclaimed. "She is my best friend—we share our most intimate secrets together—but she, like me, is an alcoholic and we often get drunk together. I just left her before I came to see you. She acknowledged my courage in coming to see you and said she should come too," she continued.

One needs the courage to trust one's own inner creativity and to realize that counselors, in essence, "step into" the other person's private world during an interview. In this example, alcohol dependence was identified in an indirect manner by taking a risk.

Dreikurs continually encouraged his trainees to make guesses or, as he called it, to "dig gold mines" early in the interview. They may simply appear in the margin of a counselor's notes as hypotheses to be further explored. Even when a guess is "wrong," that too helps the person to further refine the issue, even if it's reacting *against* or *clarifying* the hypothesis.

Although the following sections will explore the various components of the interview (i.e., life tasks, family constellation, early recollections), Powers and Griffith wisely suggest that a lifestyle assessment is not a "systematic collection of a heap of tiles; it is the imaginative reconstruction of a pattern which allow each tile of information to be fitted into the context of the whole. This context, furthermore, is a pattern of movement in line with what Adler recognized as the 'great line of action' of the 'whole of human life . . . from below to above, from minus to plus, from defeat to victory.'" [3]

The content related to family atmosphere, values, ordinal position, and early recollection in this chapter is included to provide individuals with a knowledge base to make sense of the lifestyle process. For lifestyle cannot be understood if the user lacks the holistic view of the individual within the social context of his/her family of origin.

Powers and Griffith focus their overall interpretation on the following seven key features of the child's environment:

1. Masculine and Feminine Guiding Lines and Role Models—"This is the way men are, and the way women are . . . therefore, this is what is going to unfold for me as a man or as a woman."

2. Family Atmosphere—"This is what I have to expect and prepare for in my dealings with others."

3. Family Values—"These are the issues of central importance, on which I must be prepared to take a stand."

4. Other Particularities (including the ethnic, religious, social, and economic situation)—"It is possible for me to make a place in the broader community on these terms and to this extent."

5. Birth Order Position—"This is where I stand and must stand amongst others in order to maintain my bearings."

6. Genetic Possibility/Self-Assessment—"These are my personal limits and possibilities for making a place amongst the others."

7. Environmental Opportunity/Openings for Advancement—"This is what is open to me in life, and this is what stands in my way." Such a global overview can be of assistance as we now explore the various components of the Lifestyle Interview. [4]

The Developmental Phases of Adlerian Counseling

Rudolf Dreikurs[5] delineated the phases of an Adlerian counseling relationship in four developmental sequences:

1. the establishment of a *relationship*,

2. a *psychological investigation* (including a lifestyle assessment),

3. psychological disclosure (*interpretation*), and

4. *reorientation* and re-education.

Mozdzierz and associates point out that the phases of therapy are "neither linear nor sequential steps in a progression. The four component phases are ingredients that are constantly interacting and needing attention with one component having more focus at one time and the others more at another time."[6]

Specific therapist role functions in the four phases of Adlerian therapy as adopted from Mozdzierz and associates are outlined as follows:

A. Establishing a Relationship

1. Mutual friend—caring, concern, involvement, and the capacity for empathic, humanistic identification.

2. Partner/collaborator—working together while paradoxically recognizing that ultimately only the client alone can change his or her life.

3. Confidante—purveyor of respect, trust, confidence, and good faith. Faith, hope, and love[7] or Roger's[8] "unconditional positive regard" apply here; also acts in accordance with established professional code of ethics.

4. Model—the therapist living a way of dealing with life's challenges through courageous trust in and openness to what life has to offer; also modeling effective skills of communication; also living with authenticity or congruence.[9]

5. Environmentalist—nurturing the therapeutic climate just as the natural resources of the world need care and attention; have an office that nurtures; also respect the privacy and confidentiality of the client.

    Most counselors will identify this phase through the important term "rapport," stressing the core conditions of helping that Carkhuff and associates[10] have so aptly demonstrated, such as: (a) unconditional positive regard—putting no strings on the relationship (i.e., "you would be an 'OK' person if you would only . . ."), (b) genuineness—being two real persons, not a "healthy" therapist and a "sick" patient, (c) empathy—accurate perception of the person's "world," including his/her emotional subjective "feeling tone" towards their environment, (d) self-disclosure—freely volunteering relevant personal information, and (e) concreteness—talking about specific concerns rather than vague abstractions (e.g., "you're hurt because your mom distrusts you" as opposed to "you're upset"). Carkhuff terms this phase "facilitation," the foundation or cornerstone upon which the relationship is built. It is also during the relationship building phase that both the counselor and the client agree on future counseling procedures and goals. Clients experiencing interpersonal conflicts often have difficulty forming close relationships, making the counseling process an important first step toward social living. Therefore, counselors must continually "win" or "earn" the confidence of their clients, making the relationship phase an ongoing task.

B. Psychological Investigation

1. Wide-Angle and Multifocus Observer—expanding the often narrow and restricted vision of the client; assisting in making connections between past, present, and future actions; understanding and appreciating cultural diversity and different lifestyle influences and backgrounds.

2. Lifestyle Interpreter—focusing on an individual's family constellation and early childhood history combined with a summary of early recollections or memories; helping the client understand his or her private logic.

3. Explorer—assessing the three life tasks Adler[11] identified as being the work task, the social or friendship task, and the love task. To these Mosak[12] added the task of self-esteem and the spiritual. The therapist also identifies the strengths and weaknesses of the client. "Adlerian explorers not only invite their clients on a journey through what has been and is, but also through the infinite possibilities of what can be. An exploration of options for growth and development, and an exploration of the road and choices/options that lead to a more productive and constructive future are two forms of exploration that facilitate client movement toward the future."[13]

C. Psychological Disclosure

1. Interpreter—giving the client "another set of glasses" with which to view the world; an explanation of the patient's behavior in relation to or in terms of his or her goals, intentions, purposes, private logic, or movement.[14]

2. Translator/reframer—assisting the client to understand other people, life, and the issues involved with social living; "reframing" perceived negatives to strengths wherever possible.

3. Creator of meaning and understanding—often created by suggestion, arrangement and rearrangement, connecting and disconnecting, focusing and clarifying, defining and redefining.[15]

4. Confronter—focusing on discrepancies between what a person is saying versus doing, feeling versus thinking, or between what another person says about the same situation.

   In the interpretation phase, corresponding roughly to Carkhuff's action stage, basic "life-others-self" attitudes are shared with the individual. The constant emphasis is on goals or purposes rather than "why" people act the way they do. Here the individual's "private logic" is discussed, including important implications for present and future activities.

   Confrontation concerning discrepancies between actions and words, or between ideal and real goals is also employed. Specific examples relating to one's current means of accomplishing desired goals are also obtained, and the person begins to experience greater personal insights relating to his or her goals and intentions.

D. Reorientation and Reeducation

1. Encourager—O'Connell's[16] model of encouragement includes stopping, looking, and listening through demonstrated interest, clarifying, being nonjudgmental, giving feedback, looking for useless goals in behavior, and the development of a sense of humor. "Encouragement is the realization that every deficit can also be an asset: for every negative in life . . . there is also a positive, adaptive creative response that the individual makes."[17]

2. Dialectician—understanding such paradoxes as, in human behavior, a strength can be a weakness and a weakness can be a strength; moving from "either-or" dualities and dichotomies to "both-and."

3. Other roles include resource person, "fellow pilgrim," "expert" who puts clients in charge of their own lives, comforter (from the Latin word meaning "to make strong"), educator, and humorist.

Henry Stein[18] adapts the four developmental phases into the following twelve stages of creative psychotherapy, including: (1) empathy (relationship), (2) information, (3) clarification, (4) encouragement, (5) interpretation and recognition, (6) knowing, (7) group and marathon (if needed),

(8) doing different, (9) reinforcement, (10) social interest, (11) goal redirection, and (12) support and launching.

The following section addresses various life tasks that everyone confronts one way or another. The authors also provide important links to health in their discussion of these perceived five life tasks.

Wellness and the Five Life Tasks

More than half and as many as two-thirds of all premature deaths in the United States are due to health factors that can be modified. However, while over 75% of health care dollars are spent to treat people with chronic diseases, less than 1% of federal funds and 2% of state funds are spent to prevent these diseases from occurring. The total costs of illness increased from 5% to 12% of the gross national product in the 30-year period from 1960 to 1990.[19]

Holism. Adler describes the importance of holism in understanding the individual. He noted that "it is always necessary to look for . . . reciprocal actions of the mind on the body, for both of them are parts of the whole which we should be concerned." In studying characteristics of healthy people, Maslow concluded that striving toward self-actualization, growth, and excellence is a universal human tendency and overarching life purpose. Wellness is a way of life oriented toward optimal health and well-being in which body, mind, and spirit are integrated by the individual to live more fully within the human and natural community.[20] Changes in one area of wellness affects other areas, in both positive and negative directions. Healthy functioning occurs on a developmental continuum, and healthy behaviors at one point in life affect subsequent development and functioning as well.

Myers, Sweeney and Witmer rearrange Adler's life-tasks in a slightly different sequence.

LIFE TASK 1: SPIRITUALITY

Spirituality is defined as an awareness of a being or force transcending the material aspects of life that gives a deep sense of wholeness or connectedness to the universe. A distinction is made between spirituality, a broad concept representing one's personal beliefs and values, and *religiosity*, a narrower concept that refers to institutional beliefs and behaviors that is part of the broad concept of spirituality. Religiosity is a public matter, often expressed in group religious participation, whereas spirituality is more a private issue that may or may not be expressed publicly.

Positive thoughts, hardiness, generalized self-efficacy, and optimism have been strongly correlated with well-being and resistance to stress. Both positive thoughts and optimism are components of spirituality. Spiritual support may have "a stress-buffering effect." There is a significant positive relationship between spirituality, mental health, physical health, life satisfaction, and wellness.

Here is a creative description of God written by Danny Dutton, age eight, of Chula Vista, California via the Rhode Island Episcopal News.

> One of God's main jobs is making people. He makes these to put in place of the ones that die so there will be enough people to take care of things here on earth. He doesn't make grown-ups. Just babies. I think because they are smaller and easier to make. That way He doesn't have to take up His valuable time teaching them to talk and walk. He can just leave that up to the mothers and fathers. I think it works out pretty good.

God's second most important job is listening to prayers. An awful lot of this goes on, as some people, like preachers and things, pray other times besides bedtime. God doesn't have time to listen to the radio or TV on account of this. As He hears everything, not only prayers, there must be a terrible lot of noise going into His ears unless He has thought of a way to turn it off.

God sees everything and hears everything and is everywhere, which keeps Him pretty busy. So you shouldn't go wasting His time by going over your parents' head and ask for something they said you couldn't have.

Atheists are people who don't believe in God. I don't think there are any in Chula Vista. At least there aren't any who come to the Episcopal Church.

Jesus is God's Son. He used to do all the hard work like walking on water and doing miracles and trying to teach people about God who didn't want to learn. They finally got tired of Him preaching to them and they crucified Him. But He was good and kind like His Father and He told His Father that they didn't know what they were doing, to forgive them and God said OK. His Dad (God) appreciated everything He had done and all His hard work on earth, so He told Him He didn't have to go out on the road any more. He could stay in Heaven. So He did. And now He helps His Dad out by listening to prayers and seeing which things are important for God to take care of and which ones He can take care of Himself without having to bother God with. Like a secretary, only more important, of course. You can pray anytime you want and they are sure to hear you because they've got it worked out so one of them is on duty all the time.

You should always go to Sunday School because it makes God happy, and if there's anybody you want to make happy, it's God. Don't skip Sunday School to do something you think will be more fun, like going to the beach. That is wrong. And besides, the sun doesn't come out at the beach until noon anyway.

If you don't believe in God, besides being an atheist, you will be very lonely because your parents can't go everywhere with you, like to camp, but God can. It's good to know He's around when you're scared of the dark or when you can't swim very good and you get thrown in real deep water by big kids. But you shouldn't just always think of what God can do for you. I figure God put me here and He can take me back any time He pleases.

Or consider the five-year-old child in kindergarten who was excited about the drawing she had just completed. "What is that?" the teacher asked. "Why, it's a picture of God," she replied. "Silly girl—don't you know no one knows what God look like," the teacher confronted. "Well, they will when I'm finished with this drawing," the child confidently proclaimed.

LIFE TASK 2: SELF-DIRECTION

Self-direction is the manner in which an individual regulates, disciplines, and directs the self in daily activities and in pursuit of long-range goals. It refers to a sense of mindfulness and intentionality in meeting the major tasks of life. The patterns of behavior and methods of adjustment to life that make up self-direction are sometimes referred to as "positive personality traits" that give one a stress-resistant personality. Subsections include:

1. **Sense of worth** is variously referred to as "self-concept," "self-esteem," and "self worth." A person who has high self-esteem is excited by new challenges and seeks self actualization. Positive self esteem is a preventive factor for illness, because it enhances recovery from illness and all well-being. In virtually all studies of positive mental health, the key factors that emerge are a positive self-concept, a sense of autonomy, social support, and an internal locus of control or sense of self-efficacy. Self-esteem is a more significant predictor of life satisfaction in individualist countries, such as the United States, than it is in those with a

collectivist orientation, where relationship harmony seems to be more closely related to self-esteem in predicting life satisfaction.

2. **Sense of control**—people experience positive outcomes when they perceive themselves as having an impact on what happens to them and experience negative outcomes when they perceive a lack of personal control. Perceived control is associated with emotional well-being, successful coping with stress, better physical health, and better mental health over the life span. Having an internal focus of control has been associated with lower levels of anxiety and depression and higher levels of self-esteem and life satisfaction. Higher levels of perceived self-control predict healthier behavior, including exercise participation and weight control, and in turn are affected by participation in positive health practices such as exercise.

Ellis noted that people have a tendency to disturb themselves through the perpetuation of their irrational beliefs, the major ones being (a) I must be loved or approved of by everyone, (b) I must be perfectly competent and productive, (c) it is a catastrophe when things go other than the way one might wish, (d) life must be absolutely fair, and (e) it is better to avoid life's difficulties than to take responsibility for changing them. People who have realistic beliefs are able to accept themselves as imperfect.[21] Adler referred to "internal beliefs" as one's private logic that in turn guides both the feelings and the behaviors of the individual. The greater the discrepancy between one's private logic and reality, the greater the potential for unhealthy behaviors in response to life events. Accurate appraisals of the self and the social environment are essential to positive mental health.[22]

3. **Emotional awareness and coping**—to experience and positively manage one's emotions is one index of healthy functioning. Many individuals are limited in their ability both to experience and to express joy, anger, affection, and related human emotions. Thus the quality and quantity of relationship events within their lives are limited.

Negative emotions such as anxiety and depression are associated with immune system suppression and a consequent increase in the potential for illness. Hostility has been shown to be a major contributor to high blood pressure, coronary artery disease, and death, particularly among people with a Type A personality. Conversely, the appropriate expression of negative emotions combined with the presence of positive emotions seems to strengthen the immune function.

Our deepest fear is that we are powerful beyond measure.
It is our light, not our darkness, that frightens us.

We ask ourselves;
'who am I to be brilliant, gorgeous, talented and fabulous?'
Actually, who are you not to be?

You are a child of god.
Your playing small doesn't serve the world.
There's nothing enlightened about shrinking so that
other people won't feel insecure around you.

We were born to make manifest the glory of god that is within us.
It's not just in some of us; it's in everyone.

And as we let our own light shine. we unconsciously
give other people permission to do the same.

Our presence automatically liberates others.

—1994 Inaugural Speech, Nelson Mandela

4. **Creativity**—intellectual stimulation, including problem solving and creativity, is necessary for healthy brain functioning and hence quality of life across the life span. The need to think soundly is innate and composed of several traits, including the need to know, the need to learn, the need to organize, curiosity, and a sense of wonder. Effective problem solving also correlates with reduced anxiety and depression, increased stress hardiness, and overall psychological adjustment. Creativity has been identified as a universal characteristic of self-actualizing people, all of whom demonstrate originality, expressiveness, imagination, inventiveness, and problem-solving ability. Creativity is optimized in individuals with high self-esteem and has a positive effect on life satisfaction, mental health, and overall wellness.

5. **Sense of humor**—especially when accompanied by laughter, humor causes the skeletal muscles to relax. Humor also boosts the immune system, increases heart rate, stimulates circulation, oxygenates the blood, "massages" the vital organs, aids digestion, and releases chemicals into the brain for enhancing a sense of well-being. Humor has been associated with reduced depression and pain relief, higher levels of self-esteem and lower perceived levels of stress, more positive and self-protective cognitive appraisal when dealing with stress, and a greater positive response to both positive and negative life events. Humor also allows cognitive shifts that help individuals gain insight into their personal problems, increase social cohesion, defuse conflicts, and reduce feelings of hostility. However, humor that has a put-down component is related to health problems, whereas a positive sense of humor enhances healthy aging. Humor promotes creativity, improves negotiating and decision-making skills, improves individual and group performance, relieves stress, and bestows a sense of power.

6. **Nutrition**—there is a clear relationship between what we eat and our health, moods, performance, and longevity. The eating and drinking habits of Americans have been implicated in 6 of the 10 leading causes of death, including the fact that 1 in 3 Americans is considered to be overweight.[23] Factors such as loneliness, poor physical health and lack of meaningful social contacts result in lower dietary quality.

7. **Exercise**—regular physical activity is viewed as essential in preventing disease and enhancing health and is "a key ingredient to healthy aging." Exercises increases strength as well as self-confidence and self-esteem. There is a significant correlation between physical fitness and positive emotionality as well as enhanced cognitive functioning. Exercise training has been shown to significantly decrease state-trait anxiety scores, decrease mild depression, reduce stress, and beneficially affect a variety of chronic illnesses.

8. **Self-care**—three aspects of self-care constitute this dimension: safety habits that we learn to protect ourselves from injury or death; periodic physical, medical, and dental checkups; and avoiding harmful substances, both those that we might ingest and toxic substances in the environment.

9. **Stress management**—stress affects both psychological and physiological functioning and has a specific depressant effect on immune system functioning. People who are stress-resistant experience more positive and beneficial immune system responses, greater resistance to psychosocial stressors, and more internal locus of control. They also experience more positive mental health and greater physical health. Stress management is the ability to identify stressors in one's life and to reduce or minimize stress by using strategies of stress reduction. The negative effects of stress can be reduced or eliminated through self-regulatory strategies such as biofeedback and relaxation techniques, social support, and behavioral/environmental methods such as assertiveness and communication skills training, changing mistaken ideas, problem solving, and exercise.

10. **Gender identity**—gender identity, a basic, existential conviction that one is male or female, refers to subjective feelings of maleness or femaleness and is culturally constructed or defined. Satisfaction with being a male or a female and a sense of confidence or comfort in being male or female affect one's subjective feelings of gender identity. Gender role identity, in contrast to gender identity, reflects one's identification with the social prescriptions or stereotypes associated with each sex, to which an individual may or may not conform rather than the introspective, self-definition of one's gender. American women more readily report their illnesses than do men, use medical and mental health systems more frequently than do men, and outlive men by an average of seven years.

11. **Cultural identity**—culture may be broadly defined as "multidimensional concept that encompasses the collective reality of a group of people." Psychological stress and behavioral deviance are culturally defined and are often explained in culturally specific religious or spiritual frameworks. Happiness is explained in a Western context as being positively correlated with independence and an internal locus of control. In Eastern societies, the subjective evaluation of happiness places greater emphasis on relationship harmony and interpersonal contentment.

LIFE TASK 3: WORK AND LEISURE

Work and leisure challenge or engage our senses, skills, and interests, frequently absorbing us in activities in a state of consciousness called "flow." This is an optimal state in which an individual loses awareness of self and time while being highly engaged in the task at hand. Excitement and joy are enhanced while anxiety and boredom are minimized.

Work satisfaction is based on challenge, financial reward, coworker relations, and working conditions. It is one of the best predictors of longevity as well as perceived quality of life. People who view their career as a calling tend to experience the highest work satisfaction. Recognition from others in the work environment increases sense of control for men, whereas earnings have a greater effect on psychological well-being for women. The meaning of work and time commitments related to work must be balanced in a healthy individual with time, energy, and satisfaction devoted to family and friends. In a study of working women, it was found that those who work had first or equal priority to their home life and had higher depression and role conflict scores than did those who put their relationships first.

Leisure activities, including physical, social, intellectual, volunteer, and creative, have a positive effect on self-esteem. Life satisfaction also is influenced by *leisure congruence*, defined as the selection of leisure activities consistent with one's personality type. Participation in certain types of leisure activities, notably exercise, is an important means of reducing the effects of stress by providing social support and through developing psychological hardiness.

> Work as if you don't need the money.
>
> Love as if you have never been hurt.
>
> Dance as if no one is watching.

LIFE TASK 4: FRIENDSHIP

The friendship life task incorporates all of one's social relationships that involve a connection with others, either individually or in community, but do not have a marital, sexual, or familial commitment. Empathy, cooperation, and altruism are all manifestations of social interest. Those who regularly devote time to helping others are as likely to experience health benefits as those who exercise or meditate. Adler frequently confronted his clients that they were too preoccupied with themselves. "Go out and do something for someone else" was his advice. Alternately, dissatisfaction with close friendships are more likely to avoid health damaging behaviors, such as smoking, drinking, and not using seat belts, and are more likely to consume a nutritious and healthy diet. The degree to which a person's basic social needs are met through interaction with others is positively correlated with both physical and emotional health and provides a buffer against stress. Friendship satisfaction is among the strongest predictors of positive self-esteem. Friendships also prevent feelings of loneliness—people who are socially isolated with few friends, and people who have few social contacts are much more likely to die from various diseases than those who have happy, fulfilling social lives.

LIFE TASK 5: LOVE

Healthy love relationships include

1. the ability to be intimate, trusting, and self disclosing with another person;
2. the ability to receive as well as express affection with significant others;
3. the capacity to experience or convey non-possessive caring that respects the uniqueness of another;
4. the presence of enduring, stable intimate relationships in one's life;
5. concern for the nurturance and growth of others; and
6. satisfaction with one's sexual life or the perception that one's needs for physical touch and closeness are being met, or both.

The life task of love necessitates having a family or family-like support system that has the following nine characteristics:

1. shared coping and problem-solving skills,
2. commitment to the family,
3. good communication,

4. encouragement of individuals,

5. expression of appreciation,

6. shared religious/spiritual orientation,

7. social connectedness,

8. clear roles, and

9. shared interests, values, and time.

For those who answer "no" to the question, "Do you have anyone who really cares for you?" the risk of premature death and disease from all causes is three to five times higher. Mortality rates are consistently higher for divorced, single, and widowed individuals of both sexes and all races. It is interesting that people who are unhappily married or in negative relationships are less healthy than those who are divorced, whereas divorced people have higher rates of heart disease, cancer, pneumonia, high blood pressure, depression, alcoholism, traffic accidents, homicide, suicide, and accidental death than do people who are married. Divorced people also have poorer immune system function and are less resistant to disease. These effects are not limited to any one culture. A study of Chinese adults showed that those with the greatest marital maladjustment experienced more psychiatric symptoms, had lower scores on measures of purpose in life, and perceived their health as poor. Committed relationships provide protection against physical and mental illness, increased longevity, and a greater sense of well-being. College students perceiving their families as healthy had lifestyles promoting health and wellness. Adolescents living in families that are more cohesive experience lower depression scores and also report experiencing fewer stressful life events.

In summary, an exploration of how a person is doing on basic life tasks is an important first step in the interpretation process. There is also an impact on one's basic health to the level of satisfaction/competency relative to basic tasks of living.

Family Atmosphere

Family constellation theory and the projective use of early recollections are two of Adler's most significant contributions to psychology. In this section, family atmosphere will be examined. Specific subtopics will include birth order research relative to personality and the projective use of literature in lifestyle assessment.

Shulman and Mosak use the following three qualities in describing family atmosphere: *mood, order*, and *relationships*. Mood refers to the overall emotional tone present within the family. It is most often the expression of one or both parents. Specific contrasting qualities of mood are *calm/ anxious, placid/excitable, friendly/hostile, hopeful/discouraged*, and *cheerful/unhappy.*

Order relates to the structural hierarchical relationships within the family. Patriarchal, matriarchal, authoritarian, pampering, and inconsistent discipline or limit-setting are all examples of structural relationships. Frequent changes either by moving, divorce, or death of a parent all affect family stability. Specific contrasting qualities of order affecting an individual's lifestyle include: *orderly/chaotic, democratic/authoritarian, consistent/inconsistent, logical/arbitrary, clarity/confusion*, and *ethical standards/"might makes right."*

Relationships are defined as the consistent forms of interaction present within the family. Power struggles, approval or disapproval, withholding love, openly affectionate, and "double-blind" messages ("Come here and I will slap you" versus "Why are you so afraid to get close to me?") are all relationship examples. Contrasting relationships issues affecting one's lifestyle include: *intimate (affectionate)/distant, cooperative/competitive, accepting/rejecting, understanding/blaming, openness/ concealed feelings*, and *harmonious/conflictual.*[24]

Parental Influence

One or both parents or parental figures are infinitely important in the development of a child's own view of the world. The first masculine and feminine adult role models and their interrelationship are reflected in the parents. One of the highest correlates to adult marital happiness is still the young child's own perception of his or her own parents' marital happiness.

Since modeling and imitation have been shown to be key factors in learning theory, parental models can be of a positive or negative impact. "I vow never ever to treat my own children that way" is a frequent conclusion based upon negative parental role modeling.

Shulman and Mosak provide the following parental behavior and probable responses by the child:

1. Accepting—positive self-image

2. Rejecting—negative self-image, or may look elsewhere for acceptance

3. Authoritarian—submits, seeks to please, rebels, or seeks power

4. Laissez-faire—seeks guidance and limits

5. Available—feels closer to parent

6. Unavailable—feels isolated or looks elsewhere

7. Consistency—more trust

8. Overprotection—fearfulness or resistance to limits

9. Excessive strictness—seeks to please, rebels, or covertly rebels

10. Lack of faith in the child—tries to prove self to parent and/or loses faith in self[25]

It is important to avoid a "stimulus-response" type of fatalistic parental conditioning model. Many children continue later in life to blame their parents with a "He made me this way" or "She caused me to be _____." Certainly accepting, nurturing, available, and warm parenting styles are highly correlated with children's later mental health. But that does not mean that parents cause their children to be happy or unhappy. Ultimately it is the child's own personal response or decision that dictates his/her own happiness or unhappiness.

An example is a classic study by psychiatrist James Anthony[26] when exploring children of schizophrenic parents. One childhood decision was to incorporate the mental dysfunction and later to become hospitalized. These children were defined as being made of *glass*, as they too emotionally shattered and became schizophrenic. A second childhood decision was to be functional on a normal basis but that under stress they become neurotic. This was defined as a *plastic* child, who "dented" under duress.

But the final type of child of schizophrenic parents was described as being made of steel. These children used their parents as an example of what they would not be. Such children all had a private place somewhere in their environment. For example, it may have been building model planes in the basement, or an attic where one would read or keep a journal, or some other similar place to which one could retreat when his or her parents "went crazy." A second characteristic of such children was that they actively sought out other adult role models such as teachers, neighbors, and priests or ministers. Thus, the last type of child succeeded despite a horrible parental atmosphere.

A similar phenomenon was described in an Associated Press newspaper article. It focused on what researchers are calling child "transcenders," children who succeed despite severe and abusive family atmospheres. Consider the following case history of Elizabeth as reported by Karen Northcraft, a psychiatric social worker:

Abandoned by her mother, raised in a small, West Virginia town by an abusive aunt and a lecherous uncle, Elizabeth didn't seem to have a chance. But when her impoverished family couldn't even provide a bathtub and a school counselor complained she was dirty, she made the swim team so she could get a daily shower.

Too poor to ever dream of owning a clarinet or violin, she joined the school band anyway, playing whatever instrument the school had to offer.

Elizabeth told Northcraft of bone-breaking beatings by her aunt, who had once stripped her naked and dunked her in a vat of scalding water. She told of the night when she was eight, that her uncle got into her bed and sexually molested her for the first time in what would be five years of assaults. Her aunt often told her that her mother had sold her for $25.

Elizabeth gained admission to college and was told she was dyslexic and should drop out. But she worked her way through school, earned a graduate degree and became a family therapist.[27]

The critical turning point for Elizabeth came in the fourth grade. One of her secret joys was her long blond curls. But when her aunt shaved her head, the deep well of pride, anger, and determination buried within her broke through. She was then able to reject what her aunt was saying and to emotionally "insulate" herself from her. Northcraft believes that "life for 'transcenders' is often short, sharp, and brutish, but they do well in situations anyone else would find crushing."

Research indicates that such transcenders are smart, resourceful, and independent thinkers. They succeed because they are able to seek out other role-models and make personal decisions to rise above their adversity.

Thus, it is important to note the particular conclusions that are reflected in a child's early recollections to determine the "life is _____; others are _____; therefore _____" formative conclusions a child makes about the family atmosphere.

The Naming Process

Much insight can be gained by asking the client how he or she came to be named. Who decided? Was he or she named for a special person? What different nicknames has the person been called through his or her life? What specific reactions does the individual have about such names? What new name does the person want (or have they actually obtained)?

Such background issues provide important clues as to such environmental issues as power of influence, religion, politics, and so forth.

For example, consider the name of the co-author, Daniel Gene Eckstein. His biblical heritage is reflected by having parents who were ministers in the Salvation Army and who named him after Daniel "in the lion's den" from the Old Testament. He vividly remembers as a child his mother telling him, "As a child, you will be called 'Danny'; as an adolescent, 'Dan,' and as an adult 'Dr. Daniel.'" It was only when the co-author celebrated his fortieth birthday and began asking people to change the "Dan" to "Daniel" that he remembered his mother's accurate prediction.

The middle name "Gene" remains a mystery despite having asked his parents of the origin. Consequently, it is seldom used.

The last name "Eckstein" is both a source of pride and some indication of family values. The German translation is "cornerstone," prompting an adolescent friend to joke, "We always knew you were a blockhead, Eckstein." When *Roots* was a mini-television series, the co-author began to search for his own German ancestry. At a restaurant named "Gotlieb's" in Greenwich Village, New York City, the co-author mentioned that "Gotlieb" was his father's middle name. "Beloved of God" was the owner's translation.

When the co-author questioned the restaurant owner about the possibility of a Jewish heritage, he was told: "Oh yes, haven't you heard the story of your Eckstein family? When they fled Germany, half the family denied their Jewish heritage and settled in Pittsburgh while the other half affirmed their Jewish ancestry and settled here in New York." Indeed, the co-author's grandfather was born in Pittsburgh, and when asked about possible Jewish heritage, he responded with, "It's best for you not to know or ask about such things."

It was a source of family concern when the co-author changed the pronunciation of his last name from "Eckstine" to "Ecksteen" to reflect his own pride in the Jewish tradition.

Concerning nicknames, he was also dubbed "Dumbo" as a child for his large ears, and "Dynamo Dan" as a participant in the 1968 Coaches All-American football game.

Thus, the three names reflect much of his cultural, religious, and family values. The naming process can be considered by counselors as a projective technique in and of itself.

Family Values

Family values are generally established by both parents if they were both in the home. They reflect what is prized, esteemed, and sought after as primary motivators. There is no "escaping" the judgment (positively or negatively) for a child. Consider, for example, a common source of stress relative to a parental (family) value of "religion," which frequently is synonymous with being in church or synagogue every week. When confronted that a person was not in church Sunday at 11:00, the individual replied: "But Mom, my cathedral is nature—I worship God outside" is simply unacceptable and thus rejected as an acceptable value by many parents. "You are to worship in the 'cathedral of the hardwoods' rather than the 'cathedral of the redwoods'" was the mother's unspoken communication. There is no neutrality on the issue of a family value. A sibling is either "in" or "out" on such an issue. Too often children feel a conflict between being one's self and losing parental approval versus compromising one's beliefs for such acceptance.

Often a child confronts what Walker and Belove[28] describe as a loyalty dilemma in which the parents model values directly opposed to the child's beliefs. Nonetheless, the child still wants to please and be accepted by them both.

Core family values are generally reflected in the family motto. These are frequent parental injunctions or proverbs such as "children are to be seen and not heard"; "never betray a family member"; or "go to church often, get married, and have several children."

Powers and Griffith provide a partial list of some of the following most frequently identifiable family values: *education, religious observance, honesty, loyalty to family, order, deference to authority, obedience, independence, doing your best, being best/first, thrift, distrust of "outsiders," manners, service to others, achievement, perfectionism, not complaining, not losing face,* and *doing one's duty* (the "right" thing).

They conclude that "family values refer to standards that are held up before all the children, with the implication (or explicit statement) that, 'These are the things that are important in this family, whatever others may think or do in other families.'"

This means that family values operate as imperatives. "None of the children can ignore them; on the contrary, we see each child taking up a position toward them, whether in support or in defiance, either overtly or covertly. They are the issues that all children in the family had to deal with in the formulation of their lifestyles."[29]

Birth Order (Family Constellation)

One of the most influential factors to be considered in the development of a person's lifestyle is family constellation, the order of birth of children living within a family and the dynamic relationship between siblings and other members of the family group. In the life-pattern of every person, there is the imprint of one's position in the family with its definite characteristics. It is the child's subjective impression of his or her place in the family constellation—that much of a future attitude toward life depends.[30]

From the moment of birth, the child acts in a way in which he or she hopes to achieve significance or superiority in the family. Actions that are not productive in achieving these goals will be discarded and replaced by new behaviors aimed at the same goals.

An understanding of a child's classroom behavior can be helped by an exploration of the characteristics of the family constellation. The relationships that the children form within the family contribute greatly to their personality development and to transactions in the world outside the family. In the family each child develops his or her frame of reference through which (s)he perceives, interprets, and evaluates the world.[31]

This early relationship with other members of the family establishes a personal approach to others in an effort to gain a place in the group. All strivings are directed towards achieving or maintaining a feeling of security, a sense of belonging, and a certainty that the difficulties of life will be overcome and that he/she will emerge safely and victoriously. A child cultivates those qualities by which he or she hopes to achieve significance or even a degree of power and superiority in the family constellation. Note that:

With the birth of each child the situation changes. The parents may become older and more experienced or more discouraged if they have had difficulties with their first child. During each child's formative years the financial situation of the family may have changed, the parents may have moved to another neighborhood or city or even country, or their marital status may have changed. These and other possibilities may affect one or the other. A sickly or physically-challenged child, a child born just before or after the death of another, an only boy among girls, an only girl among boys, an obvious physical characteristic, an older person living in the home, or the favoritism of the parents toward a child—all these may have a profound effect on the child's environment.[32]

The following section explores the birth-order characteristics for the following five ordinal positions: *first, second, middle, youngest, only,* and *adopted*.

There are certain characteristics that are common to each of the sibling positions within the family constellation; however, the characteristics represent a composite, so not every detail will apply in all cases. We are making guesses aimed at probabilities. It is also important to note the difference between ordinal position and psychological birth order. For example, a person may have been chronologically sixth in a ten-person family, but psychologically perceived him/herself to be the first-born in a subgroup of three siblings. So, counselors should always ask clients, "Did you personally perceive yourself to be a first, second, middle, youngest, only, or adopted child? For what reasons?" Much criticism of birth order and lack of significance in research studies is partially due to limiting the scope of the inquiry to "ordinal" position and not "psychological" birth order.

Some general characteristics of various ordinal positions include the following:

FIRST-BORN CHILD

The oldest child has a unique situation in a family. Being born first entitles such a child to the parents' undivided attention, at least until another sibling is born. Usually an oldest child will conform to the parent's standard because he or she doesn't want to lose their favor. Such children tend to be very responsible because of their desire to meet the adult standards of their parents. When another sibling is born, they often initially feel "dethroned." Usually because they are bigger and more capable, the threat of the new arrival will diminish with the passing of time. However, if the second child is very close in age to the first, there is a chance that the second might be more capable than the older. The situation of the second sibling permanently dethroning the first is most frequent when the older child is a boy followed very closely by a girl. Her accelerated rate of human growth and development makes such a "dethronement" more possible. Other frequent characteristics include preference for authority, dislike for change, conservative viewpoint, being "responsible" for the other children, ambitious, achievement-oriented, and having a tendency to be bossy with peers and relate better to adults.

SECOND-BORN CHILD

Adler noted that second-born children often make the best counselors because they are keen observers and they can often relate to the "underdog" role. Such children come in on "the second act of the play." Having a "lap car" or a "moving rabbit" ahead of them often stimulates more rapid development.

Second-born are often keen observers. Co-author Roy Kern uses the following vivid example in his workshops:

First-born: "Mom, can I go out tonight?" Mother: "No, son. It's a school night and you must do your homework—you know the rules."

First-born: "Aw, Mom—come on—you never let me have any fun!" (stomps off—second-born observing all the while.)

Two days later, the second-born approaches the mother.

Second-born: "Mom, what are you doing? You're knitting—that's just great. Why, I've even got on the socks you knitted for me last month." He then follows with "Mom, I know it's a school night, but my friends just called me to go out for a pizza. I've finished all my homework—it would really mean a lot to me if I could go just for one hour, but I will understand if you say no."

And the answer usually is "Yes, of course," much to the chagrin of the oldest.

The second child has somewhat of an uncomfortable position in life. Mostly, the child also takes a steam-engine attitude, trying to catch up with the child in front, often feeling under constant pressure. It is not unusual to see these youngsters move right on past their older and more perfectionistic-minded first-borns.

The parents, however, are more calm and relaxed with a second child, less strict, and less preoccupied with child-rearing. The second child is usually more socially oriented, more aggressive and competitive, and quite often rejects rules and regulations.

The second child may exhibit these characteristics:

1.   Never having the parents' undivided attention.

2.   Always having in front another child who is more advanced.

3.   A feeling that the first child cannot be matched, which disputes equality.

4.   Acting as if in a race—hyperactive and pushy.

5.   If the first child is successful, more likely to feel uncertain and doubt one's own abilities.

6.   Being the opposite of the first child (if the first child is dependable and "good," the second may become undependable and "bad").

7.   Less concerned about winning adult approval than about winning peer approval.

8.   The child may frequently be a rebel.

MIDDLE CHILD

The middle child will usually try to overtake the first as a result of what Harold Mosak calls the "Avis Complex" ("because I'm second I'll try harder"). Usually the middle child will choose to compete in areas in which the oldest child is not proficient. If oldest children are good students, athletes, or models of good behavior, then middle children will probably be poor students, uninterested in athletics, and discipline problems; however, they might be good musicians, artists, or strong in an area where the oldest isn't skilled. Whereas the oldest child is the "center of the universe." the subsequent children must "slip in on the second or third act."

Middle children tend to be sensitive to injustices, unfairness, feelings of being slighted or abused, or of having no place in the group. When a younger sibling is born into the family, the middle child often feels dethroned, because of the new competition from the youngest child. The middle child also has a standard bearer in front and a pursuer in the rear and is surrounded by what is often perceived as competitors.

Such children may have a tendency to:

1. Feel they have neither the privileges of the youngest nor the rights of the oldest child.
2. Hold the conviction that people are unfair to them.
3. Feel unloved.
4. Become extremely discouraged and a problem child.
5. Replace their family if they do not feel as if they belong by becoming overly involved with a peer group.[33]

YOUNGEST CHILD

Youngest children have the unique situation that they have never been dethroned. They are generally the most powerful person in the family because of the many ways of getting the parents and other siblings to do things for them. Youngest children frequently are not taken seriously because they are the smallest, and as a result, they may be spoiled by others. However, it should also be noted that youngest children should have good sibling models from which to observe and learn.

1. Get more attention from the family.
2. Do not get as much parental pressure as their older siblings.
3. Are punished less.
4. Retain the baby role and place others in their service.
5. Feel often like an only child.
6. Usually have things done for them.
7. Have most decisions made for them by others and personal responsibility taken away from them.
8. Are not taken seriously.
9. Become the "boss" in the family.
10. Often ally her/himself with the first child.
11. Attempt to excel and overtake the older siblings.[34]

ONLY CHILD

Single ("only") children usually develop in one of two basic directions: either they will try to meet the adult level of competence or they will remain helpless and irresponsible as long as possible. Usually single children will have better relationships with people much older or much younger than they are, rather than with their peer group. Single children may refuse to cooperate when their every wish is not granted. They are similar to youngest children in that neither have ever been displaced. Single children are often loners, not very sharing-oriented, and may expect a "special place" without having earned it. They have also never had a sibling rival.

Other possible characteristics include being self-centered, feeling insecure because of being reminded, "you are all we have"; may become too adult-centered and have difficulty relating to peers; usually accepts the values of the parents; and are often ambitious and achievement-oriented.

The benefit of being a single child is that usually when "he or she speaks," a parent is there to listen (in contrast with five or more siblings in which a sibling is lucky to be heard). Greater financial resources from parents are often available because there is only one child.

ADOPTED CHILD

An important issue relates to the parental attitude regarding the decision to adopt a child. For example, many parents overprotect and/or pamper adopted children by means of a "We couldn't have any of our own, but this child will have the finest of everything" attitude. Another issue involves whether there are other siblings biologically born to the parents. "In" and "out" groups of siblings often result from such a situation. Of course, the advantages surrounding an adoption include the child's having been planned and desired by the parents and the adoption agency's having conducted a thorough investigation of the home environment prior to the child's placement in the home.

In large families there can be several subfamilies. Parents usually have less time to spend with each sibling, so there is often very little for which the siblings may compete.

Joan Drescher[35] has written a creative book for children entitled *The Birth Order Blues* in which she describes the phenomenon that so often happens in children—that each birth order feels the other positions are more favorable than their own. In a humorous way, she illustrates some of what most children say in a very concrete manner about their respective benefits and liabilities of the respective positions. Table 1 summarizes her own words from the child's perspective.

Table 1

Oldest—Advantages

You get to stay up later & talk to grown-ups.

You get to see a TV show others can't.

You get to bring in the cheese & crackers when company comes.

Because you're born first, you always get to go first.

Oldest—Disadvantages

We get the blame when everything goes wrong.

Too bossy.

Other children invade my room. They get into my clothes & records & secret stuff.

If you're born first, you get old first.

Middle—Advantages

You get to be older & younger at the same time. Sometimes I'm a little sister and sometimes I'm a big sister.

Middle—Disadvantages

I get my brother's hand-me-down bike instead of a new one.

It's like being the baloney hidden in a sandwich, or the hole in a donut.

People don't look up to you like they do with the oldest, or say you're cute like the littlest. You're just plain in the middle.

I get squashed in the middle.

Youngest—Advantages

My brothers & sisters teach me things, like how to skateboard.

My friends & family are my very own cheering squad.

Youngest—Disadvantages

I get worried that no one will notice me, so I make sure everyone knows when I'm around.

I didn't even get recorded in the baby book. I guess everything I do is a rerun.

You get everyone's old toys & clothes, and the older kids boss you around like crazy.

You are lucky if there's any space left on the refrigerator door for your pictures.

Only—Advantages

You do get to have your own room, but when it's a mess, you can't blame anyone else.

My pictures get the whole refrigerator door, and I'm the only kid opening presents in our house.

Only—Disadvantages

When it's dark, there's no one to talk to.

There are no brothers & sisters to ask advice when you don't want to ask your parents.

Adapted from Joan Drescher's *The Birth Order Blues*. Viking Press, NY: Penguin of Penguin Books,1993.

Eckstein explored 151 empirical articles showing significant differences between birth-order and personality variables. Here are his research findings.

Empirical Studies Indicating Significant Birth-Order-Related Personality Differences

Daniel Eckstein

Abstract. The formative influence of birth order on a person's core personality is one of Adler's most significant contributions to psychology. The author presents an initial exploration of 151 empirically-based articles on statistically significant birth-order differences. The results provide a starting point for counselors to begin to form hypotheses concerning dynamics in an individual's personality formulation.

Introduction. So important is the impact of birth order on a person's core personality that Freud's and Adler's initial choices of patients, and the theories developed on this clinical evidence, were profoundly influenced by birth order (Ansbacher & Ansbacher, 1956). For example, Freud, his mother's undisputed favorite and a typical firstborn, was conscious of his social status, valued authority and power over his peers, and once wrote that "the unworthiness of human beings, even of analysts, has always made a deep impression on me." (139)

Adler, conversely, was influenced by his status as a second son to discount Freud's "firstborn'" notion of the Oedipus complex (with its overemphasis on parent-child relations). In elaborating on the psychological significance of birth order, Adler saw his patients as individuals struggling for power and a sense of competence (the fate of many younger siblings).

Siblings raised together are often as different in their personalities as people from different families. In *Born to Rebel*, Sulloway (1996) argued that birth order explains why siblings are so different. Siblings use physical advantages in size and strength to gain a competitive edge. Sulloway asserted that, over time, strategies perfected by first-borns spawn counterstrategies by later-borns. The result is what Sulloway called an "evolutionary arms race" (p. 15) played out within the family.

> Childhood and the family are central to the story of human behavior because they provide the immediate causal context for these developmental scenarios. Childhood is about the search for a family niche. The first rule of the sibling road is to be different from one's brothers and sisters, especially if one happens to be a later-born. Sibling diversity is testimony to the powerful role that the environment plays in personality development. Although evolutionary principles guide this process, the story is one of seamless interactions between genetic potentials and environmental opportunities. (Sulloway, p. 118)

Purpose. The focus of this article is to provide a summary of some of the empirical support relating birth order to personality characteristics. I do not purport to present an exhaustive discussion of the percentage of studies reporting statistically significant and non-significant results; rather, the focus is on identifying studies that contain statistically significant results between personality differences and birth-order typologies and reporting descriptive data in terms of variables that differ according to birth order.

Methodology. In terms of methodology, Light & Smith (1971) introduced the term vote-counting to describe the procedures researchers use to collect and to report data. Their three suggested categories would be to report articles that (a) show significant differences in birth-order studies, (b) those that yield negative instances (i.e., negative correlation between a particular attribute and birth order when other results are showing positive correlations), and (c) those studies that yield non-significant results. A limitation of this article is that statistically non-significant research studies are not reported. However, the purpose of this article is not to provide a meta-analysis but rather to provide an initial overview of some of the existing literature. Thus, this article provides a response to the critic who says, "There is no statistical support for the relationship between birth-order differences and personality characteristics."

The following research focuses primarily, but not exclusively, on articles from 1960 to 1999. All articles reported statistically significant levels at or beyond the .05 level. It should be noted that, because of a lack of empirical validation, information such as Tolman's family constellation information has not been included.

Consistent with other Adlerian-based studies, the empirical birth-order studies were grouped into the following four major categories: *oldest, middle, youngest,* and *single* (only). I acknowledge that all first-borns are single children for a certain time and that additional categories such as second-born do exist, but the above four categories are the most widely documented in the literature. For each of the four types, I have presented a table showing common characteristics identified for that type and identifying the articles (as numbered in the bibliography) that indicated each characteristic.

Oldest. At least two researchers attributed each of 26 different characteristics to the oldest child (see Table 2). The six most frequently appearing attributes were (a) highest achieving, (b) highest IQ, (c) greatest academic success/fewest academic problems, (d) highest motivation and need for achievement, (e) over represented among learned groups (e.g., college students, faculty), and (f) most affiliative under stress.

Middle. At least two researchers attributed each of 6 different characteristics to the middle child (see Table 3). The three most frequently appearing attributes were (a) fewest "acting out" problems, (b) sociable, and (c) greatest feeling of not belonging.

Youngest. At least two researchers attributed each of 14 different characteristics to the youngest child (see Table 4). The three most frequently appearing attributes were (a) greatest overrepresentation of psychiatric disorders if from a small family, (b) empathetic, and (c) tendency toward alcoholism.

Single. At least two researchers attributed each of 13 different characteristics to the single (only) child (see Table 5). The four most frequently appearing attributes were (a) most need for achievement, (b) higher achievers than all but oldest children, (c) most likely to go to college, and (d) most behavior problems.

Conclusion. Adler (as cited in Ansbacher & Ansbacher, 1956) stressed that "the golden rule of individual psychology is that everything can be different" (p. 56). Thus, birth-order personality differences are not meant to stereotype people into rigid either-or categories. Such information should be coupled with other issues such as gender, age differences between siblings, blended families, death of a sibling, family atmosphere, family values, and early recollections to form a comprehensive picture of the individual. Psychological birth order (i.e., when a child feels like a first-born despite being the third-born) is also not addressed in this survey.

Nonetheless, I do identify 151 empirically based studies reflecting significant birth-order personality characteristics. Counselors can use birth-order personality differences to begin to form initial hypotheses, or, as Dreikurs (1971) stressed, to dig psychologically relevant gold mines in the exploration of family (or family equivalent) dynamics in one's personality formulation.

This study has offered a brief summary of the birth-order findings prior to the year 2000. I recognize that the vote-counting technique which has been employed in this study does not provide the magnitude of the relationships and, furthermore, can provide misleading findings if the statistical power is less than .50 in a particular study (Hedges & Olkin, 1980). The contribution of this study is that it presents a summary of birth-order information which may provide a basis for other reviews of the literature such as narrative reviews, annotated bibliographies, and meta-analyses.

Table 2 Birth-Order Attributes of Oldest Children

High achievers (5, 25, 45, 67, 75, 85, 99, 112, 127, 139, 149)

Highest IQ (4, 17, 18, 19, 26, 39, 58, 102, 144)

Greatest academic success/fewest academic problems (1, 4, 17, 18, 25, 58, 120, 123, 148)

Highly motivated, high need for achievement (7, 45, 47, 58, 113, 118, 119, 126)

Overrepresented among learned groups (4, 5, 18, 55, 57, 67)

Most affiliative under stress (62, 72, 92, 121, 131, 147)

Least conventional sexually (58, 61, 68, 135, 140)

Most affiliative (1, 41, 58, 81, 98)

Greatest fearfulness in new situations (35, 58, 66, 88, 135)

Earliest sexuality (58, 61, 68, 135, 140)

Mature behavior (33, 4, 114, 146)

Easiest influence by authority (16, 58, 89, 135)

Conformist to parental values (45, 58, 73, 84)

Dependent on approval of others (58, 59, 73)

Most likely to be a leader (52, 67, 128)

Most vulnerable to stress (72, 121, 126)

Highest self-esteem (37, 58)

Self-disciplined (58, 84)

Responsible and conscientious (45, 58)

Competent and confident (55, 58)

Conservative toward change (45, 58)

Highest number of U.S. presidents (58, 143)

Highest percentage of Type A behavior and coronary heart disease (74, 107)

Highest percentage of frightening dreams (90, 91)

Women overrepresented in leadership positions (45, 46)

Higher narcissism (39, 76)

Note: Numbers refer to entries in bibliography found in Appendix III.

Table 3 Birth-Order Attributes of Middle Children

Fewest "acting out" problems (58, 60, 125, 124)

Sociable (44, 45, 58, 100)

Greatest feeling of not belonging (45, 58, 93)

Successful in team sports (58, 134)

Relates well to older and younger people (44, 58)

Competes in areas not attempted by oldest (45, 133)

Note: Numbers refer to entries in bibliography found in Appendix III.

Table 4 Birth-Order Attributes of Youngest Children

Overrepresentation of psychiatric disorders if from small families (13, 14, 17, 58)

Empathetic (58, 59, 131, 136)

Most likely to be an alcoholic (10, 11, 21, 22)

Act as single child if seven-year difference (64, 126, 137)

Characteristics of oldest in anxiety and fear if five years younger than next oldest (35, 58, 66)

Most popular (43, 58, 95)

Highest representation among writers, especially autobiographers and family historians (23, 29, 58)

Overrepresented in activities involving social interplay (43, 58, 100)

Highest self-esteem (58, 77)

Lowest IQ (17, 58)

Cognitively specific (58, 65)

Spoiled (45, 58)

Most affiliative (12, 95)

Most disturbed at losing a parent during childhood (40, 82)

Note: Numbers refer to entries in bibliography found in Appendix III.

Table 5 Birth-Order Attributes of Single (Only) Children

Most need for achievement (7, 47, 58, 113, 119)

Highest achievers except for oldest children (4, 18, 32, 69, 102)

Most likely to go to college (15, 144, 146, 149)

Most behavior problems (33, 77, 114, 146)

Lowest need for affiliation (36, 49, 116)

Most need for affiliation under stress (62, 72, 121)

Highest percentage of Type A behavior and coronary heart disease, as oldest child (74, 107)

Selfish (49, 126)

Most likely to have psychiatric disorders (17, 137)

Most likeable next to youngest child (1, 19)

Most cooperative (49, 126)

Most trusting (49, 135)

Strongest gender identity/least androgynous (20, 135)

Note: Numbers refer to entries in bibliography found in Appendix III.

References

Ansbacher, H. L., & Ansbacher, R. R. (Eds.). (1956). *The individual psychology of Alfred Adler*. New York: Basic Books.

Dreikurs, R. (1971). *Social equality: The challenge of today*. Chicago: Henry Regnery.

Freud, S. (1960). *An outline of psychoanalysis*, rev. ed. New York: Norton.

Hedges, L., & Olkin, 1. (1985). *Statistical methods for meta-analysis*. New York: Harcourt, Brace, Jovanovich.

Light, R. J., & Smith, P. V. (1971). Accumulating evidence: Procedures for resolving contradictions among different research studies. *Harvard Educational Review*, 41, 419–471.

Sulloway, F. J. (1996). *Born to rebel*. New York: Pantheon Books.

Guidelines for Sibling Ratings

The interrelationship of people allows an opportunity to extend the information that the individual has given in data collection portions of the lifestyle process. The way in which this happens is that behaviors are retained in an individual's repertoire because they are useful means of dealing with others. If a behavior lacks utility, it is soon dropped in favor of other actions. One has only to note the behavior of a child of deaf parents discarding the sound of crying yet retaining the physical manifestations of crying. In the same way we retain what works for us as children in our later lives.

The following ratings are used as examples of utility of behaviors and are taken from the ratings section of the lifestyle investigation guide. People rating themselves as highly sensitive and easily hurt use this set of behaviors in a special way. One guess about the use of this behavior would be that the individual exerts a great deal of control over his/her environment. Few persons would verbally attack an individual who is easily hurt or sensitive. In this way an individual may exert profound control over a situation or an environment. Such individuals have found a way to limit access to themselves by others and limit the types of feedback about behaviors which the environment has to offer. Therefore, being sensitive and easily hurt generates a socially powerful position rather than a socially weak position.

Another descriptive characteristic could be a high rating on considerateness. An individual who is considerate is by many standards a desirable person to interact with in social situations. But if the behavior is over-used, it can be an attention-getting mechanism. Being considerate can be used by an individual with a need to be the center of attention, as shown by the "model husband." The "model husband" is considerate, kind, gentle, etc., at all times except when drinking. At this point he becomes suspicious and argumentative in demeanor. How can such apparently opposite behaviors co-exist in one individual? A person can employ socially useful and socially useless behaviors to effect their overall goal-directed behavior. The situation of drinking or not drinking merely represent two occasions to be the center of attention which are affected by differing methods at each respective time. Being considerate is one side of a two-faced coin. While in a drunken state, being argumentative attains the same objective of being noticed.

Sibling ratings indicate the specific way an individual found significance with his or her siblings and/or children in general.

The Use of Literature in Lifestyle Assessment

Favorite stories, fairy tales, television characters, etc. are other useful ways to find out about one's formative experiences. Literature has had a decided influence upon Adlerian psychology in general and on lifestyle assessment in particular. For example, Adler noted that:

Our knowledge of the individual is very old. To name only a few instances, the historical and personality descriptions of the ancient peoples, the Bible, Homer, Plutarch, all the Greek and Roman poets, sagas, fairy tales, and myths, show a brilliant understanding of personality. Until recent times it was chiefly the poets who best succeeded in getting the clue to a person's lifestyle. Their ability to show the individual living, acting, and dying as an indivisible whole in closest context with the tasks of his sphere of life rouses our admiration for their work to the highest degree.[36]

Adler also wrote that:

Someday soon it will be realized that the artist is the leader of mankind on the path to the absolute truth. Among poetic works of art which have led me to the insights of individual psychology, the following stand out as pinnacles: fairy tales, the Bible, Shakespeare, and Goethe.[37]

Eckstein describes how he integrated the projective use of literature and lifestyle assessment in a graduate counseling course. A student described the impact of literature on her personal "pilgrimage" in the following manner:

The word "pilgrimage" evokes in my mind images of ancient pilgrimages across northern Spain to the sanctuary at Santiago de Compostela. These pilgrimages are superbly described in James Michener's Iberia. In the year 1130, a French priest, Aymery de Picaud, who lived along one of the pilgrim routes, described the incredible dangers faced by the pilgrims. But for those who made it, the glories seem worth the hardships. It was said that only those who made this terribly hazardous trip to Compostela truly deserved to be called pilgrims. Thus a pilgrimage symbolizes to me a mixture of pain and pleasure.

In a sense, literary experiences can be compared to a pilgrimage. Literature encompasses all of the thoughts and emotions common to man. Written words have the power to reach into the darkest recesses of my mind and force me to take a look at the unlovely thoughts that lurk, as did the robbers who lay in wait for the pilgrims, just beneath the surface. Written words also have the power to bring to my awareness the parts of my mind that are bathed in the sunlight of love, sunlight such as the pilgrims experienced as they overcame each difficulty to demonstrate an expression of their devotion. Each word that I absorb brings me a little further along the path, with roadblocks and detours scattered along the way, leading me to my ultimate destiny.[38]

The woman then concludes her own summarizing literary pilgrimage as follows:

With grief for Bambi I did weep;
An appointment at Treasure Island I did keep.
I entered the magic land of Oz;
For the miserable poor, I glorified in Robin Hood's cause.
The Bible was a lamp unto my feet:
Les Misérables my anger did heat. Rebecca's misery in Gothic gray
Was lightened by a Shakespearean play.
I felt with Admiral Perry the bone-chilling cold;
I galloped with Revere on his midnight ride so bold.
I gloried in the myths of ancient Greece and Rome,
As on the magic carpet I traveled from home.
I watched in the night with the Highwayman's black-haired Bess;
And trekked with Daniel Boone in the untamed wilderness.
The legends of Beowulf, Roland and El Cid
And the poetry of Longfellow in my heart I hid.
I journeyed with Frost down the road not taken;
and marveled at the essays of Francis Drew;
The Robe my faith did renew.
I traveled Death's journey with Thanatopsis;
And so thus ends my "novel" synopsis.

What do all these past readings mean to me in a psychological sense? They have become a part of me because in my development as a human being, these books, and many others, have stirred my blood. My mind was, and is, like a sponge soaking up knowledge. Every book has the potential power to change my mind and to alter the direction of my development.[39]

Thus, another means of exploring one's childhood is to ask about important stories, proverbs, Bible verses, or key teachings of the child's own particular religious beliefs. Like early recollections, there is a selective and projective nature to such memories which are a valuable potential "window" into the inner early childhood formative events.[40]

The Number One Priority and the "Top Card"

The number one priority is determined on the basis of the person's answers to the questions "What is most important in my quest for belonging?" and "What must I avoid at all costs?" Kefir[41] originally defined four number one priorities: *comfort, pleasing, control* and *superiority*. Dewey[42] also credits Rudolf Dreikurs and William Pew with the same four priorities. She notes that although it is often difficult for an individual to determine his or her own lifestyle, the relative order of priorities is generally recognizable.

The following compares the four priorities with what is to be avoided at all costs:

Number one priorities:	To be avoided at all costs:
Comfort	Stress
Pleasing	Rejection
Control	Humiliation
Superiority	Meaninglessness

Although people seldom give up their number one priority, it is possible to become more aware through insight and to "catch oneself" being overinvolved in each priority. Kefir and Corsini propose that a quick assessment of a client's lifestyle and core convictions could be accomplished by a clinical investigation of the person's number one priority. The priorities are further defined as follows:

Comfort. Self-indulgence and immediate gratification characterize the comfort priority. The price for pleasure is often in diminished productivity, since they will not risk frustration and do not want responsibility. Being able to delay immediate gratification is necessary for such vocational fields as medicine and graduate school, as they require many years of training prior to completion. Some stress is also helpful in providing a positive motivator. For example, it is a grain of sand that motivates an oyster to form a pearl. Undue comfort is often correlated with lethargy and diminished risk-taking.[43]

Pleasing. Pleasers often are challenging in respecting themselves or in receiving respect from others. The price the pleaser pays is stunted growth, alienation, and retribution.[44] Pleasers are good at tuning in to what others want and need. Pleasers are characterized by an "external locus of control" using Rotter's[45] term where one's happiness is in someone else's hands. Pleasers especially have difficulties in the political arena because there is always someone who disapproves of their actions. Pleasers often choose perfectionistic role models with whom they vainly jump through countless hoops, almost always in vain, as the "Good Housekeeping Seal of Approval" simply will never be granted.

Control. There are two sub-types of control: control of others and control of self. By striving for, and perhaps even attaining control, the negative consequence is that feelings of challenge and resistance in those around them are often evoked. Control of self is characterized by being "on edge," "uptight," and "hyper." Diminished spontaneity, creativity, flexibility and an inability to "go with the flow" are additional emotional costs for overcontrol.

Superiority. Being competent, being right, being useful, being a victim, or being a martyr are some of the specific manifestations of superiority. Firstborns often expect to be "number one" and are subjected to a feeling of meaninglessness when "dethroned." Such strivings also lead to undo competitive behavior. There is a profound parable relative to getting to the top described in Trina Paulus' *Hope For the Flowers*. It is a story of an aggressive caterpillar who literally steps on top of others in his single-minded quest to get to the top of a "caterpillar pillar." His own awakening occurs when his former partner appears to him as a brilliant yellow butterfly. He then leaves the vertical pillar to begin his own metamorphosis by being willing to let go of his former self, or "die," to enter a cocoon for his own transformation.[46]

The "price" paid for superiority is over-involvement, over-responsibility, fatigue, stress, psychosomatic illnesses, and uncertainty about one's relationships with others.

Steve Cunningham adapted Eckstein's lifestyle animal typologies and created what he called one's "Top Card." *In Positive Discipline in the Classroom*, Jane Nelsen and Lynn Lott creatively adapted his "Top Card" to the #1 Priorities. Specific strengths and potential blind spots or liabilities of one's early style are illustrated in the chart on pages 106–107.

The Five Animal Types representative of the five lifestyle traits:

- Aggressive—Tiger;
- Conforming—Chameleon;
- Defensive—Turtle;
- Individualistic—Eagle;
- Resistive— Salmon

If you'd like to avoid:	Then your top card is:	And perhaps you:	Assets:
Rejection and Hassles	Pleasing (Chameleon)	Act friendly. Say yes & mean no. Give in. Worry about what others want more than your needs. Gossip instead of confronting directly. Try to fix everything & make everybody happy	Sensitive to others. Have lots of friends. Considerate. Compromiser. Non-threatening. Likely to volunteer. People count on you. Usually see positives in people & things
Criticism, Humiliation, and Ridicule	Control (Eagle)	Hold back. Boss others. Organize. Argue. Get quiet & wait for others to coax you. Do it yourself. Stuff your feelings. Cover all the bases before you make a move.	Good leader & crisis manager. Assertive. Persistent. Well organized. Productive. Law abiding. Get what you want. Able to get things done & figure things out. Take charge of situations. Wait patiently.
Meaninglessness, Unimportance, and Stupidity	Superiority (Lion)	Put down people or things. Knock yourself. Talk about the absurdity of life. Correct others. Overdo. Take on too much. Worry about always doing better. Operate on "shoulds."	Knowledgeable. Precise. Idealistic. Get a lot done. Make people laugh. Receive a lot of praise, awards & prizes. Don't have to wait for others to tell you what to do to get things done. Have a lot of self-confidence.
Stress and Pain	Comfort (avoidance) (Turtle)	Make jokes. Intellectualize. Do only the things you already do well. Avoid new experiences. Take the path of least resistance. Leave sentences incomplete. Avoid risks. Hide so no one can find out you aren't perfect.	People enjoy being around you. Flexible. Do what you do well. Easy-going. Look out for self & own needs. Can count on others to help. Make others feel comfortable.

Problems:	Someone can be a friend to you by:	What I really want is:
Invite revenge cycles & others to feel rejected.	Telling you how much they love you.	To do what I want while others clap.
Feel resentful & ignored.	Teaching you a lot.	For others to like me, accept me, and be flexible.
Get in trouble for trying to look good while doing bad.	Showing approval.	
Not having things the way you want them.	Showing appreciation.	For others to take care of me & make hassles go away.
Reduction in personal growth.	Letting you know you won't be in trouble if you say how you really feel.	
Lots of sense of self & what pleases self.		
Lack spontaneity.	Saying "OK."	To be in control even though others can be better, smarter.
Social & emotional distance.	Giving you choices.	
Want to keep others from finding weak spots.	Letting you lead.	To get respect, cooperation & loyalty.
Invite power struggles. End up sick.	Asking how you feel.	
Avoid dealing with issues when you feel criticized.	Giving you time & space to sort out your feelings.	For others to have faith in me & give me permission to do what I want.
Get defensive instead of open.		
Sometimes wait for permission.		
Critical & fault finding.		To have choices & go at my own pace.
Overwhelmed, overburdened.	Telling you how significant you are.	To do it best.
Invite others to feel incapable & insignificant.		To get appreciation & recognition from others & a spiritual connection.
Seen as a know-it-all or rude & insulting & don't know it's a problem.	Thanking you for your contributions.	
Never happy because you could have done more or better.	Helping you get started with a small step.	To be told I'm right.
Have to put up with so many imperfect people around you. Sometimes you don't do anything.	Telling you that you're right.	
Suffer boredom.	Not interrupting.	For things to be as easy as they look.
Lazy, lack of productivity.	Inviting your comments. Listening quietly.	To be left alone.
Hard to motivate.		
Don't do your share.	Leaving room for you.	To have my own space & pace.
Invite special attention & service.	Showing faith.	
Worry a lot but no one knows how scared you are.	Encouraging small steps.	I don't want to argue.
Lose out on the contact of sharing.		
Juggle uncomfortable situations rather than confront them.		
Wait to be taken care of instead of becoming independent.		
Invite others to feel stressed.		

From *Positive Discipline in the Classroom*, Revised 3rd Edition by Jane Nelsen, Ed.D. and Lynn Lott, M.A. and H. Stephen Glenn, Ph.D., copyright © 2000 by Jane Nelsen, Lynne Lott and H. Stephen Glenn. Used by permission of Random House, Inc.

Early Recollections Interpretation Guidelines

When we have a pretty clear picture of what an individual's early life was like, we move into the area of early recollections. These ERs are essential to lifestyle analysis because they are used to validate our hypotheses of how an individual views self, other people, and life in general based on the family constellation information.

According to Barker and Bitter, human memory serves and reflects the individual's movement, providing a perceived continuity to experience and focusing an emotional interest on present activity. Adler's discovery of the projective quality of early recollections (ERs) gave him a positive approach to the exploration of the personality. As adolescents or adults most people retain 6 to 12 memories from early childhood which, when reviewed, comprise a personal narrative of one's life. Adler believed that a person's earliest memory was especially significant, offering an instant view of the individual's fundamental attitude(s). All memories were distortions to some extent as they are personal interpretations of reality, filtered, interpreted, and stored by the individual for future use.[47]

Although some psychologists argue that children remember almost nothing before the age of conscious recall, usually pegged as three or four, Nora Newcombe has been steadily accumulating evidence that nonverbal memories do exist and may affect behavior, thoughts, and feelings years later.

While verbal ability seems an essential part of conscious memory storage and retrieval from about ages of six or seven on, Newcombe's studies of younger children suggest that early memories are stored by a different process—probably more sensory than narrative. At ages three to five, the prefrontal cortex, the verbal center that's known to be heavily involved with memory storage and retrieval, is only partially developed. This may be why early memories are seldom consciously retrievable.

Newcombe has found that three to five-year-olds have measurable neurophysiological responses when shown photographs of people they once knew, but don't consciously recognize. When hooked to lie detector-like instruments that measure perspiration and skin conductance response, children responded more often to photos of former preschool classmates than to kids they'd never known.

If, as Newcombe's research suggests, early memories are stored by a different process, it's not such a big leap to assume that there's no expiration date on these memories, and that, below the level of our awareness, they respond to reminiscent stimuli years later.[48]

The following are some that one might consider to gain a better understanding of the meaning of early recollections. Roy Kern, Susan Belangee, and Daniel Eckstein have summarized ER interpretation guidelines in the following section called "Rose-Colored View of the World."[49]

ROSE-COLORED VIEW OF THE WORLD

Adler believed that through life experiences, we create events/beliefs in systematic ways that relate to lifestyle. It is as if we are looking at the world through rose-colored glasses. We view the world in a certain way. We then venture out looking for experiences that validate our view of the world. It is also analogous to how we put on socks (e.g., always left foot first, then right foot). We only remember those things that fit and have meaning to our lifestyle.

Adler indicated that a technique the clinician could use to assess the individuals "Rose Colored Glasses View of the World" was to employ the early recollection technique. Adler stated that early recollections (ERs) are reminders one carries with him/her that identifies one's limits and meanings of life's circumstances. Dreikurs referred to early recollections, or ERs, as "the music behind the words." We see ERs as representing the unedited content of memories we carry with us that confirm our immaculate perception of how we attack life's problems. To follow we have presented to the reader some important questions, procedures, and suggestions as to how the clinician may implement this technique created by Adler some eighty years ago.

TYPICAL QUESTIONS AND ISSUES RELATED TO ERs

One question frequently ask by individuals who are somewhat suspicious of the approach is the statement that we usually are only going to remember the most discouraging events in our early childhood and thus how can one make any sense out of the person's total lifestyle. We generally have three types of ERs reported to us by clients. There are those that are uncomfortable, traumatic, or discouraging, those that are enjoyable, and those that are ambiguous. Thus there is no evidence to confirm that we only remember the most distasteful events in our lives.

Another frequent question is "What if you remember something because your parents told you about it?" Adler would have said that this was not an ER, but rather a report. Reports usually do not have feelings associated with them.

If someone says they can't remember anything, Adlerians would propose that this is not a movement by the client toward resistances, but rather poor goal alignment between the client and the therapist. At other times when an individual has difficulty remembering ERs it could be due to some form of unreported trauma in the client's life. If it seems to be neither of these we suggest that you have the client create early recollections. A research study by the first author shows that these ERs are as valuable as those generated by the client from one's real life experiences.

What if the clinician is confronted with the ultimate threat to one's self-esteem and a therapist, which is: "What if I collected the ERs and still cannot make sense of them?" Our response is do not panic! Other possible techniques the clinician may employ to elicit additional information are to ask the following questions.

- Think of your favorite story or passage in the Bible or other significant religious book. What is it?
- What is your favorite cartoon?
- What is your favorite fairy tale?
- What is your favorite comic book character?
- A final valuable projective technique that works well with children is to request the child to identify three of their favorite animals in the jungle.

Since we believe in purposeful behavior, we assume that the client remembers the above materials because it fits with one's belief system or lifestyle. In other words, a person regardless of the stimulus statement will put on and apply his/her rose colored glasses on whatever you ask them to discuss. One must keep in mind when analyzing projective information that the information reported by the client may be viewed from two distinct perspectives. First, the information provided by the client is reflecting events when their lifestyle/belief system is getting them in trouble and not working for them. We have also found that when the client reports information that is extremely positive, we have found it is useful to view this information as how life is when their chosen lifestyle and belief system accompanying their lifestyle is working for them. In other words, one set of ERs may give you information on what life is like for me as well as information on how I would like it to be.

WHY USE ERs?

To follow are some of the major reasons we believe ERs are important when employing this projective technique:

1. They give us, as clinicians, clues about a client's lifestyle or cognitive belief system, which the client uses to keep himself/ herself out of trouble as well as in trouble.

2. They can help you understand the best way of interacting with the client. For example, if the ER's reflect a controlling style of dealing with life's problems the clinician may wish to

present information in a more tentative way. For example: I could be wrong but could it be ...?

3. ERs provide you and the client insight on how one solves major problems related to life's tasks (work, social relationships, and intimate relationships).

4. They can be used as tools to educate people on how their thinking helps them solve problems.

5. ERs can provide the clinician with important information on the connection between one's belief system and somatic illnesses.

6. Over the years the first author has had times when he would complete a total lifestyle interview with the client and then collect the ERs and find that his hunch as to the lifestyle of the individual was in contradiction with the ERs. Thus we believe ERs can serve as a validating process for the lifestyle interview. When you get conflicting information between ERs and other interview information trust the ERs.

How to Collect Early Recollections?

Presently there are numerous ways in which Adlerians collect ERs with their clients. To follow is our suggested approach and the one that has been employed to teach graduate students for the last 25 years. To follow are the steps that we believe one could use as ways of acquiring valuable data related to the ERs process.

1. Inform the client that you will be recording information on paper to conduct this segment of the interview. Begin by stating "Now that we have objective information about your lifestyle, I want to get at more subjective information on how you solve life's problems. One technique I use to do this is called an early recollections technique. What I want you to do is to think back as far as you can remember, preferably before the age of 10, and tell me an early memory or recollection of an event that has a feeling associated with it."

2. As the client provides the information on the ERs, it is important for the clinician to reframe from using clarification questions that may lead the client. The clinician is most interested in receiving as much unedited information as possible. Any attempt by the clinician to ask too early in the process to clarify information may interfere with the process.

3. When the client has finished recalling the memory, the clinician should then ask, "What was your feeling during that point in time?"

4. We believe, if the client does not identify a clear affect word, it is permissible for the clinician to probe or clarify. If the client still cannot identify a feeling word, then the clinician may question if the ER is a report versus an early recollection.

5. Next, ask the client to take a snapshot of the most vivid part of the memory and have him/her tell you what the snapshot is. You might wish to use this statement. "Now I'd like you to focus on the most vivid part of that memory. If you were to take a picture or snapshot of the most vivid part of that memory, what would it be?" or "If you could freeze a frame of that ERs that you just gave me what would it be?"

6. Record this on paper and then request the client to identify the most vivid feeling associated with this snapshot or freeze frame.

7. Generally we suggest that the clinician collect three to four ERs that include the foregoing procedure. For us, however, the rule of thumb is, if four does not give you enough information, collect as many as needed.

A Summary of the Process

- Collect 3-5 early recollections
- ERs before age 10
- Vivid memory with a feeling
- Snapshot/Freeze frame of ERs with a feeling associated

How to Make Sense of What You Just Collected

Again, each Adlerian has adopted his or her own special way of assessing ERs. To follow are some guidelines we have found most helpful.

- Headline—one line that answers the question: What does the ER say?

- Look for the reoccurring themes and feelings in each of the ERs or the other projective techniques used. For example, mistakes that are consistent in each of the ERs may indicate the importance of controlling life by following the rules, not making mistakes, being right, or it could reflect a person with high expectations.

- How detailed are the ERs? This may give cues as to the importance order or rule-focused behavior in a person's life.

- Number of people involved—note people that are present in the ER as well as those people who are left out of ER (i.e., early recollections only included females or two brothers were included, but the third brother was left out/why)? Other questions from this information according to theory are it is one indicator related to social interest. We have also found that individuals not mentioned in the ERs helps us understand gender issues and parental and sibling issues.

- Are the ERs remembered in color? This has been a important cue that a person is quite visual and thereby chooses certain types of careers or acquires much of their data on problem solving from visual cues.

- Finally, what parts of the ERs are accentuated (non-verbal behavior, tone of voice)? We, as Adler, believe that organ dialect is an important cue related to understanding the lifestyle of the individual. All behavior is movement regardless of how miniscule it appears to the naked eye or the unskilled ear.

To follow are additional guidelines and suggestions that might be helpful for clinicians using the early recollections technique.

- Give more emphasis to initial recollections than the latter ones. Similarly, more importance should be placed on "less spectacular" events. For example, almost everybody would remember their house burning down, but how many people would remember "sitting in the corner by myself stacking blocks?"

- Always get both the content and the affective feeling concerning the ER. After an individual shares a memory, always ask: "And how did you feel?"

- ERs will change before and after counseling just as the individual's attitude about the environment, others, and self change.

- Don't be afraid to guess about the meaning of ERs. If you're correct, the person will let you know by means of a "recognition reflex," a slight smile, or nod of acknowledgment. If you're incorrect, he or she may look confused or puzzled. But even when you're "wrong," the person has still defined himself or herself even if it's to disagree with a particular interpretation.

- Separate ERs may be considered as individual beads comprising a necklace. Finding unifying themes provides the string that couples or explains seemingly inconsistent, separate ERs.

- Shulman and Mosak note the following common thematic topics found in ERs: dethronement (the birth of a younger sibling or another person entering who takes center stage), surprises, obstacles, affiliation, security, skill tasks dependency, external authority, self-control, status, power, morality, human interactions, new situations, excitement, sexuality, gender, nurturance, confusion, luck, sickness, and death. The second part of the ER, the subject's feeling and identifying what was most vivid about the ER, gives valuable insight into what the person concluded about the event, the "therefore . . ." Shulman and Mosak provide the following list of representative response themes: observer, problem-solving, compliance or rebellion, a call for help, revenge, suffering, manipulation, seeking excitement, pretense, denial, resolve, competence, social interest, activity, distance-keeping, cooperation, overconfidence, self- aggrandizement, criticism, and feeling avoidance.[50]

- Powers and Griffith summarize ERs utilizing the three major factors of sequence, similarity, and symmetry. "Sequence means the arrangement of the entire set of early recollections, and the relationship of each to the ones before and after it in the series. Similarity means a repetition of (or a variation upon) ideas or themes in applying various early recollections. . . . Symmetry means correspondence between two early recollections as they balance one another, or are juxtaposed as if to represent two sides of an issue."[51]

- Other general guides for ER interpretation are summarized by Adler in Ansbacher and Ansbacher:

  1. Much comes to light through the choice of presentation of a "we" or "I" situation.

  2. Much, too, comes to light from the mention of the mother.

  3. Recollections of dangers and accidents, as well as of corporal and other punishments, disclose the exaggerated tendency to keep in mind particularly the hostile side of life.

  4. The recollection of the birth of a brother or sister reveals the situation of dethronement.

  5. The recollection of the first visit to the kindergarten or school shows the great impressions produced by new situations.

  6. The recollection of sickness or death is often linked with a fear of these dangers, and occasionally with the attempt to become better equipped to meet them, possibly as a doctor or a nurse.

  7. Recollections of a stay in the country with the mother, as well as the mention of certain persons like the mother, the father, or the grandparents in a friendly atmosphere, often show not only a preference for these persons, who evidently pampered the child, but also the exclusion of others.

  8. Recollection of misdeeds, thefts, and sexual misdemeanors that have been committed usually point to a great effort to keep them from occurring again.[52]

- In seeking common interpretive elements for both ERs and dreams, Adler's advice is important:

  We need to warn ourselves that we cannot explain a dream without knowing its relationship to the parts of the personality. Neither can we lay down any fixed and rigid rules of dream interpretation. The golden rule of individual psychology is: "Everything can be different." We must modify each dream interpretation to fit the individual concerned; and each individual is different. If we are not careful, we will only look for types or for universal symbols, and that is not enough. The only valid dream interpretation is that which can be integrated with an individual's general behavior, early memories, problems, etc. In each case the contents of the dream should be gone over with the patient and as many associations elicited from him as possible.[53]

So, we cannot interpret dreams without first knowing the dreamer.

- Kaplan suggests that the following ten questions be answered relative to ERs:

  1. Who is present in the recollection?
  2. Who is remembered with affection?
  3. Who is disliked in the recollection?
  4. What problem(s) is (are) confronted in the recollection?
  5. What special talent(s) or ability is (are) revealed in the recollection?
  6. Is the recollection generally pleasant or unpleasant?
  7. What is the client's level of activity in the recollection?
  8. What emotion does the client feel and/or show pertaining to the recollection?
  9. What does the recollection suggest to you about the client's social interest?
  10. What fictional goal(s) is (are) implied in the recollection?[54]

Explanatory Style and ERs

Nichols and Feist compare Seligman's relationship between explanatory style and a person's ER's. Seligman suggests that whenever people face uncontrollable negative events they construe the causes of these events in three relevant dimensions. They may (1) attribute the cause to either themselves (an internal explanation) or to the situation (an external explanation); (2) evolve a stable explanation if the cause persists across time or an unstable explanation if they see the cause as transient; and (3) acquire either a global or a specific explanation, depending on whether they believe the cause affects numerous outcomes or is limited to a single event. People who use stable, global, and internal explorations to attribute the causes of negative events have an optimistic explanatory style, whereas those who habitually construe unstable, specific, and eternal causes for negative events manifest an pessimistic explanatory style.

Their findings are that subjects with an optimistic explanatory style, compared with pessimists, recalled earliest recollections that received higher scores on the following six variables.

1. Optimists were likely to include other people in their earliest recollection, whereas pessimists typically made no mention or infrequent mention of others or recalled others only as an afterthought.

2. Subjects with an optimistic explanatory style tended to perceive themselves as active. They often included events in which they participated with others in activities in which they were most effective and competent. Conversely, pessimists frequently presented themselves as followers, observers, and victims. Because they saw themselves as passive, their ERs seldom presented descriptions of attempts to control a situation; instead, pessimists were more likely to reveal stories in which they were controlled by their environment.

3. Optimists recalled clearer and more distinctive events; that is, they usually presented descriptions that contained identifying characteristics, such as the specific appearance of other people, the location of the event, their own motivations, or a combination of these characteristics.

4. Optimists were more likely than pessimists to report sustained interpersonal interactions in their earliest recollection. In contrast, pessimists were more likely to recall ERs in which their involvement with others was only moderate or sporadic or in which they observed the interaction of others but were not involved.

5. ERs of optimists contained themes of personal competence and mastery of the environment, whereas those of pessimists included stories of failure in the attempts by themselves or others to gain mastery. Optimists seem to view themselves as masterful, competent people who tend to remember past successes rather than failures. When they did recall failures, they appeared to view them as temporary setbacks, confined to one case, and not their fault.

6. Optimists recalled more pleasant ERs than did pessimists.[55]

ERs and Metaphor Therapy

Richard Kopp describes the relationship between ERs and metaphor therapy, which he defines as follows:

A metaphor creates a resemblance between two different things. The term is derived from the Greek, meta meaning "above" or "over" and pherein which means "to carry or bear." Thus, metaphor carries meaning from one thing or place to another. For example, when Romeo says "Juliet is the sun," Shakespeare is suggesting that there is a resemblance between certain qualities of the sun and Juliet. Linguists refer to the sun as the "vehicle" of the metaphor, and Juliet as the "topic."

Metaphors occur frequently in everyday speech, especially when one wants to express emotionally charged content. For example, one person may convey a feeling of helplessness in the face of a series of life events, saying, "I'm sinking in quicksand," another states, "We're in a tug of war," to represent her struggle with a friend. Note that the metaphor-maker employs an image (i.e., sinking in quicksand, a tug of war) as the "vehicle" to communicate meaning about a "topic" to which the image refers (i.e., a feeling of helplessness in the face of life events, a personal relationship). Note also that the metaphor is false as a literal statement, that is, people are not actually sinking in quicksand or shooting themselves in the foot.[56]

ERs are metaphoric representations of the recollector's current lifestyle. For example, consider the memory of looking at one's seventh birthday cake and being afraid of not being able to blow out all of the candles. Kopp observes that "the fear of not being able to blow out all the candles" is viewed as a metaphor for not being up to the task, suggesting that, in his current life, the client fears he will not have the power, strength, or ability to be successful. The occasion of his birthday and all the candles on the cake are metaphoric representations for growing up and/or being a grown-up (or a "real" man) in a grown-up world.

Based on an understanding of these metaphoric movements and meanings, we might formulate the following tentative guesses regarding the client's lifestyle beliefs:

I am fearful and weak.
I fear that I will be inadequate and fail when challenged with life's tasks.[57]

Here is a developmental summary of how Kopp uses a structured interview to identify and then to apply insights relative to how the memory can be impacting one's present and possible future behavior.

1. After having identified a current challenging solution, the client is asked to identify how (s)he is most stuck.

2. Having described the difficulty, the client is then asked to identify a recent time this occurred.

3. The client is then encouraged to become more aware of the event by picturing it as vividly as possible, "who? what? and where" was it happening? And then to identify the various emotions associated with the experience.

4. Next the client is asked to identify and to describe an ER associated with the above experience. The counselor writes down the memory exactly as reported by the client.

5. Having identified and described such an early childhood experience, the client next is asked, "If you were to take a snapshot of the most vivid moment in the memory, what image stands out most?"

6. The client is then asked to describe if the memory could be changed in any way, how would it be changed? (The counselor also records this word for word.)

7. After describing the desired change, again the client is asked to discuss what stands out the most vividly in the changed memory.

8. The counselor then reads the memory to the client and asks if any connections can be made between the ER and the current challenging situation.

9. After discussing any connections between the two events, the counselor then reads the ideal "changed" version of the memory. The client is then asked if any problem-solving strategies from that "changed ER" can be applied to the current dilemma.

Kopp concludes his commentary of his creative process that he adapted from Marlis Anderson by noting that:

> By creating connections between the memory and current problem, aspects of the early memory become "vehicles" that carry meaning from the early memory image to the current situation. Metaphor therapy's approach to early recollections opens creative possibilities for change. This experiential method utilizes the imaginal and metaphoric dimensions of the lifestyle and thus complements the cognitive focus of the traditional Adlerian approach.[58]

The ER Interactive Discussion Technique

Mansager and associates developed the ER Interactive Discussion Technique for use with groups of adolescent substance abusers.

A. Gathering of ERs—They have a four-step process in the group exploration of each participants ERs.

   1. *Focusing on the issue.* The counselor starts by asking something similar to, "So, tell me, again, why you like to get high [or drunk]? What's something in our life that goes better for you because you do [get high or drunk]?"

   2. *Identification and awareness of the emotion.* Teens are asked to think of the last time the "hassle" (which is diminished by getting high) occurred. This will typically bring out specific examples about a fight with a parent, a failed test, a disastrous [or "smooth"] date, for example. The teens are asked further, when they think of this incident, if they can sense the emotion anywhere in their body.

   3. *Recording the ER.* They are asked to write down, on a prepared paper, the first recollection they can think of, whether or not it seems related to the previous discussion. The instruction is completed by asking them to note their age, the focal point of the memory (as if it were a "freeze-frame" in their favorite movie), the feeling attached to the focal image, and the reason for the feeling.

   4. *Collection and interpretation.* The papers are then collected from the members and are reviewed for themes before the next session. If time permits, the papers will be reviewed quickly so the counselor can clearly understand what has been written. If the counselor has questions, these can be answered while the teens are still available.

B. Clients' Guesses about Generic ERs
    In the next group session(s) a review of the previous work is undertaken. The teens are asked what they remember about how children tend to view the world. They are also asked, in general, if they recall the ERs they wrote the previous week. This discussion helps place the teens back into a frame of reference regarding the "glasses" worn by individuals based on their ERs. Clients are then invited to discuss the recollections typical of other teens.

C. Clients' Guesses about Each Other's ERs
    Next, the group members will be instructed to listen respectfully as the group members' own ERs are shared. The person whose ER is being read is to listen silently to the reflections and feedback of the peers on questions asked of them by the counselor.

D. Giving/Receiving Feedback about Accuracy of Guessing
    After the feedback is given, the teen, whose ER has been shared, is given an opportunity to provide feedback to the peers; correcting, "owning" or "disowning" what has been put forward by the others, questioning their comments. Thus, the adolescent can share whether or not the descriptions seemed accurate.[59]

To embellish your understanding of the early recollection process the following reprint of an article is included. The article includes creative ways in which seven recognized Adlerians gain a deeper understanding of early recollections reported by clients.

Early Recollections: Mining the Personal Story in the Process of Change

Michael Maniacci, Bernard Shulman, Jane Griffith, Robert L. Powers, Judy Sutherland, Renee Dushman, and Mary Frances Schneider

Adlerian therapy is rich in its use of personal narratives. Narratives are the basic material of the life style assessment, with Early Recollections enjoying a privileged reputation as useful vehicles for encouraging therapeutic insight and change. Shulman & Mosak (1988, pp. 63–64) state,

> Adler drew many inferences from ER; the subject's attitude toward life, hints about why a particular line of movement in life was chosen, indications of compensatory devices developed to cope with felt inadequacies, evidence of courage or its lack, of the preference for direct or indirect methods of coping, of the type of interpersonal transactions preferred, of the presence or absence of social interest, of the values assigned to affiliation, competence, behavior, status concerns, compliance and rebellion, security issues—in short, of the stance the subject adopts in order to cope with the challenges of life.

This article demonstrates five methods for employing Early Recollections (ERs) during the process of therapeutic change. Using one client's set of ERs, the article discusses and demonstrates

1. the traditional Adlerian interpretation of the Early Recollections, written by Michael Maniacci (research conducted by Bernard Shulman);
2. the Psycho-Clarity Process, discussed by Robert L. Powers and Jane Griffith;
3. the Willhite approach, offered by Mary F. Schneider;
4. the art therapy approach, presented by Judy Sutherland; and
5. the use of psychodrama, discussed by Renee Dushman.

The article includes client responses to each of the four interventions. In closing, Michael Maniacci discusses how these approaches offer flexibility of intervention and process for both therapist and client.

MARTHA'S EARLY MEMORIES

Martha, age 44, came to therapy because she was unhappy with her career as a nurse. She gave permission to experience four methods of mining her Early Recollections in therapy and then offered to engage in dialogue regarding the effects of each method. The following memories form the set of Early Recollections used throughout the article.

> **Early Recollection One.** I am about age four and I am alone in the study of the most lovely home in which our family ever lived. This house was so special. I called it the castle—it was brick and it had this wonderful study where I played. The study had a large bay window of leaded glass and below these windows was an upholstered window seat. My dad's elegant wooden desk sat in this study. Anyway, this was my favorite place to play. So in this memory, I am in the study, I have put on the Peter Pan record . . . the only musical that I knew existed . . . and I am singing at the top of my lungs. As I sing, it is as if I am totally transported into the play. I can see it in my mind's eye and I am Mary Martin, playing Peter Pan, flying around and singing the "I've Just Got to Crow" song. I am using the window seat as I sing. I run along it and fly off into the room. I am making believe that I am Mary Martin flying. I am sure I nearly wore out that record. The feeling I had was utter joy . . . the love of the music

coming out of me and the love of that wonderful musical . . . the love of that experience of both music and story joined in an art form. Most Vivid: The joy of singing. Feeling: Joy.

Early Recollection Two. I am maybe five years old and I am sitting with my cousin Julie on the front porch of my home. The home is across the street from a fire station. Julie is a baby . . . maybe six or eight months old. She is on my lap. We are enjoying the beautiful spring day. The doors of the fire station are open and we can watch the fire men washing and working on the trucks. She is happy. I am happy and very peaceful. I am aware of how lovely it is to hold her and how sweet the Spring air smells. Most vivid: The sense of touch. Feeling: Peaceful love.

Early Recollection Three. Another one with Julie. I am age five. I have placed her in my doll buggy and we are out taking a walk down the street—the same street as the fire station. It is a beautiful day, sunny and warm. I am pushing Julie and she is happy, smiling. I am happy too. It is nice to be together going out and exploring the neighborhood. Most vivid: Exploration with Julie-taking a walk. Feeling: Love.

Early Recollection Four. It is summer and I am five. I am with my family and my cousins and we have come to the hospital to visit my aunt. (My aunt had polio and was in quarantine for a year.) I remember that this was to be a big important visit. We are all together going to do this visit and there we are all of us kids, my sibling and my cousins, we are looking up at a woman who I saw leaning out of a window. She only has the use of one of her arms—the right one. She is waving and smiling. I didn't remember that she was my aunt. But I do remember that she looked beautiful and that her bath robe was a rainbow of pastels—mostly baby blue. I waved back thinking she was very pretty and wondering why she had to be up there. Most vivid: Waving at her and thinking she was beautiful. Feeling: Wondering and sort of awe.

Early Recollection Five. I am six and very hungry. I can smell that something smells good in our house. So I go into the pantry and I see a large baking dish filled with blueberry coffee cake. It is still warm. I think I'll have just a taste of it. I take one piece and I think it is so good and I am so hungry. Then I just keep coming back and nibbling at it. I nibble long enough to have taken a good fourth of the baking dish. I get a terrible stomach ache and throw up. I still really don't like blueberries.

Early Recollection Six. I remember I am very young about two or three and my grandmother is sick. (I now know she was dying of complications of diabetes). She has a big hospital bed in our house. I don't like the sick smell and it seems very dark—like the drapes need to be opened. I remember that I am supposed to be playing with my grandmother-keeping her company. My mother is there in the room--off to the side watching us. I really do not like being there. The smells are stinky. My mother gets me to carry a bed pan of my grandmother's urine into the bathroom. I do it just fine. My mom is praising me and I act like this is okay, but inside I hate being here. I don't want to be carrying this pan of urine. It stinks. Most vivid: The darkness and the smell. Feeling: Uncomfortable.

Early Recollection Seven. I am age three and this is in front of our first apartment. We are on the lawn. My dad is in his graduation robes and he is swinging me around in a circle. It is fun. I like that he seems happy and that he has some time to play. I feel glad to be with him and a little dizzy from the spinning. He must have been graduating from medical school. Most vivid: The spinning. Feeling: Playful.

THE TRADITIONAL APPROACH TO EARLY RECOLLECTIONS

In this section Michael Maniacci provides a brief overview of the traditional approach to Early Recollections. These comments are followed by Bernard Shulman's traditional interpretation of Martha's early memories. Since Dr. Shulman only had access to Martha's early memories and not other lifestyle information, his comments reflect only the interpretation of the Early Recollections.

Comments on the Traditional Approach. The traditional approach to lifestyle assessment and interpretation grows out of the work of Rudolf Dreikurs (1967) and has been expanded upon by a number of people, such as Harold Mosak and Bernard Shulman (e.g., Shulman & Mosak, 1988). In this process, after an initial interview, one or two sessions are spent formally interviewing the client in a systematic manner. Either the data collector or a colleague (if multiple psychotherapy is practiced) then summarizes the data during a third session, typically in the presence of the client. The client provides feedback during the process and either modifies or corrects the interpretations. These summaries are then neatly typed and presented to the client.

While this practice is not always followed, it is the dominant approach. One advantage in using this technique is that it allows the psychotherapist to quickly catch up to the client's style. When it is done early and in this systematic manner, the psychotherapist knows what is going on rather quickly. Another advantage is that the client, presented openly with the psychotherapist's assumptions about the dynamics of the case early and in a collaborative manner, is free to amend, correct, or even disagree at any time. This sort of clearing the air can be a good way to solidify the collaborative process: "Here is what I think is going on. What do you think?"

The approaches discussed in this issue can be implemented at any time after the traditional approach. This method does not preclude them, it simply uses them after some agreement is reached about what seems to be the dynamics of the case.

Another advantage this approach gives is that many clients feel more hopeful when the issues are outlined and presented back to them early in the process. They have more faith in the therapy process, the therapists, and their future when they can see a "road map" for what may be going on. For many clients, mutual exploration is not what is needed when they start therapy. They need a more solid grounding, a touchstone, that they can return to time and again to get reoriented during the psychotherapy process.

The Traditional Approach Applied to Martha's Memories. Martha is a 44-year-old female who is seeking a career change. No other information is available on this individual. There are seven memories, all elaborated into narratives. The bare bones of the Early Recollection (ER) can be teased out of the narrative and interrupted for core constructs. The narrative style and content suggest additional material over and above the recollection itself.

> ER One. The first memory is an idealized incident. The recollection is one of being alone, singing, running, jumping, with her own fantasy. She creates a beautiful experience for herself. The elaboration is about how special everything is . . . the house is special . . . the room is special. She is concerned with the aesthetic quality of everything she looks at. She is announcing, in the narrative, what makes her happy. And the theme of feeling happy or unhappy is more a part of the narrative than it is of the bare bones of the recollection. This person will probably seek out people who will make no demands on her. People who will allow her to create her beautiful place.

> ER Two. She is a spectator viewing the activities of others, in this case, all men. Men work or do whatever men do, and she watches. The narrative is again idealized. She pays great attention to the weather, for example.

> ER Three. She is exploring and enjoying herself. She is appreciating the beauties of life and, again, she idealizes the situation.

> ER Four. She is with a group of people, the family, and has limited interaction with them. The memory is of the woman leaning out of the window . . . relationship at a distance. She elaborates again that this is going to be a special day . . . again, she pays attention to the aesthetic details of the situation.

ER Five. In this recollection, it is harder to pick out the recollection from the background. Again, she is alone. The narrative shows her awareness of the aesthetics of the situation and, perhaps, a disregard of other values.

ER Six. She has to put up with an unpleasant situation and she is being asked to accept a responsibility. She accepts it as a duty, but she hates it. She does it because she is asked to do it. She does it to please others, not because she enjoys doing a service for others. It is interesting that this is a situation that literally stinks . . . again she is influenced by the aesthetics of the situation. "I really don't like this." This is the only memory in which her mother and grandmother appear and there is no emotional closeness in this memory. People are taking care of each other, but it is not pleasant.

ER Seven. This is the first recollection of her father. Men are more fun than women. You can at least have fun with a man. They are the source of pleasure and attention.

The narrative style is one of aesthetic perception which may become a coping method and may be used as a safe-guarding or a self-enhancing tactic. The aesthetic style is a perceptual style, a cognitive style. This style or sense can be used as a way of safeguarding with others and/or as a way of judging what is really good. It could be used as a form of superiority, it could be a reason for saying no to situations.

She keeps her distance from people. She could enjoy life if people wouldn't make demands on her . . . if she could live her fantasy. She is more of a spectator than an active participant. She'll do the job even if she doesn't like it. She needs some happy time so that she can enjoy life.

Martha's Responses to the Traditional Approach. Martha marveled at the accuracy of the traditional approach. Among the many reactions Martha had to the material are the following comments:

This is stunning! This doctor is a mind reader. I need to take a look at all of these issues, but the biggest issues—the zingers—that came out of this interpretation are the ones about relationships, and art. My job as a nurse has trained and reinforced the distance and lack of communication that was present in my family. All this caretaking without the closeness. It is closeness and good communication that I yearn for. Secondly, the artistic issue—I was very artistic as a child. . . . I am very artistic as an adult. But this sense that is so primary in the way I see the world . . . well, I hide it. I do not know where to put it in my life. I was thinking of leaving nursing for art school . . . that is one of the reasons I came to therapy. I know I have this aesthetic perceptual style—that is so on target—but I don't know how to use it well in my life. I need to find that out.

This process was stunning. I like having the comments written down so I can go back to them and mull them-it challenges me to ask myself some hard questions.

EARLY RECOLLECTIONS AND THE PSYCHO-CLARITY PROCESS

In this section, Robert Powers and Jane Griffith highlight the basic elements of the Psycho-Clarity Process. Martha offers some comments on an initial experience of one aspect of this process.

Early Recollections and the Psycho-Clarity Process. We have chosen the term *psycho-clarity* to characterize our work with clients (Powers & Griffith, 1987). In the Psycho-Clarity Process, our effort is directed at helping clients *see clearly* what they are, in fact, *doing* (thinking, feeling, acting) and the price they pay for it, and to uncover with them those interfering ideas that predicate erroneous movement. With the assumption that the client is sovereign, and that healing is only possible when movement is understood, our method is to ask clients to explain themselves to us. By this means both we and the client come to understand; then healing can begin. In articulating this process we think that we have been faithful to Alfred Adler (Ansbacher & Ansbacher, 1956a, p. 293), who said:

> This incontrovertible clarification of the errors in a life style, certainly no easy task, persuades and produces the new life style, which is actively adapted, not entirely to the existing reality, but to the growing, becoming reality.

Because the Psycho-Clarity Process relies upon a mutual evolution of therapist and client toward understanding the meaning of client movement, the task the editors set for us—namely, to interpret a set of Early Recollections of a person unknown to us, without context and client engagement—is particularly uncongenial. Adler (Ansbacher & Ansbacher, 1956a, p. 352) cautioned that the "worth and meaning [of Early Recollections] . . . cannot be rightly estimated until we relate them to the total style of life of the individual in question, and recognize their unity with his [or her] main line of striving towards a goal of superiority."

Therefore, we have instead chosen to use the present opportunity to discuss, first, what we have found to be the most significant aspects of Early Recollections, and, second, to offer a method for integrating these interpretations into a summary, titled, in our work, "The Pattern of Basic Convictions." (For a verbatim account of an exploration of Early Recollections with a client and the resulting summary, see "The Case of Janice," Powers & Griffith, 1987, pp. 197–217; 265–270.)

When working with clients to interpret Early Recollections, we focus on five aspects of these recollections: context, content, gender, movement, and evaluation.

The *context* for the set of Early Recollections is, of course, the family constellation (presumably explored and evaluated by therapist and client before the work on Early Recollections begins). Context can assist in gauging the significance of the reported age of the client at the time of the recollection. This may be, for example, the client's age at which he or she entered school, or the age at which a sibling entered the family.

The *content* of the recollections is our next focus. It must be remembered that the Early Recollection belongs to the client and is to be respected as it stands. We mention this because therapists may, in unawareness and in their enthusiasm, intrude upon the recollection, making personal assumptions about the memory. (These assumptions often begin, "It must have been . . ." or "You must have felt . . .") We are, of course, interested in the entire content, and we pay attention to any details which appear to be unnecessary to the unfolding of the story. (Such details strike us as significant since they did not have to be included for the story to cohere, and yet, there they are. To what purpose?)

Next, as we have asserted elsewhere (Powers & Griffith, 1987, p. 189), no issue has more importance in social life than that of *gender*; therefore, in any discussion of recollections we are aware of gender. For example, sometimes persons of the client's sex are present more often than persons of the other sex; sometimes the other sex does not appear at all; sometimes one sex is portrayed one way (powerful, for example) and the other sex is portrayed antithetically (weak). There are even times—Oh, happy times!—when the sexes are portrayed in cooperation and solidarity.

The next aspect we attend to is *movement*. According to Adler, "all is movement" (Ansbacher & Ansbacher, 1956a, p. 195), and this aspect of recollections tells us what clients are prepared (or not prepared) to do, and how others act upon (or with) them. We look at clients' relative effectiveness or ineffectiveness, at their physical positions in relation to others (above? below?), at clients' degree of activity and initiative, and at the extent of clients' participation and cooperation.

Finally, we look at a client's *evaluation* of the situation, expressed in the feeling reported by the client at that point in the action identified by the client as the most vivid moment. These five categories of concern and inquiry may seem to be too many foci to bear in mind during the exploration of Early Recollections; however, with practice, one learns to move with ease from one consideration to another.

In pulling together the many meanings that emerge from discussing a set of Early Recollections to form a single, coherent statement of basic convictions, we have found that step one is noting the *sequence* of the recollections and the ways in which each is related to the next. Step two is noting *similarities* among them, and step three is noting their *symmetries*.

Reviewing the sequence of the recollections allows therapist and client to fix the recollections in their minds as they process each one and state conclusions reached. During this process the (unconscious) artistic arrangement in which each memory was recalled and recited is revealed, and client and therapist can more easily discern how this arrangement highlights major themes, through repetition (similarity) or juxtaposition (symmetry), and minor themes, shown in those memories that stand alone. Rehearsing the sequence also helps therapists envision the recollections as if these were their own, a practice that heightens empathy and understanding.

Once sequence, similarity, and symmetry have been established, therapists have a scaffold to support the summary of interpretations. One can begin with symmetries, such as one might find in memories of the way the world ought to be versus the way the world is (illustrated in what we call Paradise and Paradise Lost memories), or in memories of the way women are versus the way men are, or in memories of the way I (the client) am versus the way others are. Or, one can begin with similarities, as in, for example, summarizing two or more recollections that state a point of view about what happens to me (the client) when I act on my own. Sometimes these are cautionary tales that convey the message that I dare *not* act on my own, but must have the care and protection of others. In another set of recollections, two or more might illustrate that I (the client) am entitled to inhabit a world of my own, a world I conjure to escape life's demands or to find comfort in the face of those demands (an interpretation that might be verified in antisocial uses of alcohol, for example, or in other forms of excitement and satisfaction).

Our interpretation and summary of Early Recollections in a way that is encouraging and useful to our clients depends upon our successful collaboration with them in a mutual effort to understand their movement, and upon our then being willing, on the basis of this common understanding, to translate their metaphorical speech into common language.

We think that in the work we have outlined here therapy and clarity diverge. Psychotherapy emphasizes the process of treating the client from the outside in, while our hope for psycho-clarity is that it is a process that helps clients attain a state of seeing clearly—from the inside out.

Martha's Responses to the Psycho-Clarity Process. Martha has just begun to experience elements of this process in therapy; her comments on attending to the sequencing of the ERs include:

> My therapist and I went through the sequence over and over and I kept putting myself back in those situations, one after another in the order of my remembering. All of a sudden it hit me—this is the story of my life. I began in this wonderful home surrounded by music. I went out on adventures with family members. Sometimes I overdid things. I worked hard as a caregiver. And I found joy and play with a man. I am there again. I just bought a condo with the very same set of windows and window seat that was in that study! I have just begun to fill my life with music and art. I am leaving excessiveness and stressful caregiving and I am . . . I can hardly believe I am saying this . . . I am dating a man who is a wonderful partner, a playful guy. The sequence makes sense.

THE WILLHITE TECHNIQUE

In this section, Mary Frances Schneider discusses the steps involved in the use of "The Willhite" as a process for encouraging a client's creativity regarding future movement. Martha provides her responses to the technique and discusses her reaction to each step of the process.

The Willhite Technique: Reframing Early Recollections. Willhite (1979) published the first article which focused on mining the cognitive material of the early memories through the use of the technique of reframing. Reframing is a process in which the client is asked to recreate the Early Recollection toward their self-ideal. As a therapeutic tool, refraining is a process that encourages clients to begin to contemplate and voice the values that are likely to form the substance of their creative movement toward more satisfying ways of being.

The Willhite process consists of five steps which work the narrative of the Early Recollection.

Step One. The therapist collects the client's Early Recollections.

Step Two. The therapist prepares the Early Recollections for discussion by placing the original ERs on the left side of a page and numbering each sentence of each ER. In session, the client then reworks each original ER to construct what Willhite calls the "Self-ideal."' The Self-ideal is a narrative reframe of the original ER content. After creating the Self-ideal narrative, the client is asked to identify the affective component of each sentence in the original ER and the Self-ideal ER. Willhite (1979, p. 111) states:

> I always have the client dictate the Self-Ideal frame by frame (comparing it to the Self-Concept while doing so) so that each column has the same number of action-emotion components. This format prevents the client from skipping over those portions of the Early Recollection which are indicative of anxiety and/or denial. At the conclusion of the Early Recollection the client gives me a word or phrase which is descriptive of the overall feeling of the memory. I also get an overall feeling to write in as the last frame of the Self-ideal, so that the two are graphically analogous. I number the frames for convenience.

When clients cannot identify a feeling for a sentence frame, Willhite has the client use the words—"a fact"' (Willhite, 1979, p. 112) in the place of a feeling. When the client has completed the task of labeling the feelings, Willhite helps the client "search more deeply for a believable feeling.. and] realize that this part of the memory has been purposively discounted or repressed" (Willhite, 1979, pp. 112-113).

Step Three. The client is asked to "list the emotional sequence" (Willhite, 1979, p. 113). Willhite believes this is the "interfactional style and perception of life . . . it is the emotional set-up which . . . [can lead] to a self-fulfilling prophecy that invariably confirms one's expectations about life" (Willhite, 1979, p. 113).

Step Four. Willhite (1979, p. 114) states:

> At this point it is very helpful to have the client describe a current interfactional problem with which he/she is having difficulty. Going beyond the statement of the problem, the client also describes how he/she imagines the episode will unfold and what the conclusions will be. . . . I write the client's description out word for word (on paper), separating it into thought-units, and add the emotions appropriate to each unit. Now the client has revealed in detail how his/her private logic is going to be put to work to reach a negative or unhealthy outcome. . . . I fit the episode into a format involving the same number of frames as the Self Concept and the Self-ideal. This usually involves compressing the data. Occasionally there is an apparent gap in the sequence; I simply ask the client to fill it in.

Willhite then compares this "Private-Logic-at-Work" sequence with the "Self-Concept" sequence.

Step Five. Applying the Self-ideal to the problem. Having constructed the Self-ideal, the client is invited to use these feelings and strategies in the problem-solving process. As Willhite says,

> This set-up has also been created by the client and is available to get [the client] out of the self-fulfilling emotional bind. . . . The key to the behavior change is the identification of the emotions or feelings involved. . . . It is this identification of feelings permitting the shift to new behaviors

which is the strength of the Willhite method. I have found that people don't change until they are given an alternative backed up by the feelings that are consistent with their private logic. (1979, p. 120)

These five steps form the core of "The Willhite." They are demonstrated with Martha in the next section.

Martha's Response to the Willhite Method. The following passage describes how Martha and her therapist worked each step of the method. Martha's comments on some of the steps are included.

Step One: Collecting the ERs. Martha dictated her Early Recollections. The therapist recorded them in the traditional manner.

Step Two: Creating the Self-ideal. The therapist typed out the ERs on the left side of paper and numbered each sentence of each memory. During the next session, Martha chose to write out her own "Self-ideal" responses and feeling statements to each of the E's. For completion of the exercise, Martha focused on four of the ERs, which appear in Figures 1 to 4.

The client felt deeply moved by this refraining exercise. She cried many times during these constructions. Her comments after completing the reframe work of step 2:

> This was very helpful in several ways. First, the task asked me to put myself on the line about how I would really make changes-about my own values . . . taking leadership of myself. I felt challenged and relieved at being able to "be myself" in these situations. I see many patterns very clearly . . . there was little direct communication in my family. I was such a pleaser. Women were voiceless . . . there was no such thing in that world as 'asking for what you want." As I did this exercise I realized that I could not change significant others, but with the people who are active in my current life, I can communicate clearly. I know that often I just slip into silence . . . use this old pattern. I realize how much I need to ask questions, how I need connection and information and humor . . . and why I have actively cultivated, in my adulthood, relationships with the cousins who I loved. This exercise helped me claim how much I need to be clear about what I need. I feel so sad for my mother and her mother . . . there was such devotion to work, but no warmth, connection or sharing. They had an old-world work ethic. I know that they wanted me to survive and for them working hard was the way to survive. But their sad, lonely lives make me know how much I need connection, joy and sharing . . . not just work. This exercise points me to my future . . . where to go with my life . . . how I most want to be. This material dares me to do something different . . . to act on my values . . . I loved it and it was scary.

Step Three: The Sequence of the Memory. The sequence of the memory work was conducted during the next session. Martha selected ER Four, which she felt had the greatest implications for her career questions. With the therapist she listed out the emotional sequence of the memory. Willhite holds that this sequence "is an emotional set-up which [the client] has created—leading to a self-fulfilling prophecy that invariably confirms one's expectations about life" (Willhite, 1979, p. 113).

Figure 1. Early Recollection Two: Self-Concept and Self-Ideal

Self-Concept

1. I am five and I am with my cousin Julie on the front porch of my home. (Relaxed)

2. My home is across the street from a fire station. (Excited)

3. Julie is a baby, six or seven months old. (Maternal love)

4. She is on my lap. (Maternal love)

5. We are enjoying the beautiful spring day. (Contentment)

6. The doors of the fire station are open and we can watch the firemen washing and working on the trucks. (Excitement)

7. She is happy. (Maternal love)

8. I am happy and very peaceful. (Maternal love)

9. I am aware of how lovely it is to hold her and what a sweet spring day this is. (Maternal love)

Feeling:
Nurturing love

Self-Ideal

1. I am five and I am sitting with my cousin Clara on the front porch of my home. (Peaceful)

2. My home is across the street from a fire station. (Interested)

3. Clara is a few years older than I am. (Admiration)

4. Clara is sitting next to me and we are swinging on the porch, swinging and laughing. (Joy)

5. We are enjoying each other on this beautiful spring day. (Joy)

6. The doors of the fire station are open and we decide to go over and help the firemen wash and work on the trucks. (Interest and involvement)

7. Clara and I are happy and laughing and joking with the firemen. (Joyful belonging)

8. I am so happy to be with Clara. (Joy)

9. I am aware of how much fun it is to play with Clara and how sweet the spring air smells. (Sisterly love)

Feeling:
Playful love-attachment

Figure 2. Early Recollection Four: Self-Concept and Self-Ideal

Self-Concept

1. This is summer and maybe I am age five.

2. I am with my family and my cousins and we have come to the hospital.
   (Interested)

3. (My aunt had polio and was in quarantine for over a year.)
   (Confused)

4. I remember that this was supposed to be a big important visit.
   (Interested)

5. We are all together going to do this visit.
   (Apprehensive)

6. And there we are, all of us kids, my sibling and my cousins, looking up at a woman who is leaning out of a window.
   (Wondering)

7. She only has the use of one of her arms. The right one.
   (Wondering)

8. She is waving and smiling.
   (Wondering)

9. I really didn't remember that she was my aunt.
   (Wondering)

10. But I do remember that she looked beautiful and that her bath robe was a rainbow of pastels . . . mostly baby blue. (Appreciation)

11. I waved back thinking she was very pretty and wondering why she had to be up there.
    (Wondering)

Overall Feeling:
Confused and appreciative

Self-Ideal

1. This is summer and I am five.

2. I am with my family and my cousin and older cousins and we have come to the hospital to visit my aunt.
   (Interested)

3. My mother explains to us that my aunt is in quarantine because she has polio—she would explain.
   (Ask for information and feel sadness)

4. My parents would tell us how much my aunt misses her children and how important this visit is.
   (Getting the story and feeling sad)

5. We would let my aunt know that we care and that we want her to get well. (Express my caring)

6. We would all be waving and saying encouraging things . . . and if Clara is there, we'd be telling her jokes.
   (Joyful, Encouraging, Connected)

7. I see her arm, my mom has explained how polio affected it. How she can't use it and I feel sad for her.
   (Empathy)

8. I see her waving and smiling.
   (Appreciative)

9. I am sad to realize that a person in our family is going through such suffering.
   (Empathy)

10. I appreciate her beauty and so does Clara, we talk about her beautiful robe and how she looks like a princess.
    (Appreciation, Connection)

11. As I wave to her, Clara and I talk about how beautiful she is and ask about how long she is going to be there.
    (Appreciation, connection)

Overall Feeling:
Informed, clear, empathetic and connected

Figure 3. Early Recollection Six: Self-Concept and Self-ideal

Self-Concept

1. I remember I am very young . . . two or three and my grandmother is sick.
   (Uncomfortable)

2. She has a big hospital bed in our house.
   (Uncomfortable)

3. I don't like the sick smell and it seems very dark like the drapes need to be opened.
   (Claustrophobic)

4. I remember that I am supposed to be playing with my grandmother . . . keeping her company.
   (Uncomfortable)

5. My mother is there in the room . . . off to the side watching us.
   (Unsure)

6. I really do not like being here.
   (Uncomfortable)

7. The smells are stinky.
   (Sickening)

8. My mother gets me to carry a bed pan of my grandmother's urine into the bathroom.
   (Sickened)

9. I do it just fine.
   (Stressful, accomplishment)

10. My mom is praising me and I act like this is OK but inside I hate being there.
    (Pleasing)

11. I don't want to be carrying this pan of urine.
    (Stress)

Overall Feeling:
Uncomfortable and used

Self-Ideal

1. I am very young, three, and my grandmother is dying of complications of diabetes.
   (Sad)

2. She has a big hospital bed in our house.
   (Sad)

3. The drapes and windows are open to let in the sun and fresh air.
   (Open)

4. I am visiting with my grandmother.
   (Relaxed)

5. My mother is next to me, holding me and we are playing children's games and laughing.
   (Comfortable)

6. I like being there.
   (Comfortable)

7. There are hospital smells.
   (Cleanliness)

8. My mother asks me to help her empty my grandmother's bed pan.
   (Comfort, courage and learning)

9. We do it together.
   (Collaboration)

10. My mom thanks me and I feel good about helping.
    (Pride in Learning)

11. I feel good about helping my mom who is helping her mom.
    (Helpful)

Overall Feeling:
Connected to my mom and grandmother and helpful

Figure 4. Early Recollection Seven: Self-Concept and Self-Ideal

Self-Concept	Self-Ideal
1. I am age three and this is in the front of our first apartment.	1. I am age three and this is in front of our first apartment.
2. We are on the lawn. (Happy)	2. We are on the lawn on a sunny warm day. (Happy)
3. My dad is in his graduation robes and he is swinging me around in a circle. (Excitement)	3. My dad is in his graduation robes and he is holding me in his arms and we are surrounded by our family. (Happy and connected)
4. It is fun. (Excited)	4. It is a happy day (Happy and connected)
5. I like that he seems happy and that he has some time to play. (Happy, observing)	5. I am glad that he has time to be with me . . . with all of us. (Happy and connected)
6. I feel glad to be with him and a little dizzy from the spinning. (Happy and dizzy)	6. I feel glad to be with him. (Happy and connected)
7. He must have been graduating from medical school. (Happy)	7. Mom and dad tell us about the special graduation day. (Happy and proud)

Overall Feeling: Happy and excited

Overall Feeling:
Close and feeling the Importance of the day

Martha and the therapist discussed the problem-solving style suggested by Self-Concept sequence. These Self-Concept sequences, which appear below, are patterns that the therapist actively sought to question and to help the client change.

ER Four: Self-Concept

1. Interested
2. Confused
3. Interested
4. Apprehensive
5. Wondering
6. Wondering
7. Wondering
8. Wondering
9. Appreciation
10. Wondering

Overall feeling: Confused and apprehensive

Martha was "shocked" that these steps captured the "down side" of her style. She stated,

> This wondering style keeps me confused. I isolate myself . . . and ask myself questions. I need to bring those questions out into the world so that I can construct answers . . . so I clear up confusion and am not so alone . . . so that I can act. This really captures my problem-solving style. Contemplation without conversation leaves me blocked when it comes to action.

Step Four. Problem elaboration. The therapist asked Martha to elaborate about the work problem and what might happen if she used her usual style. Martha replied,

> I would ponder this work issue because it is so important in my life. I don't know what to do. I'd ponder changing jobs or going back to school. I am scared of making a mistake. Will I leave a career that I am good at? Then I'd get stuck. That is why I came here, I am stuck. I want to take some kind of action. I am confused about how to go about making such a big decision.

The therapist and Martha applied the problem story to the Self-Concept sequence. The results, Figure 5, demonstrate the current private logic—the thinking that supports the problem state. Martha was stunned at the way she used "confusion to slip out of taking responsibility." She realized that she does" fear making mistakes . . . something that medicine reinforces . . . be perfect. Thinking ahead is good, but too much thinking ahead is paralysis. I believe that I have done this before . . . been paralyzed in the face of important decisions."

Figure 5. Current Problem and the Self-Concept

Current Problem	Self-Concept
1. I would ponder this work issue because it is so important in my life.	1. Interested
2. I don't know what to do.	2. Confused
3. I ponder changing jobs or going back to school.	3. Interested
4. I am scared of making a mistake.	4. Apprehensive
5. Will I leave a career that I am good at?	5. Wondering
6. Then I get stuck.	6. Wondering
7. That is why I came here.	7. Wondering
8. I am stuck.	8. Wondering
9. I want to take to take some kind of action.	9. Appreciation
10. I am confused about how to go about making such a big decision.	10. Wondering

Overall Feeling:
Confused and apprehensive

Step Five: Applying the Self-ideal to the problem. Martha and her therapist applied the creative process of the Self-ideal to the work problem. The results, Figure 6, were encouraging and insightful for Martha. In this part of the exercise, Martha realized,

> I have got to decide what are the values that will form my life. I need to take the time to collect information on my most important questions and have conversations to get the whole story . . . so that I can see for myself what my options are. I realized also that I have been so black and white in my thinking. I could take artistic steps and still work as a nurse. I could phase into it . . . do more of it. I also know that I used to love my nursing . . . the caring thing . . . maybe there are ways that I could still care . . . positions that would be more caring. I can open my eyes and look and talk and try some things. I think that may be about balanced caring . . . balanced joy in my life . . . not one place where I might find joy . . . not escaping parts of life . . . but creating a whole life.

With therapeutic encouragement Martha enrolled in art class and is "inspecting the stories of art students" while painting. She has asked for a transfer to OB work. She is dating and considering how her aesthetic abilities could be expressed in her life.

Figure 6. Self-Ideal Applied to the Problem Situation

Self-Ideal	Problem Situation
1. Interested	1. Am interested in investigating work and art options.
2. Ask for information and feel about the information	2. I need to have a lot of conversations about work and an artistic life.
3. Getting the story and feeling about the story	3. I have not even started to get the story on art or to look at other work options.
4. Express my caring	4. I am caring . . . where and how do I demonstrate this? Talk to significant others.
5. Joyful connection with family and expressing encouragement	5. I need to share my questions and findings with my dearest family and friends.
6. Empathy	6. I need to feel, for myself and for others— what options feel like a whole life?
7. Appreciation	7. I need to focus on what I already love and do well . . . gratitude.
8. Empathy	8. I need to focus on caring and self care as I take action.
9. Appreciation and connection	9. I want to appreciate and connect to myself and others through my work.
10. Appreciation and connection	10. This is the most important goal.

The Willhite technique opens up avenues of potential creative action and encourages maximum input from the client in this creative process. The technique helps clients clarify the attitudes they want to claim—their own lead attitudes. Therapy encourages the client to inspect these ideas and speculate on the consequences of these ideas. Therapy encourages clients to act on preferred movement and to claim the attitudes that enhance their movement and sense of belonging in each of the life task areas.

THE USE OF ART THERAPY AND PSYCHODRAMA WITH EARLY RECOLLECTIONS

In this final section, Judy Sutherland focuses on the use of art therapy with ERs and Renee Dushman focuses on the use of psychodrama with ERs. Judy and Renee work as a collaborative team and blend the use of these techniques in their group work. This collaborative group approach is evident in their sections. Both the art technique and the psychodrama were applied to one of Martha's ERs. Martha comments on the benefits of these methods.

Art Therapy and Early Memories: An Integration with Psychodrama. In each of us there is a need to tell our story and be heard by another person. Sometimes when we tell our story the other person does not hear us or understand us—for any number of reasons. Of course a counselor is trained to make sense, to bring order out of the stories we are being told by a client. This is done with the help of the client. Integrating art therapy and psycho-drama into the therapeutic process enables a deeper understanding of the meaning one gives to life events.

Art and psychodrama can express through the language of image, symbol, metaphor, and behavior that often cannot be put into words. The processes of art-making and psychodrama both move rapidly and powerfully to the core issues of one's life by tapping into one's feelings, unknown thoughts, and lifestyle convictions. This process can lead to an inner search that often adds a rich therapeutic dimension to the Adlerian group or individual session. Therapeutic action starts with our desire for things to be different; it is this desire that opens us to understanding the meaning of the story we tell ourselves.

In Adlerian theory all perception, cognition, memory, dreams, art work, emotions, self-concept, soul, and behavior are in the service of the individual and form a lifestyle pattern (Adler, 1958, 1964). No part of the behavior is ever understood by itself or out of social context. As we become more consciously aware of the unity of our own personality, we can begin to recognize our place with others and interconnectedness with all of life, family, society, and planet. We must first be willing to look inward to follow our story, as well as outward towards conscious awareness and service in the spirit of social equality with others.

The central goal in Adlerian art therapy is to learn to come together in a group, to cooperate and create without sacrificing one's uniqueness as an individual (Dreikurs, 1986). Group art therapy can help one move from the self-focused arrangement to be uncooperative or inconsolable toward one which focuses on relationship in the life tasks of work, friendship, and intimacy.

The art process can encourage the innate potential for creativity one has as a child. The creative process is the life process, and as one becomes more creative, one becomes more courageous and more willing to cooperate in a socially useful way. This encourages a feeling of belonging and a feeling of being understood which, in turn, promote social interest.

The therapeutic process in psychodrama is training for spontaneity-creativity. Moreno (1946, p. 81) called psychodrama the "science which explores the 'truth' by dramatic methods." Grant (1981, p. 1) defined psychodrama as the "soul in action." The goal in psychodrama is to increase the person's innate capacity for spontaneity-creativity, thereby increasing his or her repertoire. It is this quality that must be "warmed up" in the group, with a goal of reducing the level of anxiety in each group member and, more importantly, increasing spontaneity (Siroka, 1982, p. 1). It is this quality, encouraged in the psychodramatic and art-making process, that can promote self-awareness. Both the artwork and the enactment are expressions of the person's inner reality or the story of one's life.

An Integration of Psychodrama and Art Therapy: Step by Step. Simple art materials consisting of colored construction paper and pastels are chosen by the group members. The art therapist directs the participants to find a comfortable place to work, to close their eyes, relax, and think about an Early Recollection. Any Early Recollection represents a single event that can be used as a projective technique for understanding the client in the here-and-now moment (Mosak, 1977, p. 67).

When ready, one participant tells the group an Early Recollection. Everyone is invited to draw that person's Early Recollection "as if" it is their own (Dreikurs, 1986). Since there is no right or wrong in art, anything produced is acceptable. The drawings can be abstract, symbolic, or representational.

When the drawings are completed, the group members come back together. Each member in turn tells the story of their drawing. "This procedure warms up the group members to many issues concerning significant relationships or the lack of them" (Peterson, 1989, p. 331). The warm-up phase provides the early stage in the process of group cohesion and allows for the expression of thoughts and feelings of each group member. "The goal of the warm-up is to bring each person into the 'here-and-now' moment so that all are psychically present" (Peterson, 1989, p. 322). Just like an Early Recollection the artwork reflects what is going on in the current life of the individual. When an individual seems to be warmed up to his or her drawing, the action takes place (Dushman &

Bressler, 1991, p. 519). That individual becomes the protagonist. He or she does not necessarily have to be the one who told the Early Recollection.

After the art and psychodrama, the group participants share in what ways they identify with the action. "The need for sharing is also magnified in art therapy because there are multiple internal psychodramas occurring simultaneously while all group members are involved in their own art making action" (Peterson, 1989, p. 323). A new work of art can be created in response to the psychodrama which might help in marking a new starting point in the protagonist's life. These drawings can be used to compare or contrast with where the protagonist was before the drama and could be given to the protagonist as a gift for further consideration at home.

When group members learn to show and tell the stories of their lives through the process of art making and psychodrama, a clearer picture of the real and imagined, of the conscious and that which is not yet understood, can emerge. With self-disclosure and group support each member has a chance to change the mistaken goals that interfere with feelings of belonging. By understanding the private logic as expressed in image and behavior and being able to make sense of it, group members can begin to connect the past to the present and see beyond self-limitations in their life stories. In the spirit of giving and receiving, everyone has an opportunity to become more intimately connected with others in the group providing yet another way to encourage the feeling of belonging and social interest.

An Example of a Psychodrama Using an Early Recollection.

In psychodrama, we can go back and forth in time and psyche (Goldman & Morrison, 1984, p. 30). This modality is the next best thing to redoing life and serves as a corrective exercise. Many clients spend a significant amount of time waiting for parents or significant others to repair or undo what the client feels to be missing in these basic relationships. Rather than waiting for others to change, in therapy the client is encouraged to learn to do for him or herself what others will not or cannot do. As these behaviors of self-care take root, the client is often able to forgive, understand, repair, or restore these challenging relationships.

Step 1 and Step 2. Selecting the Early Recollection and matching affect with a current life situation. The client selected the sixth recollection as the one that provides her with 'the most challenge' in her life. The sixth Early Recollection in this case study describes a two-year-old thinking one thing and outwardly going through the motions of accepting and performing, all the while saying to herself, "it stinks." In psychodrama, we can enable the client to put these inner thoughts and feelings into action. We ask the client to maximize—clearly feel—the main emotion in this Early Recollection. Based on this affective sense, we ask the client to select a real-life situation that has the same affect. By dealing with this current situation, we can gain more clarity regarding the way these ideas play out in the client's present life.

The client is asked to think of a current situation that comes to mind. More than likely it will have the same thematic quality as the Early Recollection. In this case, the client is asked to sort for a current situation where she feels the same unwillingness, the same sense of duty or pleasure and the same sense of "it stinks." A scene would be set up and enacted that would demonstrate the current situation. In a group, other members (auxiliaries) would be asked to play the other roles needed for the action (Dushman & Bressler, 1991, p. 519). This assumes the work is being done in a group setting. In an individual session, a monodrama can be done in which chairs or other objects are used to represent people. In this case, the client may use objects (e.g., chairs) as other characters, but then is asked to engage in role reversal . . . playing each of the other roles in the scene. There will be an enactment, an exploration of the content, sometimes a catharsis, and then an integration and closure.

Most people, when they are angry, confused, frustrated, or sad, can sense somewhere in their body a physical response. They intensify this sensation, called "organ jargon" (Griffith, 1984, p. 437). When the director is aware of a strong feeling on the part of the protagonist, that feeling will be maximized by various techniques such as saying, "Where do you feel this in your body?" or in the case of sadness, "Let it go, let the tears come." When this happens, another scene from the past is developed. This is a co-production of the director and the protagonist with the help of the auxiliaries. We may have several scenes (Goldman & Morrison, 1984, p. 9), all related to the general theme of doing something one finds distasteful, leading up to the Early Recollection of the two-year-old with the grandmother.

A scenario may develop in which the child or the mother could do something differently to have a different outcome and wind up with a feeling very different from "it stinks." Insight is arrived at through these scenes.

The director will co-create with the protagonist a final scene in which the protagonist may alter in some way what was depicted in the original scene of a current situation. What was learned from the previous scene can be utilized to try out a different way of behaving in times of incongruent behavior, doing one thing and thinking another.

Psychodrama gives us the opportunity not only to explore our lives, feelings, and viewpoints, but also to alter the way we act, feel, and behave. Dreikurs stressed Adler's position, "Trust only movement" (Shulman, personal communication, April 18, 1998). Psychodrama emphasizes the act rather than the word. We focus on the present, the here and now, and explore the past because it is important to our development. Our family constellation and Early Recollections are so important to how we formulate our lifestyle and our process. So in the action section, we work from the periphery to the core (Goldman & Morrison, 1984, p. 27), from the present to the past and back to the present, and also, from the content, explore the process of lifestyle issues—the convictions and faulty notions we form from our early experiences and family ambiance.

Adler (1958, p. 73) said, "There are no chance memories; out of the incalculable number of impressions which meet an individual, he chooses to remember only those which he feels, however darkly, do have a bearing on his situation." Thus, his memories represent his "Story of My Life," a story he repeats to himself, to warn him or comfort him, to keep him concentrated on his goal, to prepare him, by means of past experiences, to meet the future with an already tested style of action.

In the psychodrama, what we see is the person's lifestyle, the person's process. Adler's "trust only movement" concept is what Moreno, the father of psychodrama, incorporated into his psychodrama method.

After the drama, the group are asked to draw the feelings and awareness that came from the enactment. Sharing the insights to the drama and the meaning of any subsequent artwork is an integral part of the process. It allows for a reintegration of the client into the group—Adler's Gemeinschaftsgefühl (social feeling) in action. The client and the group members feel intimately connected through the exploration of the client's story. This process develops and enhances the feelings of belonging that are so important to the redirective life changes encouraged by Adler and Moreno.

Martha's Experience with Art and Psychodrama

Martha selected her sixth Early Recollection for use in both of these exercises. She was initially uneasy about the idea of drawing and performing, but with minimal encouragement she found the techniques easy to enter.

Art in Action. The process of drawing the early memory was an emotional one. Martha worked only in black charcoal on white paper even though other materials were available to her. The three black figures looked like three mountains: on the left, a large undefined figure sat in a bed. On the right, a slim undefined figure stood next to a window. In the foreground, a small undefined figure stood holding a bowl. She cried while she worked and offered several important comments on the female tradition on her mother's side of the family:

This art work makes me face these women . . . the loneliness . . . the darkness . . . depression . . . . I bet my mother wanted to jump out of that window. She never did. They didn't have lives. They never had their own lives . . . men and children . . . my grandmother was a gifted dress designer. So was my mother. My mother told me a million times that her mother could have made it . . . she had the talent. Fear kept her from moving . . . ironic, huh? Fear kept my mother from moving, too. Waste. This is all about waste. Wasted talent. No connection. Isolation. Despair. They didn't know . . . society really didn't give them choices. They couldn't see . . . didn't know women who took chances.

When asked to draw how she wanted the relationship to be, she drew three women (of different ages) sitting in a circle. The three women were connected, by a gold ribbon tied at the waist. And on their laps and surrounding their chairs, was art. The piece was done in bright colors. The background was a park with flowers and greenery. Martha's statements as she drew included the following remarks:

We are connected at our core by our love of art. How I wish we could have connected and shared these gifts. We are tied by our stunning gifts. I wish my grandmother could have had that shop. I see her teaching other women, making beautiful clothes. I see my mother loving to pass down this tradition and seeing the way fabric enters into my own art. I see us as women who use our art in our families, our homes, our gifts to others . . . but we would have to take the lead. We would have to say . . . this is who I am . . . this is how I am.

Psychodrama at Work. Martha selected the Early Recollection with her grandmother and mother for the psychodrama. She matched the incident with a work dilemma that fit the thematic and affective parameters of the ER.

I was given a work assignment that is quite large—important and meaningful work—but very much beyond my current skill level. And actually too large a project for just one person. In fact, I am actually in the process of solving this dilemma. I realized that I wanted to do the task—it is of value to me—it is really important to all people who have this specific disease. I also realized that I did not want to do it alone—it was way too much work and too important to have only one person on that job.

The role play began with the therapist playing the boss and Martha playing herself. Several different scenes were played out. Martha went through feelings of anger and frustration. She melted into tears after saying, "This is important work and it is too much for one person."

Through tears she said, "It was too much for my mother do alone. She needed help caring for Grandma. I bet her mother, a widow with 12 children needed help." Martha replayed the job scene, asking for help. She had to be clear, firm, unyielding with her boss. She asked for a co-director for the project. She was thrilled. The role play continued with her selecting "the most talented woman I know." The role play continued as Martha asked this woman to join the team. The woman agreed, but had some terms of her own. After negotiating, Martha realized the next step was to do some careful planning with her partner. Martha said, "Now I am on the line. I can do this and with this partner, I can do it with joy."

Martha played out her Early Recollection several ways. The first time, with the feeling of sad, silent isolation. The second time, she asked for help and her mother helped her. She told her mother other things about the room. That she wanted the drapes opened to the light. She wanted other people to help her mother. She wanted more talking and she wanted stories from both her mother and grandmother . . . stories about their lives. Martha said, "That is what we are doing . . . from the art picture . . . we are sitting there, tied together telling each other stories . . . the stories are our life stories."

Martha elected to do a role play in which she told her mother this memory and asked her mother for more time telling stories. Martha realized that she had a way to connect with her mother and that way was through stories. "My mother only knows how to work and serve people. She doesn't know what I know . . . that our stories are our lives. I can bring that to our relationship. That is my way to connect."

EARLY RECOLLECTIONS, NARRATIVES, AND SITUATIONS: IN SEARCH OF SITUATIONS

I have been asked to comment on the previous articles written by several distinguished contributors, some of whom have been my teachers. The contributions by Bernard Shulman, Robert Powers and Jane Griffith, Robert Willhite, Judy Sutherland, and Renee Dushman show the diversity and complexity of Adlerian practice as it exists today. Mary Frances Schneider is to be complimented for bringing them together and using their approaches with a client. And most of all, Martha deserves high praise for her patience, honesty, and the courage to explore her issues in such a rich format.

I have three main comments to share. The first relates to the issue of Adlerian practice. The second regards what I refer to as "points of entry." The third entails the concept of a "situation."

Defining What Is Adlerian. As a student of Adlerian psychology—and a practitioner, teacher, and supervisor as well—I have been both impressed and dismayed for a long time by the fact that Adler did very little to clarify precisely what he did in psychotherapy. The transcripts we have of him are in family and child guidance, in front of an audience, and therefore not obviously in the most natural of settings. Many other Adlerians have attempted to delineate what to do in psychotherapy, and have produced various papers, texts and tapes. Still, what did Adler do? He did not write enough to tell us, therefore, we are in search of a model.

Psychoanalysis, for example, is very detailed, especially as originally presented by Freud. The procedures an analyst follows are well organized (even if we don't agree with them). It is relatively easy to tell who is practicing psychoanalysis from who isn't. That allows for greater technical coherence, but less tolerance as well.

We have much more acceptance of diversity with Adlerian practitioners, for our guidelines are much less precise. This is a clear strength. Yet, much more so than with other theories, we have a tendency to "adopt" techniques from other systems. As long as the basic assumptions of Individual Psychology are not violated, this is not only acceptable, but I believe it is something that keeps our practice alive and well. Hence, every few years papers appear in our literature demonstrating how a particular theory can enrich or be incorporated into our system. This is the case with Narrative Theory.

In this system of psychotherapy, Adlerians have found a home. How warm and receptive a home it is, well, that is a matter of whom you ask. For some it is a second home. For others it is a comfortable way station. In any event, it is an opportunity to examine, compare, and contrast what we do with what we think we do, and with what we fear we ought to do or not do. If Narrative Theory does nothing else, it has accomplished a lot in providing this opportunity. I know that since reading the works of Michael White and David Epson, Bill O'Hanlon, Michelle Weiner-Davis, and Steve de Shazer, to name but a few, I have had to question many of my assumptions about the practice of psychotherapy. And that, I believe, is what we all have to do.

Points of Entry. The contributors to this section can be broken into four main categories. Two articles, one by Shulman and one by Powers and Griffith, present what I (lovingly) refer to as the traditional approach. Willhite presents (via Mary Frances Schneider) the distinctive approach that bears his name. Next is the art therapy approach, presented by Sutherland; and, finally, the psychodramatic approach, presented by Dushman. Each has a "point of entry" into the client's cognizance that differs slightly from the rest.

1. *The traditional approach.* Understanding is the key to the therapeutic work of Shulman and Powers/Griffith. Their ability to see patterns, to conceptualize dynamics, and articulate issues is wonderful. Their experience, sensitivity, and insightfulness are well known. For them, I believe the main point of entry is cognitive and linguistic. Verbal and intellectual insight is the key for this approach.

2. *The Willhite approach.* Willhite's method demonstrates that the restructuring of Early Recollections can be very powerful. I see his approach using cognitive and imaginal means as a point of entry. Thinking and imagery are keys to generating insight. The client learns a great deal about the self through restructuring recollections.

3. *The psychodramatic approach.* Asking clients to do something active and physical in their work can lead to great insight. Dushman's approach is primarily behavioral and interpersonal in its point of entry.

4. *The art therapy approach.* In this approach, Sutherland asks clients to express themselves through nonverbal, nonlinguistic means. Once again, the insight gained is sincere, profound, and moving. I believe this approach's point of entry is (primarily) imaginal and interpersonal.

Focusing on the Situation. There are many ways to get to New York. I can fly, drive, walk, run, be carried, and many more. The point is, what is the best way?

Behavior, I believe, is a product not just of the life style, but of the interaction of the life style and the situation in which people find themselves. A controller, for example, will have convictions that lead her to want control. How she controls, however, we will not know until we understand the situation she finds herself in. With those she believes she can easily and openly dominate, she probably will do so. Should she find herself in a situation in which direct, overt displays of control would not be well received, she probably will find another means of control. In the first case she might scream, while in the second she might weep. Without knowing the context, we cannot clearly comprehend the behavior.

In psychotherapy, I believe we must direct much more attention to the situation rather than focusing primarily on the client or the therapist. As therapist, I come in with my issues, both personal and professional. I may be more tired one day than the next, I may have more enthusiasm one day than the next, and in some cases, the time in a session may be flexible or not (e.g., we may have 45 minutes to work on an issue with no other appointment afterwards in case we run late; or a client may raise something "new" in the last 15 minutes of a session with a crisis session scheduled immediately following). The client may be very mature, responsible, and "easy" or may be extremely discouraged, severely ill physically, and seriously considering suicide. The client may have had a very bad day at work or a wonderful day with a lover.

These contexts will definitely influence my point of entry as much as will the client's lifestyle, my theoretical beliefs, or my latest reading. We all know this, but we seldom write about it, teach it, or research it.

Conclusion. So, to the "BIG QUESTION": Which approach do I like and think will work the best? All of them and none of them. Given the right situation, any one will work well, and given the wrong situation, none will. As a researcher once wrote many years ago, what will work when, with what type of client, under what circumstances? We still have not come very far in addressing that question, because people and situations are at least as varied and complex as the techniques we develop to change them. Depending upon the time of day, my energy level, my degree of comfort with a certain approach, and the time remaining in a session, I may use any of the four approaches, some more than others. Similarly, depending upon the client's energy level, comfort level, the type of issue he or she presents, and the client's physical capability (e.g., the art therapy approach might be contraindicated for a client with two broken arms), I might not use any of these. The mind boggles at the multitude of variables that can come into play.

That is my point. Maybe, once we get down to it, that is why psychotherapy is as much an art as a science. All of these authors are excellent clinicians—I know them all, and have received formal training from three of them. I truly believe that they too would put clinical utility and pragmatics above theoretical and technical precision. Psychology is a social science, not a natural science, and as some German scholars refer to it, it is really much more aptly called a *human* science. Humans are complex, and so is the world they are both thrown into and find themselves co-creating. We all need to be reminded of this, and I believe we do remember it in practice, even if we sometimes forget it in our writings and teachings.

Given the lack of practice guidelines for Adlerian psychotherapy, the particular point of entry will depend upon the unique situation in which I find myself. I may need to enter through cognitive, linguistic means in a directive manner. At another time, with another client (or even the same client), I may be more behavioral and interpersonal, but more laid back and nondirective. I may use the Willhite technique, or psychodrama. As long as we cannot control all the variables, we will probably forever need to be able to be flexible. We will probably all need to read other journals, see other professionals demonstrate their work, and be creative. We will need the Shulmans, Sutherlands, Willhites, Dushmans, and Powers and Griffiths . . . to demonstrate different approaches so we can be reminded that diversity is flexibility rearing its stubborn head when we might prefer regularity, consistency, and uniformity. We must forever learn and keep learning; perhaps that is the primary lesson to be taken from these clinicians.

Maybe that is why I love this field and this profession most.

RESEARCH STUDIES

In a theme issue of *The Counseling Psychologist* devoted exclusively to the theory and practice of individual psychology, Allen[60] noted that more empirical studies validating core Adlerian concepts were needed. Since that time there has been a significant increase —in Individual Psychology, the principle Adlerian-oriented journal, C. Edward Watkins, Jr.[61] has summarized core Adlerian research articles and developed a bibliography based on four core Adlerian concepts, including: (1) Birth order, (2) Social interest, (3) Early recollections, and (4) Lifestyle.

Some of his overall conclusions are that research articles in Individual Psychology have indeed flourished. From 1970–1981, birth order studies predominated; investigations of social interest have increased substantially since 1977.

A family atmosphere related study involves Chandler & Willingham's[62] research comparing perceived early childhood family influence and the patient's later established lifestyle. They found that the following five factors explained a significant portion of the variance: 1) Parent relationship/parent-child relationship, 2) Mother's characterization, 3) Father's characterization, 4) Sibling inter-relationship, and 5) Subject's childhood characterization.

Research on ERs and lifestyles has been limited but has seen increase in the past decade. Much research has been conducted on a college population exclusively or on some other type of students (elementary, high school, etc.), but more studies on actual clinical populations and the general adult population are recommended.

Three formative doctoral dissertations at the University of South Carolina, under the supervision of then NASAP President Frank Walton, led to the development of an Early Recollections Rating Scale.[63-65]

Eckstein[66] used the ERRS to empirically validate a core Adlerian idea that ERs change as a result of therapy. For example, Dreikurs[67] writes that:

The final proof of the patient's satisfactory reorientation is the change in his basic mistakes, indicated by a change in his early recollections. If a significant improvement has taken place, new incidents are recollected, reported recollections show significant changes, or are in some cases completely forgotten. (p. 71)

Eckstein's major finding was that "ERs do appear to change significantly as a result of long-term therapy." He also found that global ratings based on all combined ERs was more effective in demonstrating change than separate ER ratings, again consistent with Adler's reference to the total context (*Zusammerhang*) of the whole individual. High inter-rater reliability gave additional credence to the use of Altman's ERRS in research studies. (Changes in ERs is a needed area for additional empirical clinical studies.)

John Zarski[68,69] provides further validation of the ERRS. Dutton and Newlon[70] used the ERRS to discriminate sexual fantasies of adolescent sex offenders. They found significant correlations on the mistreated versus befriended, threatening vs. friendly, and depressing versus cheerful sub-scales. A significant difference between the means was found on the scale threatening versus friendly.

Savill and Eckstein[71] used the ERRS to demonstrate changes in ERs within a state mental hospital as a function of mental status. They found a significant change toward higher mental status and higher social interest from time of admission to time of discharge as measured by the ERRS when compared to a control group which showed no such changes. They also found a significant correlation between the ERRS, a social interest sub-scale of the NOISE-30, and the Zung scale, the highest correlation being on the "befriended/mistreated" ERRS sub-scale.

Some actual pre/post ER changes from both the Eckstein[72] and the Savill & Eckstein[73] research studies help to identify for the beginning lifestyle assessor a dramatic difference in the "feeling tone" of the ERs.

The following ER is noteworthy in that the same memory is recalled but with a much higher conclusion of social interest after nine months of therapy.

Pre

"My father put me on my sister's two wheeler—I didn't trust him—I was terrified—I screamed at the top of my lungs—felt I was too young to ride."

Post

"My father was trying to teach me to ride a two-wheeler—he was trying to teach me to ride—He then took me off, knowing I was too scared. I should have been more cooperative. Later I went back and pretended I was riding. He wasn't hurting me; Felt I should have "been more cooperative.""

Thorne[74] and Thorne & Piskin[75] administered a 200-item questionnaire to seven sample clinical populations including incarcerated prisoners, alcoholics, and chronic undifferentiated schizophrenics from a state hospital. A factor analysis of their scores yielded the following five clinical lifestyles differentiations:

1. Aggressive-domineering
2. Conforming
3. Defensive withdrawal
4. Amoral sociopathy
5. Resistant-defiant

In an effort to provide a more encouraging approach to the clinical descriptions of the five factors, Driscoll & Eckstein[76] developed a lifestyle questionnaire utilizing the following animals to represent both the strengths and weaknesses of each style: tiger, chameleon, turtle, eagle, and salmon. A revision of that questionnaire formed the basis of Eckstein's questionnaire in Chapter 3.

Substantial clinical experience with early recollections by Adlerians, and some others, has strongly established their value "as the basis of Adlerian personality assessment, or understanding of a person's life style."[77] Clearly early recollections are of extreme value in investigating "a personality".

Nomothetic research, the search for general principles, in investigations of personality, per se, theories and types of personalities, is, however, a very different kind of endeavor. Some information from early recollection analysis relevant to ascertaining the particular and unique aspects of an individual's lifestyle is necessarily lost in the quest for the common elements in personalities of subgroups of people, an enterprise from which other benefits in understanding are derived.

The authors suggest additional pre-post outcome studies with clinical populations. A longitudinal study exploring the change or constancy of ERs in general of 5, 10, 15, and 20 years is also needed.

Summary

The purpose of this chapter has been to present introductory interpretation skills in analyzing lifestyle data. Specific focus has been on the family atmosphere, the family constellation, birth order, and early recollections. Empirical research validating core Adlerian lifestyle theory was also presented. Chapter 5 explores the goal of reorientation by focusing particularly on the counseling relationship.

References—Maniacci et a.l, *Early Recollections: Mining the Personal Story*

Adler, A. (1958). *What life should mean to you.* New York: Capricorn Books.
Adler, A. (1964). *Social interest. A challenge to mankind.* New York: Capricorn Books.
Ansbacher, H. L., & Ansbacher, R. R. (Eds.). (1956a). *The individual psychology of Alfred Adler.* New York: Basic Books.
Ansbacher, H. L., & Ansbacher, R. R. (Eds.). (1956b). *Superiority and social interest.* Evanston, IL: Northwestern University Press.
Dreikurs, S. (1986). *Cows can be purple: My life and art therapy.* N. Catlin & J. W. Croake (Eds.). Chicago, IL: Alfred Adler Institute.
Dushman, R., & Bressler, M. J. (1991). Psychodrama in an adolescent chemical dependency treatment program. *Individual Psychology: The Journal of Adlerian Theory, Research & Practice,* 47 (4), 516-520.
Goldman, E. E., & Morrison, D. S. (1984). *Psychodrama: Experience and process.* Dubuque, IA: Kendall/Hunt.
Grant, R. (1981). *The psychodrama handbook.* Santa Monica, CA: Private Printing.
Griffith, J. (1984). Adler's organ jargon. *Individual Psychology,* 40 (4), 437-444.
Moreno, J. (1946). The five instruments of psychodrama. *Psychodrama* VI. New York: Beacon House.
Mosak, H. (1977). *On purpose.* Chicago: Alfred Adler Institute.
Peterson, J., & Files, L. (1989). The marriage of art therapy and psychodrama. In H. Wadeson, J. Durkin, & D. Perach (Eds.), *Advances in art therapy* (pp. 317-335). New York: John Wiley & Sons.
Powers, R. L., & Griffith, J. (1987). *Understanding lifestyle: The psychoclarity process.* Chicago: The Americas Institute of Adlerian Studies.
Shulman, B. H., & Mosak, H. H. (1988). *Manual for life style assessment.* Muncie, IN: Accelerated Development
Siroka, R. W. (1982). *Spontaneity-creativity.* Unpublished manuscript. Willhite, R. G. (1979). 'The Willhite": A creative extension of the early recollection process. In H. Olson (Ed.), *Early recollections: Their use in diagnosis and psychotherapy* (pp. 108–130). Springfield, IL: Charles C Thomas Publisher.

Endnotes

1   Rogers, C. R. *Counseling and Psychotherapy: Newer Concepts in Practice*. Boston, MA: Houghton Mifflin, 1942

2   *Ibid.*, p. 62.

3   Powers, R.L. & Griffith, J. *Understanding* Lifestyle: The Psycho-clarity Process Chicago, The Americas Institute of Adlerian Studies, 1987,21–22.

4   Ibid Dreikurs, R. *Psychodynamics, psychotherapy, and counseling*. Chicago: Alfred Adler Institute, 1967.

5   Dreikurs, R. Psychodynamics, psychotherapy, and counseling. Chicago: Alfred Adler Institute, 1967.

6   Mozdzierz, G. J., Macchitelli, F. J., and Lisiecki, J. "The Paradox in Psychotherapy: An Adlerian Perspective." *Journal of Individual Psychology* 32 (1976): 155–157.

7   Mosak, H. "Adlerian Psychotherapy." In *Current Psychotherapies*, ed. Raymond Corsini, pp. 56–107. Itasca, IL: F. E. Peacock, 1984.

8   Rogers, C. "The Necessary and Sufficient Conditions of Therapeutic Personality Change." *Journal of Consulting Psychology 21* (1957): 95–103.

9   Ibid

10 Carkhuff, R. *Helping and Human Relations*. Vols. 1, 11. New York: Holt, Rinehart and Winston, Inc., 1969.

11 Adler, A. *The Individual Psychology of Alfred Adler*. H. L. Ansbacher and R. Ansbacher, eds. New York: Harper and Row, 1956, 329.

12 Ibid.

13 Ibid., p.163.

14 Ibid.

15 Ibid.

16 O'Connell, W. *Action Therapy and Adlerian Theory*. Chicago: Alfred Adler Institute, 1975.

17 Ibid., p. 163.

18 Stein, H. "Twelve Stages of Creative Adlerian Psychotherapy." *Individual Psychology* 44, no. 2 (1988): 138–144.

19 U.S. Department of Health and Human Services, Public Health Service. *Healthy People 2000: National Health Promotion and Disease Prevention Objectives*. Washington, DC: Superintendent of Documents, Government Printing Office, 1990.

20 Adler, A., [1927]. *Understanding Human Nature*. W.B. Wolf, trans. New York: Fawcett Premier, 1954.

21 Ellis, A. *Humanistic Psychotherapy: The National Emotive Approach*. New York: Julian Press, 1973.

22 Adler, A. *What Life Should Mean to You*. A. Porter, ed. New York: Capricorn Books, 1958.

23 U.S. Department of Health and Human Services, Public Health Service. *Healthy People 2000: National Health Promotion and Disease Prevention Objectives*. Washington, DC: Superintendent of Documents, Government Printing Office, 1990.

24 Shulman and Mosak, op. cit.

25 Ibid.

26 Anthony, E. J., and Cohle, B. J. *The Invulnerable Child*. New York: Guilford Press,1987.

27 *The Arizona Republic*, Oct. 17, 1991, p. B-12.

28 Walker, M., and Belove, P. "The Loyalty Dilemma." *Journal of Individual Psychology* 38 (1982): 161–172.

29 Powers, R.L. and Griffith, J. *Understanding Lifestyle: The Psycho-clarity Process*. Chicago, The Americas Institute of Adlerian Studies, 1987, 148.

30 Dreikurs, R., Grunwald, E., and Pepper, F. *Maintaining Sanity in the Classroom*. New York: Harper Collins, 1982.

31 Ibid., p. 46.

32 Ibid., p. 59.

33 Ibid.

34 Ibid.

35 Drescher, J. *The Birth Order Blues*. New York: Viking Press, Penguin Books, 1993.

36 Adler, A. [1933]. *Social Interest: A Challenge to Mankind*. New York: Capricorn Books, 1964, 58.

37 Ibid., p. 329.

38 Eckstein, D. "The Use of Literature as a Projective Technique." *Journal of Individual Psychology 40*, no. 2 (1984):145.

39 Ibid., p. 146

40 Ibid., p. 57

41 Kefir, N. "Priorities." Unpublished manuscript, 1972.

42 Dewey, E. *Basic Applications of Adlerian Psychology*. Coral Springs, FL: MTI Press, 1978.

43 Kefir, N., and Corsini, J. "Dispositional Sets: A Contribution to Typology." *Journal of Individual Psychology 30* (1974): 163–187.

44 Dinkmeyer, D., Dinkmeyer, D., and Sperry, L. *Adlerian Counseling and Psychotherapy*. Columbus, OH: Merrill Publishing, 1987.

45 Rotter, J. *Social Learning and Clinical Psychology*. New York: Johnson, 1980/1973/1954.

46 Paulus, T. *Hope for the Flowers*. New York: Paulist Press, 1972.

47 Barker, S.B. and Bitter, J.R. "Early Recollections versus Created Memory: A Comparison for Projective Qualities" *Individual Psychology 48*, no. 1 (1992): 86–95.

48 Newcombe, N. "Early Childhood Memories." *Family Therapy Networker 24*, no. 5 (2000): 18.

49 Kern, R., Belangee, S., and Eckstein, D. "Rose-Colored View of the World" *Floridan Adlerian Newsletter*, May 2001.

50 Shulman and Mosak, op. cit.

51 Powers and Griffith, op. cit., p. 266

52 Adler/Ansbacher and Ansbacher, op. cit., p. 8.

53 Adler, A. "On the Interpretation of Dreams." *International Journal of Individual Psychology 2*, no.1 (1936): 13–14.

54 Kaplan, H. "A Method for the Interpretation of Early Recollection and Dreams." *Individual Psychologist 41*, no. 4 (1985): 525–533.

55 Nichols, C. C. and Feist, J. Explanatory Style as a Predictor of Earliest Recollections. *Individual Psychology, 50*, no. 1 (1994):31–39.

56 Kopp, R. R. "Early Recollections in Adlerian and Metaphor Therapy." *Journal of Individual Psychology 54*, no. 4 (1998):480-481.

57 Ibid

58 Ibid., p. 485.

59 Mansager, E., Barnes, M., Boyce, B., Brewster, J. D., Lertora, H. J.; Marais, F., Santos., J., and Thompson, D. "Interactive Discussion of Early Recollections: A Group Technique with Adolescent Substance Abusers." *Individual Psychology 51*, no. 4 (1995):413–421.

60 Allen, T. "The Individual Psychology of Alfred Adler: An Item of History and a Promise of a Revolution." *Counseling Psychologist 3*, (1971): 3–24.

61 Watkins, C. "A Decade of Research in Support of Adlerian Psychological Theory." *Journal of Individual Psychology 38*, no. 1 (1982):90–99.

Watkins, C. "Some Characteristics of Research on Adlerian Psychological Theory, 1970-1981." *Individual Psychologist 34*, no. 1 (1983): 99–110.

Watkins, C. "Research Bibliography on Adlerian Psychological Theory." *Individual Psychologist 42*, no. 1 (1986): 123–132.

62 Chandler, C., and Willingham, W. "The Relationship between Perceived Early Childhood Family Influence and the Established Lifestyle." *Individual Psychologist 42*, no. 3 (1986): 388–395.

63 Rule, W. "The Relationship between Early Recollections and Selected Counselor and Lifestyle Characteristics." Unpublished doctoral dissertation, University of South Carolina, 1972.

64 Quinn, J. "Predicting Recidivism and Type of Crime from Early Recollections of Prison Inmates." Unpublished doctoral dissertation, University of South Carolina, 1973.

65 Altman, K. "The Relationship between Social Interest Dimensions of Early Recollections and Selected Counselor Variables." Unpublished doctoral dissertation, University of South Carolina, 1973.

66 Eckstein, D. "Early Recollection Changes after Counseling: A Case Study." *Journal of Individual Psychology 32* (1976): 212–223.

67 Ibid.

68 Zarski, J. "The Early Recollections Rating Scale: Development and Applicability in Research." In *Lifestyle: Theory, Practice & Research*, ed. L. Baruth and D. Eckstein. Dubuque, IA: Kendall/Hunt Publishing Company, 1981.

69 Zarski, J., Sweeney, T., and Barcikowski, R. "Counseling Effectiveness as a Function of Counselor Social Interest." *Journal of Counseling Psychology 24* (1977): 1–5.

70 Dutton, W., and Newlon, B. "Early Recollections and Sexual Fantasies of Adolescent Sex Offenders." *Individual Psychologist 44*, no. 1 (1988):85–94.

71 Savill, G., and Eckstein, D. "Changes in Early Recollections as a Function of Mental Status." *Individual Psychologist 43*, no. 1 (1987): 3–17.

72 Eckstein, D. "Early Recollection Changes after Counseling: A Case Study." *Journal of Individual Psychology 32* (1976): 212–223.

73 Savill and Eckstein, op. cit.

74 Thorne, F. "The Lifestyle Analysis." *Journal of Clinical Psychology 31* (1975): 236–240.

75 Thorne, F., and Pishkin, V. "A Factorial Study of Needs in Relation to Lifestyles." *Journal of Clinical Psychology 31* (1975): 240–248.

76 Driscoll, R., and Eckstein, D. "Lifestyle Questionnaire." *In The 1982 Annual Handbook For Group Facilitators*. San Diego, CA: University Associates, 1982, 100-107.

77 Ansbacher, H. "Adler's Interpretation of Early Recollections: Historical Account." *Journal of Individual Psychology 29*, no. 2 (1973): 135.

REORIENTATION

Reorientation consists of translating the insights gained during the interpretation process into actual attitudinal and/or behavioral changes. The purpose of this chapter is to integrate lifestyle assessment into a therapeutic context. Adlerian techniques for recognizing and changing self-defeating behaviors plus encouragement to reclaim one's personal power will be the focus. Reframing and other suggested change strategies will also be defined and illustrated.

Strategies for Increasing Social Interest

To create a lifestyle, one organizes activity and feeling around a guiding line, or goal, regulating emotional and behavioral response according to criteria expressed in lifestyle convictions.[1] Such a guiding line is an overriding, coherent strategy for attaining success or safety in life. It also drives judgments about possibilities and constraints of situations; and directly influences feelings and behavior in a given situation. One can conceptualize lifestyle as *movement toward or attraction to certain situations taken to constitute success, or as avoidance or elimination of certain situations taken to constitute danger.*[2]

The lifestyle allows an individual to cope in known and familiar fashions in many life events, and to operate within a relatively or distinctly narrow range of interpersonal activity. One maintains feelings of security by behaving in known ways, in selected environments, rather than by taking risks and feeling insecure. In times of stress, rather than try new behaviors, a person typically utilizes habitual patterns of behavior. Although a lifestyle offers accustomed ways to behave in most situations, the downside is that an individual can be caught in inflexible activity and in fear of moving outside an accustomed range.

An individual may come to therapy to rid himself/herself of worry, suffering, or temptation, but seldom to change a style of activity.[3] The lack of inner freedom and interest in others is a stress justified by oversensitivity to, or overvaluation of, certain possibilities embodied in apperceptual cues. The lifestyle itself, because of self-reinforcing features, creates a stress or lack of inner freedom that can be relieved by appeal to the goal or to the temptation (the client's sympathy with the suffering) or to both at once.[4]

Social Interest and Inner Freedom

Social interest is the antidote to worry, suffering, and temptation, or the lack of inner freedom. High social interest implies a flexible ability to cooperate with others. Greater Social Interest and inner freedom can become a goal in the therapeutic process. It is a guiding line or ideal that can replace other guiding lines.[5] According to Slavik, "any therapeutic strategy which helps increase one's inner freedom contributes to one's social interest. A guiding line increasing inner freedom, decreasing worry, temptation, or suffering, enables one to become task-orientated and other-orientated. Conversely, a guiding line oriented to the welfare of others increases inner freedom and reduces one's suffering and temptation."[6]

Social Interest Strategies for Increased Social Interest

To encourage prosocial movement, there are several ways in which ideas of social interest can be used: (1) as a general strategy of encouragement; (2) in repeated confrontation of client's specific behaviors; and (3) to generate alternative conclusions to client's lifestyle convictions.[7] Encouragement is particularly useful with "highly resistant" or slow-moving clients who are not wanting a lifestyle analysis or who might deny relevance of certain lifestyle conviction derived from early ERs.

In a second strategy, the appropriate concept of social interest is used in repeated, direct confrontation of client's behaviors. Starting with a description of or a presentation of clients' usual behavior a therapist can then begin to inquire about the usual results of such behavior, and what one might do to obtain a more desirable result. Suggestions toward increased cooperation then follow.

Third, a social interest therapeutic focus can help to generate alternate conclusions in clients' lifestyle convictions and alternate behaviors. Not only do such redefinitions help to avoid resistance, to build rapport, to frame behavior as positive, and in general to aid therapy to be efficient, they encourage the client to undertake prosocial change while paradoxically "staying the same." Redefining a person's behavior, situation, or symptom in a prosocial way, taking into consideration direction of movement and lifestyle convictions, increases self-confidence and social interest. Making one's behavior useful—an experience of success—with minimum change can help promote self-confidence and social interest in clients.[8]

Interpreting
Lifestyle Using Therapist-Generated Metaphors

Shulman and Mosak note that Adlerian therapists often describe lifestyles using a single word or phrase.[9] A person whose image of self, image of life, and conclusions about behavior could be summarized as "I am small and weak; life is dangerous; therefore others must protect me; might be described as having the lifestyle of a "weak baby." Similarly, someone with the lifestyle convictions that "I am the rightful heir to my father's power; life is here to appreciate me and to serve me; therefore, I have to be the center of attention; might be referred to as having the lifestyle of a "crown prince."[10] Kopp[11] maintains that such examples as "weak baby" and "crown prince" are metaphors that are employed because they capture the essence or unity of the lifestyle. Metaphors are ideally suited to the task of describing one's lifestyle because lifestyle is a holistic pattern of living[12] and because metaphors are word-pictures that convey holistic, nonlinear meanings.

Lifestyle
Expressed Through Client-Generated Metaphors

Kopp also says that "Therapists can also grasp a client's lifestyle by tuning in to the client's metaphoric language. Client-generated metaphors can be grouped into the following categories: metaphors that represent one's image of self; those that represent one's image of others; those that represent one's image of situations (life); and those that represent one's understanding of the relationships between self and self, self and others, and self and situations."[13] Each of the metaphors described in Table 5.1 expresses the person's lifestyle movement and his or her view of self, an other, or a situation (life) or his or her view of self in relation to himself or herself, a relationship with another, or a particular situation. Table 5.1 illustrates the six categories using a female case study.

Table 5.1—Categories of Client-Generated Metaphors

Category	Example
Self	"I'm a teakettle about to explode!"
Other	"My husband's a locomotive, barging in the house."
Situation	"My life is a barren wasteland."
Relationship of self to self	"I keep beating myself up."
Relationship of self to an other	"Dealing with him, I'm trying to tame a wild lion."
Relationship of self to a situation	"I'm slowly sinking in quicksand."

Adapted from Kopp, 1995, p. 104[14]

In using metaphors to assist client insight, counselors can follow this suggested sequence by Kopp.

Step 1. Notice metaphors!

Step 2. When you say (the metaphor), what image/picture comes to mind? Or what image/picture do you see in your mind's eye? Or what does (the metaphor) look like?

Step 3. Explore the metaphor as a sensory image:

   (1) Setting (e.g. What else do you see? Or describe the scene or an aspect of the scene (associated with the metaphoric image.)

   (2) Action/interaction (e.g., What else is going on in (the metaphoric image)? Or "what are the other people in the metaphoric image saying/thinking/doing?)

   (3) Time (e.g. What led up to this? Or what was happening just before the situation in the metaphoric image?)

Step 4. What's it like to be (the metaphoric image)? Or what's your experience of (the metaphoric image)? Or what are you feeling as you (the metaphoric image)?

Step 5. If you could change the image in any way, how would you change it?

Step 6. What connections (parallels) do you see between your image of (the metaphoric image) and (the original situation)?

Step 7. How might the way you changed the image apply to your current situation?"[15]

Intervention Choice Points

Jeff Zeig contends there are five choice points for clinicians relative to client interventions.

1. The *goal*—"what to communicate?" For example, when a client says "I am depressed," there are many choices for a therapist intervention. The therapist can take a cognitive, affective, or experiential approach.

2. How to communicate the goal (*gift wrapping* as a technique)—i.e., for depression, the "gift wrapping" might be exercise, hypnosis, indirect suggestions, antidote, or a confusion technique. Hypnosis is another way of "gift wrapping" ideas. Zeig continues his creative "gift wrapping" metaphor as follows: "The patient gives a gift but in the form of a symptom. The task for the therapist is to unwrap and also to give back the gift (solution). It's like Christmas. The therapist is given a gift (problem) and then gives it back to the client (solution). Therapy is an exchange of presents."

3. How to *individualize* our gift-wrapped goal (tailoring to the uniqueness of the individual). The best therapy utilizes the client's experiential language, the noted therapist Melton Erickson, according to anthropologist Margaret Mead, "invented the specific therapy for every patient."

4. The *process*—procedure for presenting including the setup, including the intervention, and including the follow though.

5. The *posture* of clinician—personally and professionally—the lens, muscles, heart, that is within each therapist. Zeig notes: "The choice becomes to be a clinician. The position the therapist takes change the goal of therapy. It is important to choose a goal a counselor can help solve. The goal can change or the 'gift-wrapping' can change or one can change the tailoring to use gestures, antidotes. A therapist can change the process. Lastly, consider changing yourself as the therapist by bringing out something new in oneself (more humor, more content, etc.)."

Zeig notes that "Psychotherapy is more an improvisation than a science."

Five specific examples of being a competent therapist that can be developed with experience include such issues as: *competence, emotional expression-emotion "reading," experiential empathy, effective use of the body*, and *changing states*.

Just as the top three factors determine the value of real estate—"location, location, location"—Zeig states the three attributes most valuable to a therapist are "observe, observe, observe." That means paying better attention to what behavior means. Zeig uses the analogy of the Nautalius weight-building machines, which isolate and develop experiential stations by what he is calling 50-60 "psycho-aerobics" exercises. Being a therapist thus can be viewed as a *state*, which, with conscious effort, can be refined and improved as one significant variable in the therapeutic relationship.

Adlerian Reorientation Attitudes

According to Murphey, Adler was one of the first theorists to emphasize personal responsibility for one's behavior.[16] Adler stressed the patient's active, responsible role in psychotherapy when he stated, "The actual change in the nature of the patient can only be his own doing. From the very beginning the consultant must try to make it clear that the responsibility for his cure is the patient's business."[17] Powers and Griffith note that "The cure or re-orientation is brought about by a correction of the faulty picture of the world to the unequivocal acceptance of a mature picture of the world."[18]

Core Adlerian therapist attitudes include mutual trust and respect, and a client/therapist relationship based upon equality and friendliness. Viewing Adlerian psychotherapy as a "cooperative educational enterprise," Mosak stressed the client's responsibility and active role:

Therapy is structured to inform the patient that a creative human being plays a role in creating one's problems, that one is responsible (not in the sense of blame) for one's actions, and that one's problems are based upon faulty perceptions, and inadequate or faulty learnings, especially of faulty values. If this is so, one can assume responsibility for change. . . . From the initiation of treatment, the patient's efforts to remain passive are discouraged.[19]

Personal Wellness Plan

In reorientation the counselor and client work together to consider alternative beliefs, behaviors, and attitudes—a change in the client's lifestyle. Having explored and discussed one's life style Myers, Sweeney, and Witmer[20] suggest the following format for developing what they call a "personal wellness plan."

1. Identify one or two specific areas in which you would like to improve. Provide a brief discussion of how your life would be improved as a result of positive change in this life task.

    a. _____

    b. _____

2. Write a behavioral plan. Include objectives for change, methods to be used to effect change, and resources that will be used as the plan is implemented. If other people are to be involved in the plan in some way, also note that.

3. Identify specific rewards for positive steps above as well as possible punishments for not keeping your agreements.

    a. Rewards _____

    b. Punishments _____

4. Develop a series of self-affirmations that you can say and/or write for yourself that will encourage you in your self-improvement game plan.

To follow are additional strategies the counselor may employ to enhance the change process during the reorientation phase of therapy.

Suggested Sequences of Adlerian Counseling

As the counselor continues to work with the client it might be helpful to pay particular attention to the following therapeutic issues.

1. *Aligning the goal.* This includes communicating empathy for the client's own creative movement for significance, intentions, and beliefs. This may include assessing whether the goals are realistic.

2. *Discussing the role, tactics, and strategy.* Specific methods of how the client attains significance are discussed. The role generally involves how a person reaches a goal (usually lacking in some form of social interest) by using particular strategy and tactics.

3. *Encouraging creativity.* This encourages an "unfreezing" of a client who is "stuck" in a habitual mode of functioning.

4. *Confronting nonconstructive tactics.* To confront is to address discrepancies between such issues as: (a) what the person *says* versus what they *do* (Adler stressed "trust the tongue of the shoe, not the tongue of the mouth"); (b) what the person verbally says and what their nonverbals communicate; and (c) what the person says compared to what someone else tells you.

5. *Stimulating a social "strategy."* Encouraging contributions to the needs of the situation. Often clients are absorbed in narcissistic "self" oriented myopic vision. The counselor encourages a return to the original problem by considering a more socially useful approach.

6. *Reorientation.* Stimulating socially interested "tactics." The therapist now asks the client if he or she would be willing to consider other tactics that would result in an effective pursuit of one's goals including an effective resolution of the problem.[21]

7. *Exploring alternatives and obtaining a commitment for socially interested action.* The client is now made aware that insight has little value in and of itself. It is only a prelude to action. Outsight—moving ideas into action is the real aim of the process.[22] In dealing with depressed patients Adler[23] advised "You can be cured in fourteen days if you follow this prescription. Try to think every day how you can please someone."

Reorientation involves what Carkhuff[24] describes as the "action" phase of counseling. The initial therapeutic style is suggested as facilitation, being receptive and encouraging a "downward, inward" self-exploration. Conversely, the action phase is an "up and out" focus.

Homework Assignments

Specific action-oriented homework assignments may include bibliotherapy, a term derived from the Greek words *biblion* (book) and *therapeia* (healing). Popular self-help books and other audiovisual aids can be used.

Traditionally the interpretation process has included a counselor sitting down alone and writing his or her impressions based upon the lifestyle interview. However, it's also suggested that it be done more in a collaborative egalitarian relationship with the client because ultimately it is that person himself or herself who is the ultimate determiner of the "truthfulness" of any interpretive guesses by counselors.

Therefore, a suggested intervention may be, "Here are some of my ideas. How would you like to rewrite them to fit you?" Such a procedure helps to increase the psychological "ownership" of the investment and the involvement of the client himself or herself appreciating and valuing such a personal story.

Cue sorting" or ranking items from most to least importance is one specific technique that Bitter recommends to begin the interpretation process. Another is to consider the issues in their life like a "room" in which ones that are at the "top" are important and need to be attended to right away versus issues that are in the "middle of the room" that are also important but can wait somewhat, while issues in the "bottom" part of the "room" are not necessary to deal with in the immediate future.

Journal writing[25] is also an effective method for clients to record their personal feelings and reactions in a reflective manner. Stone notes that journaling shares many similarities with the process of obtaining ERs from clients.

Journaling is storytelling to ourselves . . . journaling embodies lifestyle. Journals record the "recollections" of the mind recorded over time in contrast to the "classic" epigrammatic recollections gathered in a lifestyle assessment. Nevertheless, journaling and lifestyle recollections embody the same dynamic processes. Our stories tell how we interpret life. Albeit with subjectivity, it is out reality. Our stories are as meaningful for us in journaling as any we hear or read. And the dynamic processes used in journaling and lifestyle assessments are the same as those evidenced in the novels, short stories, dramas, and poems. . . . Journaling is but a means for recording and reflecting upon the stories in our lives. Journaling provides a tool by which we can apply these stories to our lives."[26]

Seven specific action-oriented tasks that can be utilized by counselors include the following:

1. Confronting irrational and/or self-defeating beliefs. Cognitive-oriented beliefs, thoughts, and perceptions. Therapeutic interventions could include reframing, guided imagery, practicing encouraging self-talk.

2. Cognitive/behavioral including both thought and physical activities. Examples include letter writing (anger, forgiveness, acceptance, guilt, good-bye, self- and other love), keeping journals, writing likes/dislikes, goals, expectations, and relaxation exercises.

3. Behavioral. Examples are charting the frequency of behaviors, reinforcement strategies, punishment, aversive conditioning, and exercising.

4. Metaphorical/symbolic—stories, anecdotes, puns, riddles, metaphors.

5. Strategic/paradoxical tasks—paradoxical (self-contradictory meanings), prescriptions, experiences and messages.

6. Absurd/ambiguous tasks—assignment of deliberate absurd tasks with an indirect meaning or experience.

7. Social directives—tasks that involve or promote social interest, cooperation and interactions. For example, in his young adulthood cognitive therapist Albert Ellis had a fear of being rejected by women. His self-prescribed homework assignment was to be rejected by 100 women in a two-week period. "I'm doing an experiment—women have turned me down for a date this week. Will you be the next?" he humorously said to each prospective "rejector."[27]

Nikelly describes other action-oriented interpretive techniques as follows:

An effective and practical approach is to encourage the client to interpret his own behavior and then to consider alternative solutions which might prove effective. In other words, he is encouraged to search his life pattern and to suggest alternative behavior to reach his goals rather than to seek for deep and hidden drives. The therapist can sift out unacceptable or inappropriate explanations and help the client gain insight into those that are actually interwoven into his lifestyle.

Humor can be effective in helping the client relate more positively toward the therapist. . . . Humor can help to disarm the client provided that the therapist is fair and honest with him and that the humor is built upon mutual respect and trust. . . . The technique of overstatement, for example, may show the client that he is deciding (by avoiding anxiety and interaction) to see the world as a hostile jungle. 'Let's see if we can make it even worse' exposes this maneuver and yet allows for an acceptance of the person.

The Midas technique ostensibly attempts to gratify the client's psychological demands. However, since giving in to his demands never solves his basic problems, he continues to remain unsatisfied and comes to understand that his fundamental outlook and style of living must be altered so that he will no longer rely on others for attention and gratification.[28]

George Carlin's Theory of Life

The most unfair thing about life is the way it ends. I mean, life is tough. It takes up a lot of your time. What do you get at the end of it? A Death. What's that? A bonus?

I think the life cycle is all backwards.

You should die first, get it out of the way. Then you live in an old age home.

You get kicked out when you're too young, you get a gold watch and you go to work. You work forty years until you're young enough to enjoy your retirement.

You do drugs, alcohol, you party, you get ready for high school. You go to grade school, you become a kid, you play, you have no responsibilities.

You become a little baby, you go back into the womb, spend your last nine months floating . . . and you finish off as an orgasm.

Another technique includes *role-reversal*, where the person is encouraged to assume the position of "significant others" in the environment to assess the effects of his/her behavior on them. Still other techniques include what Adler termed "anti-suggestion," similar to what Viktor Frankl[29] called *"paradoxical intention."* Here the person is encouraged to do the very things that has been feared by him or her. It is also done with as much humor as possible. For example, a person afraid of losing consciousness may be asked to try "passing out." Bringing humor into the situation, the counselor then adds, "Come on now, pass out all over the place . . ." People, discovering they cannot intentionally do what they had feared would happen to them, often laugh at the situation also. Of course, the counselor then attempts to assure such persons that since it is impossible to "pass out here on purpose, then you cannot pass out any other place if you try." Frankl said such a situation "takes the wind out of the sails" of fear.

"Avoiding the client's 'tarbaby'" is a technique borrowed from an Uncle Remus story in which Briar Rabbit was all covered with tar. Anyone touching him got "stuck." So too counselors can get stuck in the client's discouragement and depression. For example, the very strength of compassion can lead counselors to be vulnerable to be caught in the client's mistaken beliefs. Consider someone with a victim attitude that says "Life has basically dealt me a 'lousy hand'"—"I have been unwanted, unloved and abused." Counselors implying "Yes, it *has* been unfair for you" while possibly having the client grateful for such sympathy are not assisting the client to develop what Frank Walton has called "psychological muscle." Counselors reinforcing such stimulus/response victim statement as "my mother made me . . ." have gotten stuck in the client's "tarbaby."

The Paradox of Change—Considerations for Counselors

Abstract changes in beliefs and behavior are fundamental goals of counseling. The following section addresses such specific concepts:

1. "Legacy," impressions—("seeing beyond Z") and the tendency of the now
2. Paradigm shifts
3. The paradox of therapy
4. "Intent and outcome"
5. Who is the "Perceiver I?"

"Impressions of the now" are formed by one's early developmental experiences. Such impressions are literally etched like an engraving on the human mind and soul. Early recollections provide a valuable prospective insight into one's formative impressions created in childhood when each person makes core decisions or conclusions about life, others, and one's self.

Such impressions may of course be either positive, or "negative," or a combination of both. These etchings create a literal groove on one's mind. Unfortunately, most people are unaware of such etchings of the mind because they are formed at such an early age when the child has no conscious cognitive awareness or "container" to know such markings on the mind.

"Impressions of the now" then lead to *legacy*, which can be defined as the resulting habitual remnants or pattern resulting from such things. Legacy is the consequence or result of impressions and forms what Shulman calls a "pre-working hypothesis."[30]

The "tendency" is the consequence of such unified, holistic, deeply grooved, largely unconscious impressions—patterns that come to characterize one's basic lifestyle. Piaget uses the term "assimilation" to refer to the process where a person filters new information through a pre-formed hypothesis—over many years, habitual ways of acting result in tendencies or predispositions of beliefs and behaviors.[32]

Although most people coming to counselors usually say they want to change, the paradox of therapy is that clients typically resist change (called accommodation or changing one's inner beliefs by Piaget) to adapt to new "external" information. Such factors as fear of change, fear of the unknown, comfort in one's predictable, breakable habitual patterns often create client resistance to have the courage to change the known for the "road less traveled" in the unknown, unexplored future.

Intent and Outcome

The difference between intent and outcome is an important change-related concept. Intent is what one says he or she wanted to happen (e.g., "I intended to be on time for our meeting"). The outcome is what actually occurred ("I was talking on the phone"). Counselors can gently confront such "I intended 'this' but a different 'that' happened" outcome occurred by asking clients to consider that what actually happened (outcome) is precisely the desired result that was wanted all along. Simply stated, an outcome is saying one thing but doing another. Or, as Adler said, "Trust only movement," further poignantly described as "trust the 'tongue' of the shoe, not the 'tongue' of the mouth."

A paradigm is a systematic organized pattern, similar to what Piaget called a scheme or schema. We all have broad categories ("computer programs") on such concepts as love, friendship, helping, self-love, women, men, work, abuse, change, and so forth. Paradigms are necessary to help organize separate, discrete disconnected bits of information. But unless paradigms are open to change or modification (accommodation), then one continually recycles through a "washing machine with dirty water and no rinse cycle." In such a case, one becomes a prisoner or slave to one's rigid, habitual unexamined patterns.

Personality disorders (i.e., borderline, narcissistic, being schizoid, dependent, etc.) are basically distorted schemes. Specific examples such as "I am enraged because I was never truly loved" are preoccupied with, "me, me, me." "I avoid intimate/close relations," or "I must be in a relationship and approved of by significant others" are representative broad conclusions corresponding respectively to the above-listed personality disorders. Cognitive therapists such as Albert Ellis identify and confront such broad overgeneralized irrational beliefs.

The Impact of Cultural Heritage

There are obviously other significant factors influencing a child besides the family. Children do not grow up in a vacuum. They cannot be understood apart from the historical, the geographical, the socioeconomic, the cultural, and/or religious influences surrounding them.

Assimilation and accommodation are cultural factors when one is in any type of minority group status. To what extent one preserves cultural and religious observances when the predominant culture surrounding a family is a consideration. Also relevant is the issue of prejudice or acceptance of the various cultures in a community.

Ivey and Simek-Downing suggested that counselors answer the following questions to start them thinking about how their cultural heritage may affect their counseling:

1. *Ethnic heritage.* With what ethnic background do you first identify? First identify your nationality—U.S. citizen, Canadian, Mexican, etc. Beyond this first answer, you may find the words *white, red, black, Polish, Mormon, Jewish,* or others coming to mind. Record these words.

Then, where did your grandparents come from? Great-grandparents? Can your trace a family history, perhaps with different ethnic, religious, and racial backgrounds? Trace your heritage in list form or in a family tree. Do not forget your heritage from the country within which you live.

2. *Are you monocultural, bicultural, or more?* Review the list you developed and pick out the central cultural, ethnic, religious, or other types of groups that have been involved in your development.

3. *What messages do you receive from each cultural group you have listed?* List the values, behaviors, and expectations that people in your group have emphasized over time. How have you personally internalized these messages? If you are aware of the message, chances are you have made some deviation from the family, ethnic, or religious values. If you are unaware, you may have so internalized the values that you are a "culture-bearer" without knowing it. Becoming aware of obvious but unconscious culture-bearer messages may become the most difficult task of all.

4. *How might your cultural messages affect your counseling and therapeutic work?* This final question is the most important. If you believe in individuality as supreme, given your family history, you may tend to miss the relational family orientation of many Asians and African-Americans. As we all have cultural histories, it is easy to believe that our way of being in the world is "the way things are and should be."[31]

Summary

A positive identification with one's own ethnic, cultural and racial heritage provides a firm base for understanding and respecting the world view of people with different ethnic, cultural and racial heritages.

Reframing: Creating New Impressions

"You seek problems because you need their gifts—there is no such thing as a problem without a gift for you," Richard Bach wrote in *Illusions*.[33] In *The Search for the Beloved*, Jean Houston notes that wounding is a core component of being able to have empathy for others.[34]

Reframing will now be further defined and illustrated.

"Reframing" an Innovative Educational Technique: Turning a Perceived Inability into an Asset

Daniel Eckstein, Ph.D.
Presented at "Breakthroughs 2001:
Ninth International Conference on Thinking,"
Auckland, New Zealand, January 15, 2001

Introduction

Early in life, people begin to form conclusions about their world. Such lifestyle core decisions can be described by Adlerian psychologists as conclusions about life in general, other people, and one's self. Such impressions may be either positive, or "negative," or a combination of both. These etchings create a literal groove on one's mind. Unfortunately, most people are unaware of such etchings (decisions) of the mind because they are formed at such an early age the child has no conscious cognitive awareness or "container" to know such markings on the mind. Thus, a person in a new learning environment "brings to the party," what Shulman calls a "pre-working hypothesis." "These events have happened to me and therefore it means that . . ." indicates the conclusions one has drawn about early formative experiences. Piaget introduced the term "assimilation" to refer to the process where a person filters new information through a pre-formed hypothesis over many years, habitual ways of acting result in tendencies or predispositions of beliefs and behaviors.

A paradigm is a systematic organized pattern, similar to what Piaget called a *scheme*. We all have broad categories ("computer programs") on such concepts as love, friendship, helping, self-love, women, men, work, abuse, change, etc. But just as some computer programs can become contaminated by a virus like the "I love you" e-mail message sent on May 5, 2000 from one computer in the Philippines to electronic systems around the world, so too one's "and therefore"—conclusions or interpretations of "defining" life events can be a positive or a negative influence in learning new concepts.

Paradigms are necessary to help organize separate, discrete disconnected bits of information. But unless paradigms are open to change or modification (a process Piaget defined as *accommodation*) then one continually recycles through a "washing machine with dirty water and no rinse cycle." In such a case, a student becomes like a prisoner or slave to rigid, habitual unexamined patterns. New learnings are inhibited by old patterned decisions about one's life.

A vivid example of a rigid scheme or paradigm involves the Swiss watchmakers. In the 1960s they had 60 percent of the world watch market and 80 percent of the profits. One day a technician invented the quartz crystal movement to keep time. Excitedly he took his invention to his Swiss superiors. "It has no moving parts—it's not a watch at all!" they ridiculed him. The quartz crystal idea was considered so unimportant that it was not even patented. Later at an international watch conference, the quartz crystal idea was openly displayed at a booth by the Swiss. Personnel from Texas Instruments and Seiko walked by the table—they liked what they saw. Their ability to see beyond the previous "this is a watch" paradigm helped created a new product. Less than ten years later, Texas Instruments and Seiko had captured 80 percent of the international watch market.

Questions to Consider

The basic construction of reframing is that the contents of one's mind are in his or her direct control. Psychologist Albert Ellis has vividly illustrated this concept by citing an example of a man standing on a street corner waiting to cross an intersection when he is bumped from behind by someone. He immediately turns to confront the aggressor—only to discover a blind woman has inadvertently bumped him. The core issue then becomes "what happens to the anger that was originally based on a different assumption?"

Contemplate the following questions:

1. How do you make up your mind?

2. Have you ever changed your mind?

3. How long did it take you?

4. What were the significant factors that led to your changing your mind?

5. How can a parent, teacher, counselor, supervisor, and/or religious person influence someone else to change his or her mind? (Example: street corner, bump, angry, blind, different reaction.)

CHANGING BELIEFS

Consider the following provocative statement—

"Nothing one person believes as an individual is believed by all people." The phenomenon of reality is based on a person's own conscious experience. Therefore, one's personal reality is based on personal perception.

This is the essence of phenomenology in philosophy. The Adlerian concept of private logic is consistent with such a philosophy in that one's own "filter" dictates one's own experience.

Unfortunately, unconscious conditioning from one's early formulative life often causes systematic biases and distortions of current functioning. The goal of the therapist first and foremost is to examine his or her formulative childhood to become more aware of the countertransference. It is hard to be compassionate about the counseling process if one does not know the experience of being a client oneself.

Too often adults are living with the ramifications of parents who felt out of control in their own childhood. Too many children, adolescents, and adult lives are guided by goals that someone else set for them early in their life. But often there is also a rejection of the very goals someone else set for the person, not because the goals themselves were not worthwhile, but because "he" or "she" set them for the person. Too few people consider what the household environment was like in which they were conceived and in which they grew up. For example, at what stage of human development were the parents at the child's conception? What were their wants, needs, motivators at that time? What were the expectations of conformity expected to be part of the surrounding community? That is not to say that community standards in and of themselves are bad or wrong. Nonetheless, many local environments are often filled with racism, sexism, anti-semitism, and other prejudices. Section II of the lifestyle interview focused specifically on such family or family equivalent issues.

Consider also the pressure of social consciousness often "demanding" conformity to cultural beliefs, values and maps to both the young child and the parent. If one accepts the notion that the sub-conscious mind is born "empty," a blank slate as it were, then the first seven years can be considered as the "formative years." Hopefully one falls in love with "mama" or her equivalent here. The next seven years could be considered the practicing and refining of that image. The first crush of Suzie or Bobbie hopefully occurs sometime here. Adolescence is often characterized by some form of rebellion in which the initial sense of self is being formed. Early and middle adulthood further refine these basic core convictions of life, self, and others.

But too often by age 40 an adult experiences a conditioned conformity. It is as if the adult is living around the parameters of what didn't work in one's early own life. For someone of that age, the therapeutic intervention might be to help the person remember the power that may have been in the rebellion around age 21. For many young adults the too frequent conformity of middle age has not set in yet at that age. That is an ideal age for manifesting the changes necessary to alter one's frequently conditioned existence later in life.

Consider the adage that "knowledge is power." Conquer the mind and robotic conditioning and there is the renewed power of transformation possible to a person. A lifestyle assessment is one specific systematic way of exploring, identifying, discussing, revising, renewing, and updating an earlier programmed, version of the self—to frame it in computer terminology. The program—life-style of the individual—has not incorporated new "technology" (wisdom, learnings from experience, and feedback from others) and it also frequently has caught a few "viruses" along the way.

Here is a common irrational belief that many people in the helping professions or on spiritual paths accept as true—"to be a counselor (priest, minister, rabbi, etc.) means one *should* be poor, or at least, not wealthy. But pleasure and comfort do not necessarily mean one is materialistic, and thus "earth bound" instead of "heaven focused." Again the therapeutic challenge is to identify, and then "unmask" and "unlearn" conditioned beliefs. Kurt Levin said the process of change is first to identify the blockage by unfreezing; step two to put in a "new" program, and thirdly, to "freeze" that new desired "updated computer program." This is the task of the therapist in the re-orientation phase of Adlerian therapy.

Consider that the human mind, until conditioned, can be liberated. Indeed a basic human privilege is that life is intended to be one's servant, not one's antagonist as is too often the case in tortured or tormented individual enslaved by the demons of their own mind's creation. One client said it this way: "My mind causes me such torment and suffering that hell would be a vacation." For anyone to be successful in changing the conditioned mind from any defeat or resulting from any disorder, the mind, like the physical body, needs comfort, rest, being held and being rocked. How does one comfort the mind?

The mind is comforted when it is allowed to rest in a state of peace. Rested, the mind, like the physical body, is then ready to resume action again. When the mind is not rested, it too is tired, gets discouraged, and wants to give up. For instance, most people have had the experience of being so tired they wanted to lie down and sleep but they couldn't because the mind is so active.

The sub-conscious mind is like a computer. Unfortunately, much of its programming is done unconsciously. Thus, insight is one specific goal of re-orientation. It can be programmed. A person cannot change something of which the indiviual is unaware. Too many people have left such notable virtues as compassion, peace, happiness, and joy out of the program. The existential decision of each person is the decision (made consciously or "defaulted" by unconscious conditioning) to become the master and not the servant of one's destiny. That involves being what the author calls being "a cue" ball vs. an "eight" personality. A cue ball is a motivator, actively knocking life around the "table"; contrast that with an eight ball personality, one who sets passively on the table waiting to get knocked by life in the "corner pocket."

The mind is the key to such liberation. Consider the saying "man is born free—yet everywhere he is in chains." And with such liberation comes the experience of peace, both internally and externally. This indeed is the very "birthright" of each person. Tragically it has most frequently been "given away" by conditioning and by irrational beliefs.

Consider the analogy of the sub-conscious mind as being "a pregnant woman." During the nine months prior to birth, what thoughts would you hope to program in the unborn child? For example, you would probably consider the child would know that it is capable of loving and of being loved. What emotional, physical and spiritual "nutrients" would you feed that developing child? From which mental "diseases" (fear, worry, self-doubts, self-condemnation?) would you help the child develop an "immunity?"

The sub-conscious mind cannot exist without input from the conscious mind. Therefore, the power to create (or to recreate or to re-invent one's perception of the world) can be altered by changing the basic "life, self, and others" messages being sent by the conscious mind to one's sub-consciousness.

Here are some basic techniques for becoming the master rather than the servant of one's life. There are, of course, countless volumes of other books on the subject. Consider this, a Forest Gump "Whitman's sampler box of candy."

Encouragement

Reframing

Relaxation

Visualizations

Affirmations

JOY AND PURPOSE

One specific intervention for training the mind is to reflect on one's purpose or mission. Consider the difference between desire and purpose. Desire resides in the conscious mind (i.e. "I desire a million dollars."). Purpose is a function of the sub-conscious mind. (My purpose in having a million dollars is to _____.") Early childhood conditioning is one adult consequence of such a belief as "I am miserable when my husband leaves." The therapeutic journey and other spiritual mindfulness practices are meant to return to the place of the origin inside the sub-conscious mind and to "house clean" as it were by focusing on purpose rather than desire.

The accurate practical first step in therapy is to establish treatment goals. Clients are best assisted by acknowledging, "My purpose(s) in coming to therapy is(are) _____. I will know I am successfully accomplishing that(those) purpose(s) by _____. Resistances or self-sabotaging strategies to thwart my purpose can or could consist of _____."

LEARNING BY CREATING NEW IMPRESSIONS

"Reverend Ike" is a popular U.S. evangelist who encourages people to get wealthy by giving money to his ministry. As an impoverished inner city child, he frequently would leave his predominately black neighborhood of Harlem in New York City and visit another part of the city where "uppity folks" were dining in fine restaurants. He would stand outside the window watching what they ate, how they acted; he imagined their feelings, their conversations, the taste of their food—all the while telling himself that someday he too, would be inside that fine restaurant.

Such positive impressions help "seed" new tendencies (learnings). Paradigms, creativity, positive change—all are the consequence of the paradox involving simultaneously maintaining the best of core established educational principles (assimilation), coupled with the openness to new learning experiences (accommodation).

REFRAMING DEFINED AND ILLUSTRATED

Reframing changes the original meaning of an event or situation, placing it in a new context in which an equally plausible explanation is possible. As used by structuralists, reframing is directed toward relabeling the problem or redefining what a person has defined in a discouraging self defeating manner.

Senoi Dreamwork Reframing. Lankton describes the Senoi tribe of Malaysia, a village in which there has been no reported armed conflict, violent crime, or insanity for the past 300 years. According to the Senoi, each dreamer must conquer the hostile spirits that frequent one's dreams. A particular therapeutic technique that anthropologists have called "Senoi Dreamwork" forms the basis of the following process: the healer begins the process by telling the dreamer to "close your eyes and let me know when you are in the dream." When this is accomplished, the dreamer is led through six typical stages: Key, Embellishment, Main, Figure, Trophy, and Quest. Then the dreamer is briefly led into the reality of the dream and aided in contacting the evil spirit. The dreamer next induces the other spirit to give him or her a gift. When, in the dream, the gift is manifest, the dreamer then proceeds to go about creating a tangible replica in the physical world. Thus, even confronted with "hostile" figures in dreams, the Senoi "unmask" or "reframe" the experience by seeking a gift. Richard Bach in *Illusions* says, "There is no such thing as a problem for you without a gift in its hands. You seek problems because you need their gifts."

Reframing and Neuro-Linguistic Programming. Reframing is an integral aspect of Neuro-Linguistic Programming (NLP). Leslie Cameron-Bandler believes that inherent within the structure of reframing is the optimistic belief that we have all the resources needed to make any desired change. She writes that:

> What is important is that when I organize my behavior as though it were true, positive change becomes easier to accomplish. Remember that we as humans never experience the world directly, but instead create maps or models of our world experience such that the only reality we ever know is a subjective reality. Adopting the above belief provides you with a terrific advantage. Since subjective realities can be altered and reorganized, we are given the opportunity to mold our realities in useful and beneficial ways.

She also relates a case study of how she used reframing with a women whose brand-new plush carpeting had actually become a source of irritation to her and her husband because she was obsessively vacuuming the carpet to remove his footprints. Cameron-Bandler describes the reframing as follows:

> I asked her to close her eyes and see her carpeted home—to see that the carpet was perfect, not a single strand of it out of place. And as she was enjoying seeing the carpet so perfect, I told her she could become aware that there was complete silence in her house; and as she listened to the silence, she could realize she was all alone with her perfect carpet. It was only now, I told her, that she would finally realize that every footprint that appeared on that carpet was a sign that her loves ones were near, and that she was with her family. So each time in the future, whenever she would see a footprint on the carpet, she could feel the closeness of her family and the love she felt toward them . . . By doing what I did, I reframed "footprints on the carpet" to trigger warm, loving feelings rather than compulsive cleanliness.

Laborde uses the following creative mnemonic to describe the reframing process:

R Recognize what is causing the unwanted behavior.

E Express appreciation to the past for past service. (This may be difficult.)

F Find out the intent, purpose, or payoff of the behavior.

R Request your creative part to find three ways to satisfy the intent.

A Agree to try the three new ways before using the unwanted behavior.

M Make sure there is agreement on the new learning, the new behaviors.

E Equality check. Will the new ways of thinking, acting and functioning in one's world create equal and cooperative relationships with others.

Cognitive Restructuring. The Cognitive Restructuring Protocol (CRP) is a procedure for reframing by rewriting self-defeating thoughts. Table 1 shows a completed CRP for an adult who experienced a temper outburst at work. The description on the left-hand side represents the client's perception of what happened during an encounter with his supervisor, whereas the right side of the CRP begins with a "camera check" that forces the client to focus on the sensory data rather than his interpretations (e.g., what a video camera would have recorded). Each separate thought can be listed on the left side, then rebutted on the right.

Table 1—Cognitive Restructuring Protocol (CRP)

Situation (A): where, when, who —
"My boss has it in for me. I'll never get promoted."

Camera check (A1): videocam view—
"My boss handing me my evaluation. Seeing one unsatisfactory rating."

Automative thoughts/images (B):

1. "He's a jerk."

Rebuttals/Reframes (B1): objective facts; feel and act; planning/ preparing/problem solving—

1. "That's labeling, He is the same person who gave me a high rating last period. I need to calmly talk it over."

2. "He has never respected my work!"

2. "I am overgeneralizing. He promoted me last year. I need to focus on a plan re: the goals we discussed."

3. "I can't take the embarrassment."

3. "I've taken a lot worse, like when Dad died 2 years ago. I need to focus on my past ways of coping."

4. *Concluding Beliefs:* "I am treated this way because"—
   a. "I am always unlucky. Bad things always happen to me."
   b. "I'm too old to compete."

4. *New Beliefs:* "I can manage this way because"—
   a1. "I am in control of each choice I make. I make opportunities happen."
   b2. "I am wiser each year."

5. *Internal Beliefs:* "Others act like this because"—
   a. "You can't trust anyone."
   b. "They are no good."

5. *New Beliefs:* "Others act like this because"—
   a1. "Most other people are like me: honest/ decent."
   b2. "They are fallible humans."

6. **Self-talk about my feelings (C)**—"My boss is making my life miserable."

6. How I **would like to think** (C1)—
"I control my feelings by changing my thoughts."

7. **What I did/said; behavior (D)**—"Told him I was furious and walked out."

7. **How I would like to behave** (D1)—Remain and talk it out with him focusing on specifics.

(Adopted from Nay, 1995)

NEGATIVE ATTRIBUTIONS

Carlson, Sperry, and Lewis note that reframing is also referred to as *"relabeling," "positive interpretation," "positive connotation,"* and *"reattribution."* "Negative attribution" is one of the most discouraging behaviors that can be exhibited. Basically it consists of projecting or attributing negative motives to someone else ("He gave the donation just to soothe his guilty conscience," "He just has one thing on his mind," or "She just is here to be seen").

Reframing recognizes the positive intention/motivation that often is behind even disruptive behaviors. For example, a mother who yells at her son to do his homework is reinterpreted as being positively motivated behaviorally illustrated by showing concern about her son. Such reframing demonstrates that there are indeed advantages and disadvantages to every behavior. By accepting the behavior, the person will often decrease the behavior.

Relabeling is similar to reframing in that an adjective that is positive in connotation is substituted for an adjective that is negative in connotation. For example, if the wife screams at her husband complaining that he is controlling, one could relabel the "negative attribution" interpretation by saying the husband is overburdened. Stanton calls such a technique as "ascribing noble intention." For example, a positive label for "jealousy" could be "caring," and "anger" could be relabeled as "desire for attention." From the individual psychology perspective, "ascribing noble intention" is an empowering, encouraging example of positive (rather than negative) attribution. Reframing does not seek to say that anger *per se* is positive; rather it seeks to find some possible positive motivator influencing such behavior.

Here are some specific examples of reframing by renaming—

Ascribed Weakness	Probable Strengths
Helplessness	Coping
Depression	Persistence
Fearfulness	Courage
Distrust	Loyalty
Denial	Nurturing
Repression	Protective of children
Delusion	Perseverance
Disassociation	Endurance
Distress	Humor
Highly emotional	Creative

again. The other half typically get angry at being misunderstood or "not being taken seriously."

Re-labeling One's Story. Sam Keen suggests retelling one's childhood story from a different perspective. For example, if one's core decision about the world is based on a novel called "tragedy," how would the story change if the title became "hilarious comedy," or a "mystery" novel seeking to solve a dilemma, or an "adventure" story filled with new twists and turns around every corner?

REFRAMING: A PERSONAL EXAMPLE

The following is a personal example from my life that illustrates a teacher's use of reframing. Almost forty years after the incident, the event still marks a turning point in my life. It was written on the eve of the U.S. holiday of Thanksgiving, a time of reflections and acknowledgment of people, things and events for which one is grateful.

Today I dedicate this personal example of reframing to "Kings" and "Queens" around the world, the true educators who help others in rediscovering something encouraging about themselves they have forgotten somewhere along the way. A "timeless" 40 year old teacher's intervention lives on today in the life of the student who has indeed used the gift of enthusiasm to encourage and to be continually encouraged by others. It will be included in the 2002 *Chicken Soup for the Teacher's Soul*.

A TRIBUTE TO MANY CROWNED AND UNCROWNED KINGS AND QUEENS

"It was the spring of 1962. I was in the seventh grade at Johnnycake Junior High School in Baltimore, Maryland—Section 7B, to be precise. In earlier years, the distinction between classes had been the 'redbirds' and the 'bluebirds' in a vain attempt to avoid labeling one class smart and the other class (mine) the 'dummies.' Still, we all knew the hierarchy of redbirds and bluebirds. So in the seventh grade the pretense was dropped in favor of "7A" and "7B."

"All my neighborhood friends were in the coveted 'A' class. As for me, I was majoring in playground. I was also a so-called honor student—as in, 'Yes, your honor. No, your honor. I won't do that anymore, your honor.'

"I was a classic left-handed, dyslexic, hyperactive boy who consistently received unsatisfactory conduct scores under the category vaguely defined as 'self-control.' 'M's' and 'n's' were indistinguishable to me, 'd's' masqueraded as 'b's' and 'p's' as 'q's.' Classes were much too long, the desks far too small, and the outdoor activities way too short. Like a prisoner about to granted a three-month furlough from his cell, I was counting down the days until June.

"The teacher for both 7A and 7B was like a giant redwood tree to me, a colossal giant, who at 6 feet 2 inches tall seemed twice as awesome from my diminished vantage point. Mr. King was the apt title of our teacher. He was kind, knowledgeable and much revered by both sections A and B—a rare feat for any teacher.

"One day, Mr. King approached my 7A friends and observed, 'There is someone in 7B who is just as smart as any of you—trouble is, he just doesn't know it yet . . . I won't tell you his name, but I'll give you a hint: He's the kid who outruns all of you and who knocks the ball over the right field fence.'

"Word of Mr. King's declaration reached me that afternoon as we boarded the school bus. I remember a dazed, shocked feeling of disbelief. 'Yeah, sure, you've got to be kidding,' I replied to my friends; but on a deeper, more subtle level, I remember the warm glow that came from the tiny flicker of a candle that had been ignited within my soul.

"Two weeks later, it was time for dreaded book reports in front of the class. It was bad enough to turn in papers that only Mr. King read and graded, but there was no place to hide when it came to oral book reports. When my turn came, I solemnly stood before my classmates. I began slowly and awkwardly to speak about James Fenimore Cooper's epic book *The Pathfinder*. As I spoke, the images of canoes on the western frontier of eighteenth-century America collided in my mind with lush descriptions of the forest and Native Americans gliding noiselessly over lakes and streams. No Fourth of July fireworks ever surpassed the explosion that took place inside my head that day—it was electrifying!

"Excitedly, I began trying to share my experience with my classmates. But just as I began a sentence to tell about the canoes, another scene of the land collided with the Native Americans. I was only midway through one sentence before I jumped to another.

"I was becoming 'hyper' in my job, and my incomplete sentences made no sense at all. The laughter of my classmates at my 'craziness' quickly shattered my inner fireworks. Embarrassed and humiliated, although I wanted either to beat up my tormentors or to run home and cry in my mother's arms, I had learned to mask those feelings long ago. Trying my best to become invisible and disappear, I started to return to my desk.

The laughter ceased at the sound of Mr. King's deep, compassionate voice. 'You know, Danny,' he reigned forth, 'you have the unique gift of being able to speak outwardly and to think inwardly at the same time. But sometimes your mind is filled with so much joy that your words just can't keep up with it. Your excitement is contagious. It's a wonderful gift that I hope you can put to good use someday.'

"There was a pause that seemed to linger forever as I stood stunned by Mr. King's words once more. Then clapping and congratulatory cheers came from my classmates as a miracle of transformation occurred within me on that great day."

IMPLICATIONS FOR COUNSELORS AND EDUCATORS

In conclusion here are some suggestions for teachers and counselors encouraging students to learn new behavior, ideas, or concepts.

1. Discouraging decisions, conclusions, or "and therefore . . ." about past events often interfere with the ability to learn new material.

2. The good news is that despite reinforcement though repetition such self-limiting decisions can be changed in an instant.

3. Reframing is one specific technique educators can use to help learners redefine or relabel self-defeating conclusions about themselves.

4. Reframing is a form of encouragement for educators. It redefines a negative into a positive interpretation. Bitter's creative examples of reframing include a woman who was worrying that she was too old to begin her college degree and was told, "In four years, you'll be 50—you'll either be 50 and further educated, or 50 and less educated." Another person recalled the shame of having thrown a bat in anger that had struck a friend in the head. Bitter's response was, "You're the kind of person I'd like to counsel me because you carry a memory of what happens when you hurt others around you."

5. The Senoi Dreamwork process helps "unmask" challenges by asking for a gift to come from it. So too creative educators can encourage students to view challenges from life in a more optimistic way to learn lessons in all aspects of the learning process.

6. Humor and laughter are often helpful ways of helping a person re-invent or reinterpret a self-defined discouraging experience. For example, one person says "The glass is half empty," another says "The glass is half full," while the third one observes "The glass is too big."

Here is how the author has reframed what he calls the 7 Destructive D's of group membership and the 7 Constructive C's.

The Seven Destructive D's of Group Membership

1. *Delay.*   "Great idea. We'll get to this _____" (tomorrow, next week, next year, whenever)

2. *Deny.*   "That's not my/our job!" "What deadline?" "The memo about the policy change—what memo? Never saw it!!"

3. *Dominate.*   By intimidation, interrogation, interruption, etc. ("I win/you lose")

4. *Discourage.*   The Blame Game. "Who wrote that report? What a ridiculous idea" or the "no good deed will go unpunished" syndrome.

5. *Defer.*   "This is really a job for _____" or "That's a great idea— we'll discuss it _____."

6. *Deflect.*   "That's not my/our job—it's more appropriate for _____," or "This is being returned for _____."

7. *Drop.*   Since we have no [time, money, resources, desire], it's time to _____. "Turn out the lights, 'the party's' over."

Reframing the 7 D's to the 7 Constructive C's of Group Membership

1. *Compromise.* "Let's see where the middle-ground between us might be."

2. *Caring.* "We missed you last meeting" or "It's so good to have you back."

3. *Compliment.* "I know it took effort to get the report to me on such short notice."

4. *Collaborate.* "Come, let us work together."

5. *Consideration* "You first," "What are your thoughts _____?" "If it's O.K. with you, I'd like to _____."

6. *Concise.* "What date should we meet again?"

7. *Contribute.* "What if I take that part of the group project?"

7. In a very personal way, Mr. King, the author's seventh grade teacher, first saw an intellectual spark of potential that has transcended a career as a professional athlete and has help inspire him to present this paper today at this prestigious conference. It's been said that "the greatest use of a life is to spend it in a cause that will ultimately outlive it."

8. Reframing an adolescent frequently accompanying drug and alcohol use as often being based on an attempt to avoid pain and hurt is another suggestion. Many resistive adolescents freely acknowledge such motivations. Educators can then suggest counseling as a different method for obtaining the necessary "psychological muscle" in coping and reducing the hurt and pain such adolescents have experienced.

9. Reframing is an excellent technique for educators of defiant or aggressive adolescents. Hanna, Hanna, and Keys (1999) suggest what they call an "instant reframe" when working with such adolescents. The bitter student who loudly proclaims that "I hate everyone and everything" could receive an "instant framed" response such as "sometimes one of the purposes or payoffs for anger is that it may be a way for you to feel better. Is it that time for you?" Rebellious defiance can also be reframed as "being honest with your emotions." Likewise, apathy can be relabeled as "an attempt to avoid being hurt again" or "not caring about anything" can be redefined as "caring about everything but worrying about nothing." An "acting out" adolescent student could also be viewed as "protesting against a perceived loss of personal freedom." The word "control" can also be relabeled as "influence."

Adlerian therapist Harold Mosak once confronted a hostile adolescent by reframing the freedom issue in a most creative way. "Do you know what a puppet is?" he rhetorically asked the female adolescent after she sarcastically nodded with a "whatever, who cares?" nonverbal shirk of her shoulder. Mosak continued, "When you pull the right string on a puppet, the right arm goes up—when you pull the left string, the left arm goes up." "But let me tell you about what I call 'a reverse puppet,'" he continued. "A reverse puppet is when you pull the right string and the left leg goes up and when you pull the left leg string, the right arm goes up—but the critical factor is that as a 'reverse puppet' someone is always 'pulling your strings,'" he concluded. Confronting the freedom being lost by the adolescents angrily reacting to others ("pulling her strings" and controlling her "like a puppet"). Another reframing follow-up intervention could be to contrast the "negative label of seeing a counselor" to "cool people often go to counselors to become more popular and respected by their peers" (or "happy and carefree" or any other goal described by the troubled student himself or herself).

10. Students experiencing a crisis can be reminded that there are two different symbols in the Chinese characters for the word crisis. The first is *danger* or *troubled water*. The other is *opportunity*, including the optimistic belief that there is a means of resolving the challenge

11.	All of us have been hurt or experienced dircouraging events in out lives.

Here is an inspirational (reframing) story about how a "cracked pot" was used to bring beauty to others.

A water bearer in India had two large pots, each hung on each end of a pole which he carried across his neck. One of the pots had a crack in it, and while the other pot was perfect and always delivered a full portion of water at the end of the long walk from the stream to the master's house, the cracked pot arrived only half full. For a full two years this went on daily, with the bearer delivering only one and a half pots full of water to his master's house.

Of course, the perfect pot was proud of its accomplishments, perfect to the end for which it was made. But the poor cracked pot was ashamed of its own imperfection, and miserable that it was able to accomplish only half of what it had been made to do. After two years of what it perceived to be a bitter failure, it spoke to the water bearer one day by the stream. "I am ashamed of myself, and I want to apologize to you."

"Why?" asked the bearer. "What are you ashamed of?"

"I have been able, for these past two years, to deliver only half my load because this crack in my side causes water to leak out all the way back to your master's house. Because of my flaws, you have to do all of this work, and you don't get full value from your efforts," the pot said.

The water bearer felt sorry for the old cracked pot, and in his compassion he said, "As we return to the master's house, I want you to notice the beautiful flowers along the path."

Indeed, as they went up the hill, the old cracked pot took notice of the sun warming the beautiful wild flowers on the side of the path, and this cheered it some. But at the end of the trail, it still felt bad because it had leaked out half its load, and so again the Pot apologized to the bearer for its failure.

The bearer said to the pot, "Did you notice that there were flowers only on your side of our path, but not on the other pot's side? That's because I have always known about your flaw, and I took advantage of it. I planted flower seeds on your side of the path, and every day we walk back from the stream, you've watered them. For two years I have been able to pick these beautiful flowers to decorate my master's table. Without you being just the way you are, he would not have this beauty to grace his house."

Each of us has our own unique flaws. We are all cracked pots. In God's great economy, nothing goes to waste. Don't be afraid of your flaws. Acknowledge them, and you too can be the cause of beauty. Know that paradoxically in our weakness, we indeed find our strength.

—Author unknown

Thus, a new reframed story is an assertive first step to changing old paradigms into new impressions.

Such positive impressions help "seed" new tendencies. Paradigms, creativity, positive change—all are the consequence of the paradox involving simultaneously maintaining the best of established, stable personality traits (assimilation), coupled with the openness to new experiences (accommodation).

Gratitude is an important concept that often needs to be reframed. Consider the following:

If you woke up this morning with more health than illness . . .
you are more blessed than the million who will not survive this week.

If you have never experienced the danger of battle,
the loneliness of imprisonment, the agony of torture, or the pangs of starvation . . .
you are ahead of 500 million people in the world.

If you can attend a church or synagogue meeting
without fear of harassment, arrest, torture, or death . . .
you are more blessed than three billion people in the world.

If you have food in the refrigerator, clothes on your back,
a roof overhead and a place to sleep . . .
you are richer than 75% of this world.

If you have money in the bank, in your wallet,
and spare change in a dish someplace . . .
you are among the top 8% of the world's wealthy.

If your parents are still alive and still married . . .
you are very rare, even in the United States.

If you hold up your head
with a smile on your face and are truly thankful . . .
you are blessed because the majority can, but most do not.

If you can hold someone's hand,
hug them or even touch them on the shoulder . . .
you are blessed because you can offer God's healing touch.

If you can read this message,
you are more blessed than
over two billion people in the world that cannot read at all.

Have a good day,
count your blessings,
and remind everyone else how blessed we all are.

The following section focuses on the critical therapeutic skill of reframing relative to facilitating change.

The Role of Counselors in the Change Process

In the Old Testament, there was what was known as a "City of Refuge" where one could go and be nurtured by others when life's challenges seemed overwhelming. In this century the natives on the "Big" island of Hawaii created a similar "City of Refuge"— even if criminally guilty of murder, if one could make it safely to that place, he or she would be safe from harm's way. In a similar manner, it is possible for clients to feel such a safe and caring environment in the presence of counselors.

The counseling process itself involves dialogue between two or more people. It is ideally conducted in an atmosphere of trust and safety; so as to provide the climate for change. Plato formulated and refined his personal philosophy through meaningful dialogue with others. Specific counseling techniques previously described such as "stroke and spit" (encouragement and confrontation), "reframing a perceived minus into a perceived plus," encouragement, acting "as if," etc., are part of the "doing" component. "Being" involves the counselor's attitude of openness, honesty, genuineness, warmth, understanding, etc.

Because we are all "encapsulated" within ourselves and our often unconscious conditioning, counselors can help provide a more encouraging and empowering "reflection" to the client of him/herself.

"Man of La Mancha" is a poignant musical about Don Quixote, a "madman" knight who battled "windmills" he perceived to be "the Great Enchanter." But in his delusional state there was a purity of spirit and an innocence of heart much like the contemporary Forrest Gump. Along with his loyal sidekick Sancho Panza, Don Quixote encounters a country inn and tavern which he perceives to be a castle. There he sees the woman of his dreams, Dulcinea. He is instantly smitten by her radiant beauty and sings to her:

> "I have dreamed you too long,
> Never seen thee, or touched, but know thee
> with all of my heart . . ".

His beloved Dulcinea quickly corrects him that her name is Aldonza and that she is "no kind of a lady":

> "I was spawned in a ditch by a mother who left me there,
> naked and cold and too hungry to cry.
> I never blamed her, I'm sure she left hoping
> that I'd have the good sense to die!
> For a Lady has modest and maidenly airs
> and a virtue I somehow suspect that I lack;
> It's hard to remember these maidenly airs
> in a stable laid flat on your back!
> If you feel that you see me not quite at my virginal best,
> Cross my palm with a coin and I'll willingly show you the rest!"

Then Don Quixote exclaims, "Never deny thou art Dulcinea," to which Aldonza replies:

> "Take the clouds from your eyes and see me as I am!
> You have shown me the sky, but what good is the sky
> To a creature who'll never do better than crawl?
> Of all the cruel bastards who've badgered and battered me,
> You are the cruelest of all!
> Don't you see what your gentle insanities do to me?
> Rob me of anger and give me despair!

> Blame and abuse I can take and give back again,
> Tenderness I cannot bear!
> So please torture me now with your "sweet Dulcineas" no more!
> I am no one! I'm nothing! I'm only Aldonza the whore!"

Again Don Quixote asserts, "And forever thou art my lady Dulcinea!" She stomps away yelling at his madness. And yet on a more subtle level a seed had been planted, a new impression germinated in this reflection of her beauty. The "perceiver I" of Don Quixote saw the woman of his dreams. The "perceiver I" (described below) of her own self-worth was of "Aldonza, the whore," but it was Don Quixote's external reflection of beauty that helped her rediscover it within herself so that at the end of the play she called herself Dulcinea. Such a profound reorientation of her own self-assessment was influenced by someone else.[35]

Who Is the "Perceiver I?"

In like manner counselors have the opportunity to be the "perceiver I" that reflects beauty, love, and harmony in a myriad of personal strengths within the client. Profound behavioral and belief shifts thus are facilitated.

Through an optimistic orientation, Carl Rogers steadfastly maintained that counselors who help create a favorable environment by sending "powerful invitations" (reflections) help clients rediscover the traits within themselves. Obviously such an idealistic perspective does not always occur in the others, however. For example, Don Quixote's self-perception was viewed as delusional by most people around him.

Robert Carkhuff[36] concluded that "counseling can be for better or worse" for clients. Sexism, racism, ageism, and other counselor prejudices negatively impact the "perceiver I" reflections being sent to clients. Consider the following different perceptions of the same person.

Eliza Doolittle to Colonel Pickering in George Bernard Shaw's *Pygmalion*:

> . . . The difference between a lady and a flower girl
> is not how she behaves but how she's treated.
> I shall always be a flower girl to Professor Higgins
> because he always treats me as a flower girl
> and always will;
> but I know I can be a lady to you
> because you always treat me as a lady and always will.

Behavioral or attitudinal change is possible when expanded "tendencies" result in new impressions of the now. "Who is the perceiver I?" basically explores specific issues of self-love (or the lack thereof). Such self-assessment can paradoxically be facilitated in a therapeutic dialogue with a caring person who genuinely "reflects" the "impossible dream" of "Dulcinea" awaiting transformation from "Aldonza."

The late John F. Kennedy frequently quoted George Bernard Shaw's "You see things as they are and you ask, 'why?' But I dream dreams that never were and ask, 'why not?'" Caring counselors can help create an environment where positive client change coupled with core stable traits or temperaments become the "possible dream."

Interpretative Motivation Modification

Nystul states that "motivation modification" as contrasted with behavior modification is an important aspect of client reorientation.[37] "The Adlerian counselor is not preoccupied with changing behavior; rather he is concerned with understanding the individual's subjective frame of reference and the identification of the individual's mistaken goal, or goal within that framework. Indeed, the behavior of an individual is only understood when the goals are identified."[38]

Adlerian theory is initially based on the client gaining insight, or a recognition into one's own style. But as Kurt Adler notes, insight alone is not enough.

In order for change to occur at all . . . the patient must learn to understand something— about his life, his relations to others, his behavior—that he did not understand before. One would say, perhaps, this is a new insight. But insight alone is not enough; there must be, in addition, a sort of artistic penetration and permeation of the patient's life attitudes with this newly understood more social behavior.[39]

Mistaken Beliefs

The "private logic" of a client often contains faulty conclusions or overgeneralizations. Utilizing the "basic mistakes" of Adler, the "irrational beliefs" of Ellis,[40] and the "cognitive deficiencies" of Beck,[41] co-author Roy Kern and colleagues compiled the following list of faulty cognitions:

1. *Casual Inference.* Making an unjustifiable jump in logic by drawing a conclusion from evidence that is either insufficient or actually contrary to the conclusion reached. ("I made an A- on the test; I am not smart.")

2. *Blowup.* Tending to exaggerate or magnify the meaning of an event out of proportion to the actual situation; generating a general rule from a single incident ("I made a mess of my relationship with Ellen. I guess you could consider me a real social bust.").

3. *All-or-Nothing Thinking.* Thinking in extremes; allowing only two possibilities—good or bad, right or wrong, always or never ("People never have a good time with me").

4. *Responsibility Projection.* Failing to assume responsibility for one's emotional state ("This course is causing me to have a nervous breakdown!"), or for one's personal worth ("If my parents had only made me study in high school, I'd have been able to qualify for college").

5. *Perfectionistic Thinking.* Making idealistic demands on oneself ("I made a D on that test; I'm so stupid!").

6. *Value-Tainted Thinking.* Couching a statement in such terms as "good," "bad," "worthless," "should," "ought," or "must" ("I must get into medical school or I won't be able to look my father in the eye").

7. *Self-Deprecation.* Focusing on punitive self-statements rather than task orientation ("I hate myself for not being able to break this habit").[42]

Once clients discover the illogical aspect of their thinking, they generally are motivated to make changes in their personal private logic that will render it more functional. According to Kern and associates, the correction of self-defeating, private logic includes the following steps:

1. Asking the client to describe only the facts of the actual situation that gave rise to an expression of the faulty thinking ("I made a 78 on my freshman composition exam") and to omit the self-defeating statement (". . . and I know I'm just going to flunk out of college"). In this way, the reality of the situation is separated from the individual's personal conclusion.

2. Asking the client to generate alternative explanations for the situation that triggered the illogical conclusion. The student making the 78 on the composition exam could have concluded, "I made a high C when I'm used to making A's, and this discrepancy is disappointing. I guess I'll have to study much harder if I am to meet my expectations."

3. The client is told to avoid being the direct object or the subject of a passive verb. In the case of responsibility projection, the personal statement is to be reconstructed in such a way that the client becomes the subject of an active verb. For example, the statement "My roommate makes me so mad when she doesn't hang up her clothes" could become: "When my roommate doesn't hang up her clothes, I become very angry because I'm telling myself that she should meet my expectations and something's wrong with me since I can't get her to do better. Clearly, my roommate is not doing it to me—I'm doing it to myself!"

4. Asking the client to design a positive course of action based on the more reasonable of his or her alternative explanations. This technique is used to assist clients to recognize the poor fit between many of their fictions and reality and to practice a more responsible kind of self-talk.[43]

One of the goals of counseling is to identify basic mistakes and to bring them to the client's awareness. It is the counselor's responsibility to discover those early, erroneously developed convictions and to help the client see how those ideas are false and how they can interfere with effective social and personal functioning. The process of psychotherapy is uncovering the basic mistakes and correcting them.[44]

Visualization is a powerful technique for changing mistaken notions, because clients often are willing to suspend the usual linear rationale mode of viewing the world and thus allow greater creativity as a valuable partner with logic. Hypnosis and trance work are closely related to the use of visualization for encouraging lifestyle change. An entire issue of the *Journal of Individual Psychology* (December, 1990) is devoted to Adlerian applications of hypnosis. There Carich, Sperry, and Fairfield also present specific induction techniques and case studies illustrating the role of hypnosis in depth personality change.

Changing Mistaken Beliefs through Visualization of ERs

According to Ling and Kottman early memories do not reflect the client's current self-image, view of the world, and style of interaction with others. When asked to describe specific incidents that took place during the early years of life, the client selects, alters, or imagines events that express the central issues and interested of his or her life. Gathering early recollections can help the counselor begin to understand the client's struggles, attitudes, hopes, and behaviors. They give the counselor clues about the direction of the client's strivings and the ways the client gains significance. Early recollections indicate the values to which the client ascribes and the dangers the client wishes to avoid. Basic mistakes, illuminated by the early recollections, represent the client's basic convictions about self, the world, and others. These ideas, which govern behavior, may or may not be within the client's awareness.

Basic mistakes are basic because they are original ideas a child develops to fulfill the needs of belonging and significance. They are considered mistakes because they are faulty conclusions drawn from a child's perspective while the child is engaged in the struggle to establish a place in the world.[45] As Dreikurs and Soltz indicated, "Children are expert observers but make many mistakes in interpreting what they observe. They often draw wrong conclusions and choose mistaken ways in which to find their place."[46]

Lingg and Kottman believe that

sometimes simply talking to the client about mistaken beliefs and bringing them to the client's awareness is enough to bring about changes in the client's self-perception. However, at other times, mistaken beliefs and private logic are so ingrained in the client's way of looking at life and self that talking about them does not bring about a change. When this happens the counselor must introduce creative ways of helping the client reexamine basic convictions in order to bring about changes. Early recollections have been used to help the client gain insight into his or her life style.[47]

By interpreting a series of ERs to the client, the counselor can hold up a mirror reflecting the patient's present attitudes and intentions. ERs represent a microcosm of the client's mistaken beliefs and private logic, active interpretation and visualization of early recollections may be an excellent tool for helping the client reconsider mistaken beliefs, it may then be possible for the client to substitute positive convictions for negative beliefs.

Lingg and Kottman describe their counseling technique as follows:

The counselor beings the visualization process with some basic relaxation techniques. . . . The counselor then asks the client to visualize the specific incident chosen to represent the particular mistaken belief. It may facilitate the process if the counselor suggests to the client to think of the early recollections as a scene in a play or television show to be watched from the perspective of an audience. The counselor then asks the client to describe the scene as it is unfolding. With eyes still shut, the client is asked to describe the feelings experienced during the interaction. In order to begin to change the mistaken belief, the counselor asks the client to visualize himself or herself as an adult actually entering the scene. The client is asked to visualize the adult self comforting the child self, telling the child self how valuable, important, and lovable he or she is. Then the counselor suggestions that the visualized adult begin to help reconsider any mistaken beliefs about what is necessary to achieve significance and belonging. . . .

The counselor then asks the client if there is anything else in the visualized interaction that needs to be changed or if there is anything else the child self needs. If the client answers affirmatively, the counselor guides the client through the process of visualizing the adult self making those changes, doing whatever needs to be done in order to help the child self feel comfortable and safe.[48]

After the client has been brought back to the present, the counselor can invite the client to reexamine mistaken beliefs and to consider other more useful ways of gaining a sense of significance and belonging. The counselor can also help the client change the working of selected negative self statements by creating more positive self-affirming rather than blaming, criticizing, and/or condemning self-statements.

Bettner and Lew[49] developed Connexions Focusing Technique© for retrieving and interpreting early recollections (ER), to link clients' presenting problems to beliefs and behaviors developed in early childhood. By utilizing the Couple Complementarily, they observe that "using the CFT procedure with both partners enables the therapist to see certain similarities in the two lifestyles." When looking at the early recollection, it is useful to visualize the stated problem as having three nonlinear interactive parts:

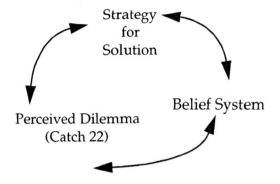

Strategy for Solution

Perceived Dilemma (Catch 22)

Belief System

1. The Perceived Dilemma (Catch 22)—the problem as the person sees it.

2. The belief system—the thoughts and beliefs which make this a problem and that determine the possible options for resolution.

3. The strategy for the solution.

Each of these parts defines and is defined by the others.

Although the original dilemmas no longer exist, the clients are still functioning with their original beliefs and strategies. It is these unexamined beliefs and strategies that contribute to their current difficulties.

Here is the authors' summary of their nine-step model.

Step 1. Have the person identify one issue by condensing it into one or two sentences.

Step 2. Follow that by asking: "What would be different in your life if you didn't have this problem?"

Step 3. Have the client give an example of a recent experience related to the presenting issue that helps identify to purposive "payoff" for the behavior.

Step 4. If possible, have the client then reproduce the feeling or tension described. Specifically focus on how and where the client experiences the challenge in his or her body.

Step 5. Ask for a childhood recollection whether or not it seems to be related to the problem. Tape record or write the incident verbatim.

Step 6. Play back or read their ER phrase by phrase. Have the client give all feelings, thoughts, and descriptive material related to each phase.

Step 7. After reviewing the entire client's additions, then examine them relative to each specific phrase with the intention of uncovering core underlying beliefs. The therapist and client together develop the material into a statement of belief. Such a collaboration helps empower the client as well as to increase the "psychological ownership" of the events core beliefs.

Step 8. Combine the belief statements into a single summary statement and review with the client.

Step 9. Summarize the information into a single extensive description, including the client's apparent dilemma ("Catch 22"), creativity, and strategies and solutions.

Distorted Thinking Styles

Negative thinking can very often be identified as distorted thinking. Becoming aware of thinking distortions makes one able to actually change negative thoughts to positive ones, effectively eliminating the depression and anxiety that these thoughts create.

Distorted thoughts can be easily identified because they (1) cause painful emotions such as worry, depression, or anxiety, and/or (2) cause you to have ongoing conflicts.

The following fifteen distorted thinking styles are examined by McKay, Davis and Fanning.[50]

1. Filtering entails looking at only one part of a situation to the exclusion of everything else.

2. Polarized thinking involves perceiving everything at the extremes, as either black or white, with nothing in between.

3. Overgeneralization reaches a broad, generalized conclusion based on just one piece of evidence.

4. Mind reading takes place when one bases assumptions and conclusions on an "ability" to know other people's thoughts.

5. Catastrophizing involves expecting the worst-case scenario.

6. Personalization results in interpreting everything around you in ways that reflect on oneself, and one's worth.

7. Control fallacies involve feeling either that the events in your life are totally controlled by a force outside of oneself, or that the individual is responsible for everything.

8. Fallacy of fairness is based on the trap of judging people's actions by personally created rules about what is and what isn't fair.

9. Emotional reasoning is the mistaken belief that everything an individual feels must be true.

10. The fallacy of change is the assumption that others will change to suit oneself if they are pressured long enough.

11. Global labeling is making a broad judgment based on very little evidence.

12. Blaming involves the belief that bad things that happen are someone's fault, either of the individual him/herself, or of someone else.

13. Shoulds entail operating from a rigid set of indisputable rule about how everyone including oneself should act.

14. Being right involves continually needing to justify a personal point of view or way of behaving.

15. Heaven's reward fallacy is the belief that if one always does the right thing, he or she will eventually be rewarded (even if doing the right thing means ignoring your personal needs).

Copeland suggests the following four-step process for eliminating distorted thoughts:

1. What emotion (or emotions) are you feeling now?
   I am feeling angry, tense, and anxious.

2. Describe, in detail, the event or situation that gave rise to your emotion. For example:
   I went to my friend Peter's house at 4:00 P.M., as previously arranged, to go for a walk and have dinner together. He was not home when I got there.

3. Describe your thoughts, and identify any distortions in your thinking.
   Because Peter wasn't there, I decided he really didn't want to spend the time with me, that he really doesn't like me and doesn't respect my feelings.

4. Refute the distortions.

There was only one piece of evidence, his not being there when I arrived, that was the basis for my distortion. The truth is, Peter and I have been close friends for a long time. All evidence indicated that he likes me a lot. An emergency may have come up, he may have gone to do an errand that took longer than anticipated, he may have misunderstood the plan that we made, or he may have forgotten that we made a plan (or I may have misunderstood)—any of which are acceptable reasons and do nothing to lend credence to my distorted thought. The best course of action for me would be to wait on his porch (doing relaxation exercises) until his return; or leave him a note asking him to call me when he gets in.[51]

Copeland also suggests "Thought Stopping" as a way of confronting one's own self defeating beliefs (Adler's "spitting in the soup" concept). Thought stopping is a simple way to bring thoughts to consciousness and eliminate them. By eliminating a negative thought, you can eliminate the emotions and feelings that go along with it.

After identifying a negative thought for target practice, the following self-reflective questions should be asked:

1.   Is this thought realistic or unrealistic?

2.   Is the thought productive or counterproductive?

3.   Is this thought easy or hard to control?

4.   How uncomfortable does this thought make me feel?

5.   How much does this thought interfere with my life?

A Sample Thought-Stopping Exercise

Bothersome Thought:
I'm afraid I'll have another deep depression and need hospitalization.

Is this thought realistic or unrealistic?
It is realistic, because I've had deep depressions before for which I needed to be hospitalized. However, the circumstances of my life have changed significantly since then. I understand depression. I have an excellent support system of health care workers, family members, and friends. I watch for early warning signs and get help early. Several related medical problems have been appropriately treated. I use relaxation techniques, exercise regularly, and carefully manage my diet. I have eliminated sugar and caffeine from my diet. There is limited stress in my life and I have learned to handle stress that is unavoidable.

Is the thought productive or counterproductive?
Definitely counterproductive.

Is this thought easy or hard to control?
At times this thought is very hard to control.

How uncomfortable does this thought make me feel?
Very uncomfortable!

How much does this thought interfere with my life?
It interferes a lot, because it makes me depressed and discouraged. Based on the answers to these questions, it is clear that I would benefit from eliminating this thought from my mental repertoire.

Second, Copeland recommends dwelling on the thought by bringing it to the level of consciousness and by focusing on it for several minutes. Next, the undesirable thought should be interrupted by means of such a powerful response as forcefully saying, "STOP!"; wearing a rubber band on one's wrist to snap when unwanted thoughts come up, pinching one's self, or digging the nails into the palms on one's hands.

Finally, a positive or assertive thought should be substituted for the negative one.

Affirmations

An affirmation is a statement that describes the way one would want his or her life to be utilizing a best-case scenario. Some examples include such phrases as:

I think and act with confidence.
I am strong and powerful.
I fully accept myself as I am.
I have many accomplishments to my credit.
I am healthy and energetic.
I deserve the time and space to heal.
I have all the resources to do what I want to in my life.
I am loved by many people.
I am a very valuable person.
I am safe and protected.
I am effective and efficient in stressful situations.
I am peaceful and serene at all times.
My relationships are happy and fulfilling.
I am in charge of my life.
I look and feel wonderful.[52]

Prior to using an affirmation, the authors recommend that the person first get in a more relaxed state. In contrast with a frequent occurrence the person affirms, "I am warming and caring" to which the sabotaging "inner critic" immediately replies, "bull ____." As the state of relaxation makes it more likely that the affirmation will be assimilated through to the individual's thought processes.

Here is an example of not taking oneself too seriously—another set of affirmations to set a "lighter" tone in this section.

Humorous Affirmations

As I let go of my shoulds and feelings of guilt, I can get in touch with my Inner Sociopath.

I have the power to channel my imagination into ever-soaring levels of suspicion and paranoia.

I assume full responsibility for my actions, except the ones that are someone else's fault.

I no longer need to punish, deceive or compromise myself. Unless, of course, I want to stay employed.

In some cultures what I do would be considered normal.

Having control over myself is nearly as good as having control over others.

My intuition nearly makes up for my lack of good judgment.

I can change any thought that hurts into a reality that hurts even more.

I honor my personality flaws, for without them I would have no personality at all.

Joan of Arc heard voices too.

I am grateful that I am not as judgmental as all those censorious, self-righteous people around me.

I need not suffer in silence while I can still moan, whimper and complain.

As I learn the innermost secrets of the people around me, they reward me in many ways to keep me quiet.

When someone hurts, forgiveness is cheaper than a lawsuit. But not nearly as gratifying.

The first step is to say nice things about myself. The second, to do nice things for myself. The third, to find someone to buy me nice things.

All of me is beautiful and valuable, even the ugly, stupid and disgusting parts.

I am at one with my duality.

Only a lack of imagination saves me from immobilizing myself with imaginary fears.

I honor and express all facets of my being, regardless of state and local laws.

Today I will gladly share my experiences and advice, for there are no sweeter words than "I told you so."

A good scapegoat is nearly as welcome as a solution to the problem.

Just for today, I will not sit in my living room all day watching TV. Instead I will move my TV into the bedroom.

Why should I waste my time reliving the past when I can spend it worrying about the future?

The complete lack of evidence is the surest sign that the conspiracy is working.

I am learning that criticism is not nearly as effective as sabotage.

Becoming aware of my character defects leads me to the next step—blaming my parents.

To have a successful relationship I must learn to make it look like I'm giving as much as I'm getting.

To understand all is to fear all.

"Stroking" and "Spitting":
Two Core Adlerian Counseling Skills

The skillful blending of encouragement and confrontation are described by Nikelly[53] as "stroke and spit tactics." Stroking is synonymous with encouragement, caring, and other "powerful invitations" for client growth. Dreikurs[54] described Adler's vivid metaphor of "spitting in the soup" by noting that a bowl of soup will not be enticing to a soup lover if someone contaminates it with spittle.

An additional analogy—when co-author Eckstein was a child, it was a rare treat when his parents would give him a sparkling ice-cold soda pop on a hot summer day. The first few sips were pure ecstasy, but frequently the command came to "share it with your brothers and sisters." Inevitably a sibling would grab the soda pop in one hand with a pack of crackers in the other. After a few "swigs" the half empty bottle would be returned to him, complete with a mixture of cracker crumbs floating on the top. Such "backwash" certainly changed the meaning of the cold drink for him. What had once been so desirable was instantly made much less gratifying.

Another technique known is *"sweetening the pot."* For example, a 37-year-old single male client was avoiding asking any women out for a date because he feared his mother would not approve of any them. The counselor's intervention consisted of having the man imagine a "great big smile of delight over his mother's face because her little boy was not going to leave home" the next time he avoided asking a woman for a date.[55]

Encouragement is a core component to "tapping creative personal power." Key factors contributing to reorientation are the client's recognition of a personal power, an ability to make decisions, and the ability to choose directions.[56] Personal power arises from a creative ability that lies in each person. "In consideration of the influence of the environment, the therapist must take into account the creative ingenuity by which events are perceived. Based on an innate striving to succeed, the influences existing in the environment, and a unique creative power, the individual establishes a personal style of living which directs thinking, feeling and acting. The creative schema through which an individual orients the self to the world is a personalized sense of meaningfulness, significance, or power."[57]

Client Resistance

The paradox of therapy is that although clients purportedly seek counseling to change, they also have a nonconscious investment in maintaining their particular symptoms for the protection it affords the self-esteem and the lifestyle. This threat to the self-esteem generates a fear of change, rooted in what Adler termed the fear of being proven worthless. He notes that "all neurotic symptoms have as their object the task of safeguarding the patient's self-esteem and thereby also the lifeline [later, lifestyle] into which he has grown."[58]

A core confrontation often involves the clients overtly stated desire for change as contrasted with his or her desire to maintain homeostasis, a balance or the status quo in order to protect one's own self-esteem.

An accurate understanding of resistance involves counselors realizing the inevitability of clients' resistance to change, the purposive nature of clients' symptoms and the misalignment of therapeutic goals.

When a therapist advocates changes by suggesting that clients stop responding to their circumstances in the ways they have assumed offer the most opportunity for success, it can easily be viewed by the client as asking them to perform against their own best interests. Thus, unless a counselor considers the private logic and apperceptions that justify and require the behavior, it is natural for resistance to follow and therapeutic directives to fail.[59]

With respect to the purposiveness of behavior, symptoms are used by clients to achieve two primary goals. They may be used to avoid personal responsibility, something Eric Berne described in "Wooden Leg" by asking the rhetorical question, "What do you expect from someone with a wooden leg?"[60] The implied answer is, "Nothing."

King notes "Clients frequently ask similar rhetorical questions demonstrating resistance to change. 'What do you expect from someone who is co-dependent? What do you expect from people who are phobic? What do you expect from persons who are depressed?' In all these cases the clients' implicit demand is to be exempted from responsibility for their behavior and the need to change."[61]

A second possible purpose of symptoms may be that a person may gain respect or sympathy due to their heroic struggles to overcome their problematic behavior. Dreikurs noted that resistance was actually a discrepancy between the goals of the therapist and those of the patient.[62]

King observes that "In the therapeutic process itself there are many occasions for goal divergence. The Adlerian therapist works to move clients toward responsibility; clients strive for exemption and evasion. The therapist advocates equality and social interest; clients pursue superiority and personal interest. This conflict between the goals of the therapist and those of the clients, often implicit and unacknowledged, forms the very fabric of therapy and contributes significantly to resistance."[63]

Milton Erickson described the process of utilization as being simply taking all that clients present—strengths, ability, symptoms, and resistance—and using that as the basis for creating therapeutic changes. For example, Erickson began a conversation with a delusional schizophrenic believing himself to be Jesus Christ by saying that "I understand you are good at carpentry."[64]

Co-author Eckstein humorously tells graduate students that the "secret" to his success in therapy is found in the following "koan" (proverb). "Take credit for all client successes—blame all failures to client resistance."

On a more serious note, client resistance is often described as a reoccurring counselor challenge. Reframing the concept resistance is a suggested first step for counselors. For example, consider resistance as "lack of goal alignment" between the counselor and the client or between what clients *say* they will do ("the tongue of the mouth) versus what they are actually doing ("movement", i.e., the "tongue of the shoe"). Rather than there being some thing "wrong" with the client, analyzing the "gap" between the counselor and the client is important. Carl Rogers defined anxiety as the "gap between the real and the ideal" and that anxiety is a type of motivator in and of itself. For example, consider the following "it is a grain of sand that motivates an oyster to form a pearl."

Both Freud and Adler described resistance in terms of a "motivated avoidance" behavior. Freud believed the avoided repressed, traumatic, childhood memories. For Adler, the avoidance originated in the lack of courage to face the challenges of life and the "fear that his relationship with he psychologist" should "force him into some useful activity in which he will be defeated."[65] This "freedom from responsibility" in facing life's demands while maintaining one's self-esteem was Adler's conception of the purpose of resistance.

Dreikurs' assessment of resistance is a misalignment of goals between the therapist and the client has become the standard definition of resistance in much Adlerian literature.[66] Therapists can be led astray when they listen to the words of the client rather than attending to the client's movement, which, Adler said is a far more reliable indication of the client's goal.[67]

Stress

Stress-related disorders have become the leading cause of the Western world's workers' compensation claims. John Carpi has poignantly described the negative consequences of stress.

> We may respond to stress as we do an allergy. That is, we can become sensitized, or acutely sensitive, to stress. Once that happens, even the merest intimation of stress can trigger a cascade

of chemical reactions in brain and body that assault us from within. Stress is the psychological equivalent of ragweed. Once the body becomes sensitized to pollen or ragweed, it takes only the slightest bloom in spring or fall to set off the biochemical alarm that results in runny noses, watery eyes, and the general misery of hay fever. But while only some of us are genetically programmed to be plagued with hay fever, all of us have the capacity to become sensitized to stress.

This new paradigm of stress demonstrates that there is a link between psychological events and physical eruptions, between mind and body. The psychological events that are most deleterious probably occur during infancy and childhood—an unstable home environment, living with an alcoholic parent, or any other number of extended crises. The new paradigm also firmly ties everyday psychological stress to such suspect complaints as ulcers, headaches, and fatigue. The new blueprint of how we respond to stress also may explain why people have different tolerances for stress. Our ability to withstand stress has less to do with whether we are strong willed than with how much and what kind of stress we encountered in the past. However, we all start out with the same biological machinery for responding to stress. Stress activates primitive regions of the brain, the same areas that control eating, aggression, and immune response. It switches on nerve circuits that ignite the body's fight-or-flight response as if there were a life threatening danger.

Looking for stress as a chemical reaction and realizing that this reaction, if strong enough, can change how we react in the future, offers the possibility of explaining many things we have witnessed regarding stress. Perhaps what we called learned helplessness is biologically programmed helplessness. Some may be unable to respond to stress because trauma has altered their biology, we can't really call that learned behavior. If this new picture of stress is not yet quite in full focus, that's because it requires the melding of disciplines ranging from genetics to psychology to medicine, and demands a new theory of mind/body interactions. But it holds the promise of entirely new strategies to combat stress.[68]

Here are some specific examples of what Carpi describes as "Stress-Stoppers."

1. **Mindfulness Meditation**—Patients can be taught mindfulness mediation, which comes out of the Buddhist tradition. Practitioners set aside 20 to 40 minutes a day when they focus on calming and becoming aware of their bodies with the aim of catching them—and interrupting them—in the act of hyperresponding to stress. Other forms of meditation use other devices to bring on moments of quiet contemplation, but all are designed to get you to focus on your body.

2. **Biofeedback**—There are three main forms of it: electromyography (EMG), galvanic skin response (GSR), and electroencephalography (EEG). By attaching electrodes to the body system that readily reacts to stress—muscles, skin, and brain waves, respectively—you can monitor your actual stress level and learn to control, even reduce it. Modern biofeedback devices give off some signal—a blinking light, a bell—that announces a high level of tension. You concentrate on slowing the blinking light or bell. Each form of biofeedback works best for specific stress-related problems. EMG biofeedback, for example, reduces tension headaches; it allows people to focus and relax the muscles in the forehead that cause head pain; GSR seems to work best for stress-induced migraines, which tend to coincide with a rise in body temperature. EEG biofeedback leads to the deepest relaxation states.

3. **What Calms You**—You have to become aware of what calms you best. This may include listening to music, going for a walk, or exercising.

4. **Relaxation Response**—One of the best-studied stress-relievers is the relaxation response, first described by Harvard's Herbert Benson. Its great advantage is that it requires no special posture or place. Sit and recline comfortably. Close your eyes and relax your muscles. Breathe deeply. To make sure that you are breathing deeply, place one hand on your abdomen, the other on your chest. Breath in slowly through your nose, and as you do you should feel your abdomen (not your chest) rise. Slowly exhale. As you do, focus on your breathing. Some people do better if they silently repeat the word one as they exhale; it helps clear the mind. If thoughts intrude, do not dwell on them; allow them to pass on and return to focusing on your breathing. Although you can turn to this exercise any time you feel stressed, doing it regularly for 10 to 20 minutes at least once a day can put you in a generally calm mode that can see you through otherwise stressful situations.

5. **Cleansing Breath**—Take a huge breath in. Hold it for three to four seconds. Then let it out v-e-r-y s-l-o-w-l-y. As you blow out, blow out all the tension in your body.

6. **Relaxing Postures**—Sit anywhere. Relax your shoulders so they are comfortably rounded. Allow your arms to drop by your sides. Rest your hands, palm side up, on top of your thighs. With your knees comfortably bent, extend your legs and allow your feet, supported on the heels, to fall gently outward. Let your jaw drop. Close your eyes and breath deeply for a minute or two.

7. **Passive Stretches**—It's possible to relax muscles without effort; gravity can do it all. Start with your neck and let your head fall forward to the right. Breathe in and out normally. With every breath out, allow your head to fall more. Do the same for shoulders, arms, back.

8. **Imagery**—Find a comfortable posture and close your eyes. Imagine the most relaxed place you've ever been. We all have a place like this and can call it to mind anywhere, any time. For everyone it is different, it may be a lake, it may be a mountain, it may be a cottage at the beach. Are you there?

9. Here are five other proven "stress-busters."

    a. Curl your toes against the soles of your feet as hard as you can for 15 seconds, then relax them. Progressively tense and relax the muscles in your legs, stomach, back, shoulders, neck.

    b. Visualize lying on a beach, listening to waves coming in and feeling the warm sun and gentle breezes on your back. Or, if you prefer, imagine an erotic fantasy or picture yourself in whatever situation makes you happiest.

    c. Set aside 20 to 30 minutes a day to do anything you want—even nothing.

    d. Take a brisk walk.

    e. Keep a Walkman handy and loaded with relaxing, enjoyable music.

10. **The Power of Understanding**—Simply knowing about stress sensitization seems to help some people.

Shulman notes that the client's fear of disapproval—of being exposed and found defective—may interfere with the counseling relationship. He listed the following defenses used by clients to "defeat" the counselor or to "save" their self-esteem:

1. Externalization: The fault lies outside me, including:

   Cynicism: Life is at fault.

   Inadequacy: I am just an innocent victim.

   Rebellion: I cannot afford to submit to life.

Projection: It is all their fault.

2. Blind Spots: If I don't look at it, it will go away.

3. Excessive Self-Control: I will not let anything upset me.

4. Arbitrary Rightness: My mind is made up; don't confuse me with facts.

5. Elusiveness and Confusion: Don't pin me down.

6. Contrition and Self-Disparagement: I am always wrong.

7. Suffering as Manipulation: I suffer to control others.[69]

All such defenses or client resistant behaviors have the potential for destroying the counselor-client relationship. Allen humorously calls this "avoiding the client's tarbaby," which he describes in the following manner:

The Adlerian recognizes all too well that as self-defeating and incommodious as a particular modus vivendi or "identity" may be, it remains, in the eyes of the client, his best bet—and accordingly, he will defend it. As dismal as his set of expectations for himself in the world may be, they at least enable him to make sense out of the "blooming, buzzing, confusion" and perhaps even entitle him to certain concessions. So, he will struggle to maintain their claim to validity.

For example, some clients attempt to annoy the counselor in order to establish the validity of his thesis that he is an unlikable person (see, even my counselor whose job it is to like all sorts of people, dislikes me). Other clients will try to discourage the counselor in order to validate the hopelessness of their position or the wisdom of their decision to do nothing about it. In effect the counselor's sense of discouragement is used by such clients as license to curse the darkness and to avoid the unpleasantness involved in the attempt to generate any light by their own efforts.[70]

The skillful use of confrontation of discrepancies coupled with the power of encouragement are two essential global Adlerian counseling skills that should permeate the entire process. Specific development approaches and Adlerian counseling techniques follow.

Excuses

Linden explores the role of client excuses as another form of resistance. He notes that

We tend to think that we give good reasons for our behavior but that other people make excuses. This is self-deception. We all make excuses because often there is a discrepancy between the goals of our private logic and the ironclad law of social living. . . . Behavior is usually result of a mixture of common sense and private logic.

An excuse is the price that private logic pays to common sense. The private logic of each of us differs, but we all want to minimize the price that such conflict costs. We hope that alibis or excuses will allow us to do what we want to do without having to pay a heavy price. . . . The greater the discrepancy between societal demands and personal goals, the more private logic is involved and the deeper the resulting excuse.[71] Since excuses are not only means of concealing our true intentions but also modes of social withdrawal, perhaps the ultimate excuse for avoiding the problems of life, the "most intensive safeguard" for not playing our part in social living is, as Adler states, "suicide."[72]

Linden believes that excuses may be classified as being first-level, second-level, and third-level excuses. First-level excuses are everyday excuses. These are immediate, situational, and often superficial excuses based in the present and may be used to justify present, past, or future actions. The primary purpose of a first-level excuse is to maintain a favorable self-image both for ourselves and others. They employ such devices as projection, semantic redefinition, reversal of cause-effect relationships, false cause, and hasty generalization.

The second strategy, diminishing, accepts responsibility but attempts to soften or water down the negative appearance of the act, to make it "seem not so bad." The strategy of "diminishing" takes two directions: reframing and reworking the standards. "Reframing" is a strategy to consciously or unconsciously hide from yourself the undesirable consequences of your actions, often claiming that one was unaware of what was going on. "Reworking" consists in either claiming that the standards for performance were vague and fuzzy or that the standards were set too high in the first place and hence are unfair.

In the third strategy, temporization, one admits responsibility for the act and that it was faulty, but one goes on to weaken accountability by appealing to extenuating circumstances. This often takes the "appeal to the people" (*ad populum*), or band wagon approach. "Others did just as poorly (or worse)." "Old people cannot remember things," etc. The goal here is to seek protection in the crowd through shared incompetence. Another "Yes-But" strategy is projection: other people or some outside force made me do it. A third form of temporization consists of "consistency-lowering strategies" thus claiming that the situation was unusual either because "we didn't try very hard" or because we lacked intent and "didn't mean to do it."[73]

Procrastinator's Creed

I believe that if anything is worth doing, it would have been done already.

I shall never move quickly, except to avoid more work or find excuses.

I will never rush into a job without a lifetime of consideration.

I shall meet all of my deadlines directly in proportion to the amount of bodily injury I could expect to receive from missing them.

I firmly believe that tomorrow holds the possibility for new technologies, astounding discoveries, and a reprieve from my obligations.

I truly believe that all deadlines are unreasonable regardless of the amount of time given.

If at first I don't succeed, there is always next year.

I shall always decide not to decide, unless of course I decided to change my mind.

I shall always begin, start, initiate, take the first step, and/or write the first word, when I get around to it.

I will never put off 'til tomorrow, what I can forget about forever.

Not all excuses are total lies. They are often merely products of our biased apperceptions. Nor are they all bad. Indeed, there are positive advantages of excuses. Excuses can and often do protect and/or bolster our self-image. "By giving an excuse, we acknowledge the validity of the standards we have violated."[74] This acknowledgement of societal standards and common sense can serve as a social lubricant, easing our relationships with others, and it can provide us social space to take further chances, further risks.

Having been a member of Weight Watchers for 15 years, Linden has heard many excuses. Here are some food-related faulty logic responses one might use according to Snyder's classification.

1. Semantic Redefinition: "And what did you do when you went to the movie?" "I bought some popcorn." "But you promised to give up eating between meals." "Oh, but popcorn is not food, it's roughage!"

2. Hasty Generalization and/or False Cause: "The reason that the dresses in the shop are so small and don't fit is because they are all being sewed by those tiny Asian women."

3. Reversal of Cause-Effect: "Anxiety about food must be inherited. My children are driving me nuts." From an Adlerian point of view, the most common reversal of cause effect is the appeal to feelings.

4. Disconnection of Cause-Effect: "I cannot understand why I am not losing weight. I walk two miles every night." "Where do you walk?" "To the Dairy Queen."

5. Hidden Agenda: Husband: "You will have to quit Weight Watchers, you are using too much hot water."

According to the husband's private logic, when the wife was fat, she displaced more area in the tub; therefore used less water to take a bath. But I know that she is thinner, there is less water displacement. She is using more hot water and thus driving up the water and heating bills.

Linden says second-level excuses are at a greater distance from social interest. First-level excuses are concerned mostly with accountability and thus preventing shame. Second-level excuses are more concerned with responsibility and often involve guilt. Second-level excuses often have recourse to the past in order to provide distance in the present and to avoid present problem solving. Sometimes they engender striving for superiority not over problems, but over people. The basic dynamic is one of withdrawal, avoidance, and the creation of a substitute goal, an excuse. This style of thinking leads us into sham battles with ourselves and "we soon reach a deadlock and become powerless to accomplish the very thing we were striving for."[75] As Mosak states, many of us do not want freedom for that would mean accepting full responsibility for our behavior and:

We prefer a "good excuse" and are willing to suffer the pains of guilt feelings. But they, too, are only a pretense. Guilt feelings are the expression of good intentions which we do not really have. They always indicate an unwillingness to face up to a situation, using the excuse of a past transgression.[76]

Guilt feelings as an excuse. Dreikurs believed that this strategy was so important that he devoted an entire article to it: "Guilt Feeling as an Excuse."[77] As children, we learn that one of the payoffs of guilt feelings is "moral enhancement."

Whatever the child may have committed, he can make a favorable impression by admitting his guilt, preferably with an ostentatious display of regret and remorse. No misdeed is really so bad when a child can convincingly demonstrate how sorry he feels. Accepting one's guilt becomes, therefore, a sign of high oral standards. (p. 233)[78]

Dreikurs summarized his distinction between guilt and guilt feelings as follows:

Guilt is unavoidable in a social order, but guilt feelings are not directly related to guilt. They are supposed to preserve conformity, but are mostly used to conceal defiance. The development of guilt feelings ... serve mainly as a proof of good intentions. They can be used to gain moral superiority. ... They permit a shift of emphasis from the important present situation to the past, thereby providing relief from responsibility for present attitudes. They provoke unpleasant experience which a discouraged individual anticipates. They prevent constructive action under the guise of remorse. (p. 239)[79]

The third and deepest level of excuses consists of the creation of fictional obstacles to avoid dealing with an imminent task. This is the level of illness. The depth of the illness will vary according to the degree of distance from social interest.

Third-level excuses lie heavily in the realm of private logic and operate without awareness. Adler says, "the patient unknowingly selects certain symptoms and develops them until they impress him (consciously) as real obstacles. Behind his barricade of symptoms, the patient feels hidden and secure." Adler then continues:

The patient declares that he is unable to solve his task "on account of the symptoms, and only on account of these." He expects from others the solution of his problems, or the excuse from all demands, or at least, the granting of "extenuating circumstances." When he has his extenuating alibi, he feels that his prestige is protected.[80]

Neurotic symptoms serve another purpose too, as a type of a "win-win insurance policy." If one fails, the symptoms provides a "perfect explanation of having botched it up" and if one succeeds in overcoming one's self-imposed obstacles, "the success is a triumph—in spades!"[81] Symptoms may be an excuse to evade tasks that one fears one may fail in or one may use symptoms to appear greater than one is. Third-level excuses, safeguarding devices, are triggered by external events in the present and are future oriented.

Adler describes some of the character traits that are developed when one moves away from social interest and are then used as excuses:

> These are: increased over-sensitivity, greater caution, rage, pedantry, defiance, thrift, dissatisfaction, and impatience. . . . To be relieved of impending demands of life, to delay the solution to a life question, or to gain extenuating circumstances then becomes the secondary ideal goal. This is demanded by the egotism of the patient and his lack of interest in others.[82]

Additional Specific Counseling Strategies

Several Adlerian counseling techniques or strategies have been described already in this chapter. These include encouragement, spitting in the client's soup, paradoxical intention, humor, and avoiding the client's tarbaby. Other strategies include:

1. Immediacy—using the present here and now interaction between the counselor and client as a "slice of life" a microcosm of one's macrocosm.

2. Acting "as if"—Adler created the "as if" technique based on Hans Vaihinger's "as if" philosophy. It can be defined as a cognitive, behavioral intervention in which the client anticipates, pretends, and/or enacts a futuristic event, belief, or desired behavior. The client can also be asked to act or behave "as if" the problem is resolved.[83] Carich concludes that the "as if" technique is a pretend intervention that alters cognitive factors (guiding fiction, private logics, etc.) and behavior as the client engages in pretend experiences.[84]

3. Catching oneself—as clients gain insight into their own goals they are invited to "catch themselves" falling into dysfunctional patterns. Often this awareness initially comes after the fact; however, as greater insight is developed, it often can even precede the actual event. Coupled then with "spitting in one's own soup," "catching oneself" is a valuable first step to awareness and then the freedom to choose an alternative behavior or attitude.

4. The therapeutic memoir technique—involves the use of childhood photographs. The selection description of specific childhood pictures is another valuable means of gathering formative childhood information.[85]

5. The push-button technique, clients are asked to close their eyes to visualize an event in their life that made them very happy. They are then asked to re-experience the good feelings they had on this occasion. Next, clients are requested to visualize an unpleasant event such as when they felt humiliated, and are again asked to re-experience those feelings. Then they are asked again to visualize and re-experience the happy incident and the associated positive feelings. The goal is for clients to learn they can create their feelings by the thoughts they choose to have.[86]

The Counselor as Philosopher:
The Philosopher as Pastor/Priest

In a sense, the presenting problems of therapy are similar to the basic philosophical and existential questions confronting all human beings. "Who am I? Why am I here? What is my purpose? What is valuable? What is ethical and moral? What is truth?" are representative questions reflecting such philosophic modes of inquiry as identity, epistemology (knowledge), and axiology (values). Therapists need to see specific presenting problems in a larger, more existential or spiritual quest for higher meaning or purpose in one's life. Such a spiritual quest is not synonymous with religion which often is associated with blind adherence to a particular set of rules. However, spirituality often includes one's own religious preferences as part of it.

Pancner and Pancner (1988) use the creative analogy of *The Wizard of Oz* by L. Frank Baum (1900)[87] to illustrate a representative pilgrim (Dorothy) and her spiritual quest along the "therapeutic" yellow-brick road. Selected passages follow:

> Twentieth century America offers a standard of living and a wealth of material goods unsurpassed by any other known civilization. And yet, in this society which is so oriented to consumption and instant gratification, happiness and balanced living seem to elude many. The rise of crime, increase of alcoholism and drug addiction, and escalating suicide rates are evidence that although people are living in a nation of plenty, many still are struggling and searching for more.

> As therapists, we may begin to sense our enlarged task and responsibility in taking the patient's symptoms as metaphor or allegory for defining and exploring broader issues and questions. Many of the patient's presenting problems can be interpreted as revealing deeper issues and discordances on the spiritual level. Although unable to do the actual changing for the patient, the therapist can be a teacher and guide

> Psychology is derived from the Greek word psyche, meaning soul and life. One of the founding fathers of psychology, William James, strongly advocated and focused on the psychological as well as the spiritual nature of man. Modern psychology has emphasized the psychological side of man, while almost entirely negating the spiritual aspect. Because the spiritual nature is not addressed in most clinical training institutes, the clinician is very hesitant to deal with this facet of a person. And yet, if the whole person is to be the focus, this spiritual area has profound impact on the personality and therefore has to be recognized and incorporated into the psychological therapeutic process.[88]

Pancner and Pancner then address the specific story of the *Wizard of Oz* and apply it as being like the journey of counseling:

> As the story opens, Dorothy, in gray, barren, arid Kansas, finds herself being sucked up and whirled away in the eye of a cyclone. She, her dog Toto, and the house are quite literally blown out of Kansas. Her fear rages as greatly as the storm. Wondering if she will be dashed to pieces, she senses she is on an uncharted, unplanned journey.

> So it is with many people coming into psychotherapy. The onset of their symptoms may be experienced as occurring quite suddenly, coupled by a feeling of having little or no control over what is happening, and being at the mercy of the unknown. With disorientation and disruption either due to symptoms or upheaval in one's environment, the orderly, predictable life-pattern is abruptly changed. The person is thrown into another dimension of dealing with altered perceptions, frightening medical intervention, perhaps physical incapabilities, and a new, uncharted "cyclone" experience is begun.

> Similarly clients find themselves dumped into an alien land of helpers. Many clients believe that their great hope of returning to the way it used to be hinges on the magic and wizardry of the therapist whom they then can perceive as guru or god. In psychotherapy, one of the initial tasks for the

therapist and patient is to define expectations and goals for treatment. At this point, many clients do not sense any power from within to solve the dilemma and lean heavily on the therapist.[89]

Reproduced from Pancner, K., and Pancner, R., "The Quest, Gurus, and the Yellow Brick Road" *Individual Psychology 44*, no. 2 (1988):82–85.

Pancner and Pancner then specifically focus on the process of psychotherapy and the relationship to the spiritual/existential task of life. Their philosophy would appear to be consistent with Teilhard de Charden who wrote that "We are not human beings having a spiritual experience. We are spiritual beings having a human experience."

> The path of spirituality parallels the course of psychotherapy in that they both explore the steps involved in knowing or discovering oneself. Both are a journey inward, and, like Dorothy's quest, usually there is intense upheaval. The path can become a long, arduous journey like the yellow brick road, having many bumps and potholes.

> Through psychotherapy, an awakening process can begin, and coming to terms with one's individuality puts one on the path of growth. As one senses more freedom, the chains of robotic deadness can be loosened and the awakening process can begin . . . In the final analysis, clients must realize they have the energy, source of power, and locus of control to live out life in a balanced way. Within a person lies the capacity to travel one's own yellow brick road, search for answers to questions and problems, and drown the witches of fear, negative thinking, and destructive living. Therapists and teachers are important for the introduction of new concepts and techniques, clarification and redefining of perceptions and current situations; however, if one continues to only look outside oneself, seeking out solutions, happiness, and balance from others, one's answers will remain obscure. It is by turning inward and acknowledging one's inner depths and resources that one realizes that answers and power come from within. At that point of discovery one realizes that outer "gurus" have clay feet, are merely mortal, and are sorely lacking in answers for another's life journey, and so, "physician heal thyself" can be aptly applied in stating, "client, heal thyself." One must become one's own wizard or guru, realizing that the power lies within, not emanating from external sources. This then is the task of the therapist: to guide patients to seek within themselves.[90]

Counselors need to be aware of the physical, mental, emotional, and existential/spiritual needs of their clients. The ultimate encouragement is for clients to discover those gifts within themselves. Despite different levels of mental health or mental illness, each person is striving for some type of significance. And, as Lovejoy[91] observes, "Though not everyone can occupy the top of every tree, there are, in fact, many trees."

Forgiveness

Forgiveness is an essential therapeutic and spiritual process. Jesus Christ was once asked "how many times should I forgive?" "Seven times 70" was his metaphor reply, meaning "unlimited." A starting point is to contrast what forgiveness is *not* with what forgiveness *is*:

Forgiveness Is Not . . .

1. Forgiveness *is not* forgetting. By forgiving the people who hurt us, we do not erase painful past experiences from our memory. Nothing we have done so far has been able to turn back the clock and remove the unpleasant incidents from our life history, and forgiveness will not do that, either. We cannot forget, nor should we. Those experiences, and even the pain they caused, have a great deal to teach us, both about not being victimized again and about not victimizing others.

2. Forgiveness *is not* condoning. When we forgive, we lessen the past's impact on our present and future, but this does not alter the fact that the injuries and injustices we experienced were painful and unfair when they occurred originally. By forgiving the people who hurt us, we are not saying that what was done to us was acceptable or unimportant or "not so bad." It was bad. It did hurt. It has made a difference in our life. In fact, true forgiveness cannot occur while we are in any way denying, minimizing, justifying, or condoning the action that harmed us.

3. Forgiveness *is not* absolution. Many of us who were raised in the Catholic religion regularly confessed our sins and then received absolution. We performed whatever penance the priest suggested, and the slate was wiped clean until we next sinned, confessed, and were absolved. Many of us still associate forgiveness with this sort of absolution, but that is not what we are expected to do when we forgive the people who hurt us. We do not "let them off the hook." We do not absolve them of all responsibility for their actions. Often "I absolve you" are words spoken from atop our "mountain" of self-righteousness and demonstrate that we have not yet healed our wounds or let go of pain from the past. Absolution is just another way to be "one up" on the people who hurt us. And that is not forgiveness.

4. Forgiveness *is not* a form of self-sacrifice. Forgiveness is not gritting our teeth and tolerating the people who hurt us. Plastering a smile on our face and "making nice" is not forgiving. Forgiveness is not swallowing our true feelings and playing the martyr, saying it's all right when it is not or getting by somehow in spite of the pain. The "grin and bear it" approach to forgiveness makes life less joyful and more difficult. Actual forgiveness has the opposite effect and cannot be undertaken halfheartedly. We either forgive or we don't. Being honest about the fact that we are not ready to forgive yet is better for us in the long run than pretending to forgive.

5. Forgiveness *is not* a clear-cut, one-time decision. No matter how sincerely we want to let go of the past and move on with our life, we cannot expect to wake up one morning thinking, "Okay, today's the day I'm going to forgive someone who hurt me," and then blithely do it. We cannot make a five-year plan that designates the first Tuesday of every third month as a forgiveness day or making a list of people who have hurt us, and systematically forgive them. Forgiveness just doesn't work that way. It cannot be forced. Forgiveness is what happens naturally as a result of confronting painful past experiences and healing old wounds.

What Forgiveness Is . . .

1. Forgiveness is a by-product of an ongoing healing process. Many of us grew up believing that forgiveness was an act to be performed or an attitude to possess, and the reason that we could not forgive was that we were not trying hard enough. But what really keeps us from forgiving the people who hurt us is that we have not yet healed the wounds they inflicted.

2. Forgiveness is the gift at the end of the healing process. We find it waiting for us when we reach a point where we stop expecting "them" to pay for what they did or make it up to us in some way.

3. Forgiveness is an *internal* process. It happens within us. It is a feeling of wellness and freedom and acceptance. Those feelings can be ours at any time, as long as we want to heal and are willing to try.

4. Forgiveness is a sign of positive self-esteem. It is no longer building our identity around something that happened to us in the past, realizing that there is more to us and more we can do. The past is put into proper perspective, and we realize that the injuries and injustices are just a part of our life and just a part of who we are better than all of us.

The religions in which we were raised presented forgiveness as a moral obligation. To be considered "good" and worthy, we were supposed to "turn the other cheek" and forgive our enemies. We believe, however, that forgiveness is instead our moral right—a right to stop being hurt by events that were unfair in the first place. We claim the right to stop hurting when we can finally say, "I'm tired of the pain, and I want to be healed." At that moment, forgiveness becomes a *possibility*—although it may not become a reality for quite some time.

5. Forgiveness is letting go of the intense emotions attached to incidents from our past. We still remember what happened, but we no longer feel intensely angry, frightened, bitter, resentful or damaged because of it. Forgiveness becomes an option once pain from the past stops dictating how we live our life today and we realize that what once happened to us does not have to determine what will happen to us in the future.

6. Forgiveness is recognizing that we no longer need our grudges and resentments, our hatred and self-pity. We do not need them as an excuse for getting less out of life than we want or deserve. We do not need them as a weapon to punish the people who hurt us or keep other people from getting close enough to hurt us again. We do not need them as an identity. We are more than a victim of injury and injustice.

7. Forgiveness is no longer wanting to punish the people who hurt us. It is no longer wanting to get even or to have them suffer as much as we did. It is realizing that we can never truly "even the score" and it is the inner peace we feel when we stop trying to.

8. Forgiveness is accepting that nothing we do to punish *them* will heal us. It is becoming aware of what we did because we were hurt and how these attitudes and behaviors have also hurt us. It is deciding that we have simply done enough hiding and hurting and hating and that we do not want to do those things anymore.

9. Forgiveness is freeing up and putting to better use the energy once consumed by holding grudges, harboring resentments, and nursing unhealed wounds. It is rediscovering the strengths we always had and relocating our limitless capacity to understand and accept other people and ourselves. It is breaking the cycle of pain and abuse, ceasing to create new victims by hurting others as we ourselves were hurt.

10. Forgiveness is moving on. It is recognizing that we have better things to do with our life and then doing them.[92]

Today

Mend a quarrel. Search out a forgotten friend. Dismiss suspicion, and replace it with trust. Write a love letter. Share some treasure. Give a soft answer. Encourage youth. Manifest your loyalty in a word or deed. Keep a promise. Find the time. Forego a grudge. Forgive an enemy. Listen. Apologize if you were wrong. Examine your demand on others. Think first of someone else. Appreciate, be kind, be gentle. Laugh a little more. Deserve confidence. Take up arms against malice. Decry complacency. Express your gratitude. Worship your God. Gladden the heart of a child. Take pleasure in the beauty and wonder of the earth. Speak your love. Speak it again. Speak it still again. Speak it still once again.

—"On This Day." 1999. *Shakthi.* 5,4, p. 18.

Force-Field Analysis as a Reorientation Strategy

Kurt Lewin[93] developed the Force-Field analysis model to assist in problem solving and planned change. In his model, the term force does not refer to a tangible, physical force; rather it serves as a metaphor for a broad range of interpersonal influences affecting the system. For example, some influences on couples might include such issues as religious beliefs/preferences; financial considerations; fear of change itself; mistrust; sex-role stereotypes; division of responsibilities (role perceptions); competitive behavior between the couple; and basic personality differences such as being introverted or extroverted.

Basically Lewin believes that there are both restraining forces and drawing forces arrayed against each other within a force field. The interaction between the restraining forces that work against change and the drawing forces that are "pushing" or motivating toward change. If the desired change is not coming about, then the restraining forces are collectively stronger than the drawing forces. Conversely, change will occur when the collective driving forces are greater. The benefit of the model for couples is that it provides a way to analyze the various "push/pull," drawing/restraining forces; it also can assist a couple in developing strategies for causing change.

The following specific activity can be utilized by counselors to assist couples. It is intended to help couples in exploring the issues involved with considering a change. For example, many times counselors are contacted because one or both members are considering separation or a divorce.

Being more aware of the issues that say "yes" as well as the factors that say "no" to any change being considered by the couple can help focus the issues. The following questions can be completed by one or both members of the couple. It is often useful if both persons are completing the form to answer the questions independently, then to compare the responses together.

FORCE-FIELD ANALYSIS ACTIVITY

1. Write down a specific issue or situation that you feel needs to be changed (e.g., moving, changing jobs, having children, separation or divorce, etc.) below.

    _____

    _____

    _____

2. List below the issues that are restraining, saying "no" to the considered change (e.g., too risky, too expensive, etc.).

    _____

    _____

    _____

3. List below all the factors that are driving or motivating you to say "yes" to the possible change (e.g., emotional pain, unhappiness, better opportunity, etc.).

    _____

    _____

    _____

4. Does this situation remind you of a previous decision or issue? If so, briefly describe the incident, including the decision and the outcome.

    _____

    _____

    _____

5. What are the benefits to you of not making this change right now?

    _____

    _____

    _____

6. What are the costs (emotional and/or financial) to you of not deciding right now?

    _____

    _____

    _____

7. Review your list of restraining forces in #2. Rank each in order of priority by assigning a rating from 10 being the highest to 1 being the lowest value in terms of importance to you. For example, "too risky" might be rated an "8" for a fairly high value to you, whereas "too expensive" may be only a "4" because of being a moderate to low issue. Now rank order your priorities with your 1–10 rating beside it.

Issue   **Rating**

_____   _____

_____   _____

_____   _____

_____   _____

_____   _____

8. Do the same thing as #7 for your driving forces. For example, "emotional hurt" might be ranked a "10," whereas "better opportunity" might be a "7."

Issue   **Rating**

_____   _____

_____   _____

_____   _____

_____   _____

_____   _____

_____   _____

9. What are your reactions/feelings/opinions to your responses in #7 and #8? How likely do you feel it is for a change to occur?

_____

_____

_____

10. What would be a specific "game plan" necessary for the change to actually occur?

a. _____

b. _____

c. _____

d. ⁹⁴ _____

SUGGESTED SYSTEMATIC SUMMARY FOR THE ECKSTEIN LIFE STYLE INTERVIEW (ELSI)

(Page numbers appearing in brackets [ ] denote location in this book where topic is addressed.)

1. **Current Functioning in the Five Life Tasks** [pp. 83–89]
    A.   Activities that bring joy to the client:

    _____

    _____

    _____

    B.   Subjective concerns/complaints/illnesses/medications:

    _____

    _____

    _____

    C.   Summarize the five life tasks:

    _____

    _____

    _____

    D.   Integrate "the question" and formulate three to four key areas of concern in the person's current life:

    _____

    _____

    _____

2. **Family Atmosphere** [pp. 80; 89–97]

    (Summarize overall impressions in the following areas.)

    A.   Issues regarding the "naming process": [pp. 91–92]

    _____

    _____

    _____

B.	Mood: [p. 89]

_____

_____

_____

C.	Order: [p. 89]

_____

_____

_____

D.	Relationships: [p. 89]

_____

_____

_____

E.	Masculine and feminine role models: [p. 90]

_____

_____

_____

F.	Parental interaction and parenting style: [pp. 90–91]

_____

_____

_____

G.	Family Values/Family Motto: [p. 92]

_____

_____

_____

H.	Psychological birth-order position and sibling ratings (list personality traits): [pp. 92–96]

_____

_____

_____

I.	Influential stories, fairy tales, television characters, myths, etc.: [pp. 102–104]

_____

_____

_____

J. Describe the impact of the person's cultural heritage: [p. 152]

_____

_____

_____

K. Any other significant factors (e.g., significant deaths, additions or subtractions to family, divorces, ethnic or community values, etc.): [p. 152]

_____

_____

_____

3. **Summarize key aspects of the early recollections** (ERs) [pp. 151–160]
    A. ER #1
        (1) Newspaper headline:

        _____

        _____

        (2) Who is liked or disliked in the recollection? In what way?

        _____

        _____

        (3) What problem(s) is(are) confronted in the recollection?

        _____

        _____

        (4) What special talent(s) or ability is(are) revealed in the recollection?

        _____

        _____

        (5) Is the recollection generally pleasant or unpleasant?

        _____

        _____

        (6) What is the client's level of activity in the recollection? (i.e., active or passive)

        _____

        _____

        (7) What emotion(s) does(do) the client feel and/or show pertaining to the recollection?

        _____

        _____

(8)   What does the recollection suggest to you about the client's social interest?

_____

_____

(9)   What specific needs or values are reflected in this ER?

_____

_____

B.   ER #2
    (1)   Newspaper headline:

_____

_____

(2)   Who is liked or disliked in the recollection? In what way?

_____

_____

(3)   What problem(s) is(are) confronted in the recollection?

_____

_____

(4)   What special talent(s) or ability is(are) revealed in the recollection?

_____

_____

(5)   Is the recollection generally pleasant or unpleasant?

_____

_____

(6)   What is the client's level of activity in the recollection? (i.e., active or passive)

_____

_____

(7)   What emotion(s) does(do) the client feel and/or show pertaining to the recollection?

_____

_____

(8)   What does the recollection suggest to you about the client's social interest?

_____

_____

(9)   What specific needs or values are reflected in this ER?

_____

_____

C. ER #3

    (1)   Newspaper headline:

_____

_____

    (2)   Who is liked or disliked in the recollection? In what way?

_____

_____

    (3)   What problem(s) is(are) confronted in the recollection?

_____

_____

    (4)   What special talent(s) or ability is(are) revealed in the recollection?

_____

_____

    (5)   Is the recollection generally pleasant or unpleasant?

_____

_____

    (6)   What is the client's level of activity in the recollection? (i.e., active or passive)

_____

_____

    (7)   What emotion(s) does(do) the client feel and/or show pertaining to the recollection?

_____

_____

    (8)   What does the recollection suggest to you about the client's social interest?

_____

_____

    (9)   What specific needs or values are reflected in this ER?

_____

_____

D. Recurring Dream

    (1)   Who is present in the recurring dream?

_____

_____

    (2)   Who is remembered with affection?

_____

_____

    (3)   Who is disliked in the recollection?

_____

_____

    (4)   What problem(s) is(are) confronted in the recollection?

_____

_____

    (5)   What special talent(s) or ability is(are) revealed in the recollection?

_____

_____

    (6)   Is the recollection generally pleasant or unpleasant?

_____

_____

    (7)   What is the client's level of activity in the recollection?

_____

_____

    (8)   What emotion does the client feel and/or show pertaining to the recollection?

_____

_____

    (9)   What does the recollection suggest to you about the client's social interest?

_____

_____

   (10) What specific needs or values are reflected in this recurring dream?

_____

_____

   (11) Global ratings and impressions of all early memories:

_____

_____

4. Common ER Themes [pp. 108–111]

(Check all that apply and briefly describe them)

_____ dethronement (the birth of a younger sibling or another person entering who takes center stage) _____

_____ surprises _____

_____ obstacles _____

_____ affiliation _____

_____ security _____

_____ skill tasks _____

_____ dependency _____

_____ external authority _____

_____ self-control _____

_____ status _____

_____ power _____

_____ morality _____

_____ human interactions _____

_____ new situations _____

_____ excitement _____

_____ sexuality _____

_____ gender _____

_____ nurturance _____

_____ confusion _____

_____ luck _____

_____ sickness _____

_____ death _____

5. Identify core family values and your perception of how the client accepted or reject them. [pp. 92]

_____

_____

_____

6. Identify and summarize the importance of the #1 priority and the "Top Card" assets/liabilities. [pp. 104–107]

_____

_____

_____

7. Create a "force-field analysis" relative to what issues impede ("no") or amplify ("yes") relative to a possible change in this person. [pp. 188–190]

_____

_____

_____

8. "Possible Mistaken Notions" and Self-Defeating Beliefs/Behavior. [pp. 168–173]

_____

_____

_____

9. Assets/Strengths/Specific Areas to be Encouraged.

_____

_____

_____

10. Reorientation (Reframing a "perceived minus into a plus") Recommendations and Suggestions. [pp. 153–165]

_____

_____

_____

11. Future Implications of Present Lifestyle.

_____

_____

_____

(OPTIONAL)

After sharing your lifestyle summary with your client, answer the following questions:

12. What were the major "recognition reflexes" or areas of agreement by your client of your summary?

_____

_____

_____

13. What were the major disagreements? How did you handle them?

_____

_____

_____

14. What were your own issues that were brought up by your client's lifestyle? (e.g. similarities, differences, judgments, etc.) What were your own reactions to your summary?

_____

_____

_____

15. Any revisions or modifications to your original summary?

_____

_____

_____

16. Any other observations or reactions?

_____

_____

_____

17.   Any other questions and/or comments, observations?

_____

_____

_____

CONGRATULATIONS!

Summary

Reorientation has as its therapeutic goal long-term client behavior or attitude change. This chapter has explored core mistaken beliefs, and specific Adlerian counseling techniques for use in lifestyle interpretations were identified. Force-Field Analysis was presented as an example of one specific structural approach to identifying both the restraining and driving forces relative to the issue of change in one's life.

The Wisdom of Yoda

When nine hundred year old you reach,
Look as good as you will not

Wars not make one great
Adventure. Heh! Excitement. Heh!
A Jedi craves not these things.

You must unlearn what you have learned.
Try not. Do or do not. There is no try.

Luminous being are we . . . not this crude matter
That is the way of things . . .
The way of the Force.

A Jedi must have the deepest commitment,
the most serious mind.

Once you start down the dark path,
forever will dominate you, destroy, consume
you it will . . .

Beware of the dark side. Anger . . . fear
. . . aggression
You must feel the force around you.

Through the Force you will see other places.
The future . . . the past, old friends long gone

Still matter not
If you choose the quick and easy path . . .
You will become an agent of evil.

Control, control, you must learn control.
Mind what you have learned
Save you it can.

May the "Force" of lifestyle assessment be with you as an evolving "Jedi" change agent. Hopefully our book on lifestyle interventions has helped you better discover your own and your clients unique "psychological fingerprints."

Endnotes

1   Shulman, B. H., and Mosak. H. H. *Manual for Life Style Assessment.* Muncie, IN: Accelerated Development, 1988.
2   Ansbacher, H. L., and Ansbacher, R. R. (Eds.). *The Individual Psychology of Alfred Adler.* New York: Basic, 1964.
3   *Ibid.*
4   Slavik, Steven. "Presenting Social Interest to Different Lifestyles." *Individual Psychology* 51, no. 2 (1995):166–177.
5   Adler, A. *Superiority and Social Interest: A Collection of Later Writing.*, H .L. Ansbacher and R. R. Ansbacher (Eds.) New York: Norton, 1979.
6   Slavik, *op .cit.*, p. 168.
7   Bishop D. R. "Clinical aspects of denial in chemical dependency." *Individual Psychology* 47, no. 2 (1991):199–209.
8   Slavik, *op. cit.*, p. 175.
9   Shulman, B. and Mosak, H. *Manual for Lifestyle Assessment.* Muncie, IN: Accelerated Development, Inc., 1988.
10 *Ibid*
11 Kopp, R. R. "Metaphoric Expressions of Lifestyle: Exploring and Transforming Client-Generated Metaphors." *The Journal of Individual Psychology* 55, no. 4 (1999):466–473.
12 Mosak, H. "Lifestyle." In H. Mosak (ed.). *On Purpose* (pp. 183–187). Chicago: Alfred Adler Institute of Chicago, 1977.
13 Kopp, *op. cit.*, p. 467.
14 Kopp, R. R. *Metaphor Therapy: Using Client-Generated Metaphors in Psychotherapy.* New York: Brunner/Mazel, 1995: p. 104.
15 Kopp, *op. cit.*, p. 470.
16 Murphey, T. "Encouraging Client Responsibility." *Individual Psychologist* 40, no. 2 (1984): 122–132.
17 Adler, A. [1964]"Superiority and Social Interest: A Collection of Later Writings." In *The Individual Psychology of Alfred Adler.* H. L. Ansbacher and R. R. Ansbacher eds.. New York: Norton 1979; 58.
18 Powers, R. L. and Griffith, J. "Enhancing the Quality of Adlerian Life: An Assessment and Reorientation." *Individual Psychology* 52, no. 1 (1996): 333.
19 Mosak, N. "Adlerian Psychotherapy." In *Current Psychotherapies*, R. Corsini., ed. Itasca, IL: F. E. Peacock, 1979, 65.
20 From Myers, J. E., Sweeney, T. J., and Witmer, J. M. "The Wheel of Wellness Counseling for Wellness." *Journal of Counseling & Development* 78, (2000): 251–266.
21 Dreikurs, R. *Psychodynamics, psychotherapy and counseling.* Chicago: Alfred Adler Institute. 1967.
22 Dinkmeyer, D., Dinkmeyer, D., and Sperry, L. *Adlerian Counseling and Psychotherapy.* Columbus, OH: Merrill Publishing, 1987.
23 Adler, A. *What Life Should Mean to You.* A. Porter, ed. New York: Capricorn Books, 1958.
24 Carkhuff, R. *Helping and Human Relations.* Vols. 1, 11. New York: Holt, Rinehart and Winston, Inc., 1969.
25 Progoff, I. *At a Journal Workshop.* New York: Dialogue House, 1980
26 Stone, M. "Journaling with Clients." *The Journal of Individual Psychology* 54, no. 4. (1998): 537.
27 Carich, M. "Utilizing Task Assignments within Adlerian Therapy." *Individual Psychology* 46, no. 2 (1990): 217–224.
28 Nikelly, A., ed. *Techniques for Behavior Change.* Springfield, IL: Charles C Thomas, (1971: 87–89.
29 Frankl, V. *The Doctor and the Soul.* New York: Bantam Books, 1971.
30 Shulman, B. *A Comparison of Allport's and the Adlerian Concept of Lifestyle.* Chicago: Alfred Adler Institute, 1973.
31 Ivey, M.B., and Simek-Downing, L. *Consulting and Psychotherapy: Integrating Skills, Theory and Practice* (2nd ed.) 1987, p. 104. Adapted by permission of Prentice-Hall, Inc., Englewood Cliffs, New Jersey.
32 Piaget, J. "Intellectual Evaluation from Adolescence to Adulthood." *Human Development* 15 (1972): 1–12.
33 Bach, Richard. *Illusions.* New York: Dell, 1977.
34 Houston, J. *The Search for the Beloved.* Los Angeles: Jeremy Tarcher, 1984.
35 Wasserman, Dale. *Man of La Mancha* (a play) New York: Tams-Witmark Music Library, 1966.
36 Carthuff, R. The Art of Helping, 6th ed. Amherst, MA: Human Resource Development Press, 1987.
37 Nystul, M. "The Use of Motivation Modification Techniques in Adlerian Psychotherapy." *Journal of Individual Psychology 41*, no. 4 (1985): 489–494.
38 Songstegard, M., Hogerman, H. and Bitter, J. "Motivation Modification: An Adlerian Approach." *Individual Psychologist* 12 (1975): 17.
39 Adler, K. "Techniques That Shorten Psychotherapy." *Individual Psychology* 45, no.1 (1989): 62.
40 Ellis, A. *Humanistic Psychotherapy: The National Emotive Approach.* New York: Julian Press, 1973.
41 Beck, A. "Cognitive Therapy: Nature and Relation to Behavior Therapy." *Behavior Therapy* 1 (1970): 184–200.
42 Kern et al. *A Case for Adlerian Counseling.* Chicago: Alfred Adler Institute, 1978.
43 *Ibid,.* pp. 21–22
44 Manaster, G., & Corsini, R. *Individual Psychology: Theory and Practice.* New York: F. E. Peacock, 1982.
45 Lingg, M. A., & Kottman, T. "Changing Mistaken Beliefs through Visualization of Early Recollections" *Individual Psychology* 47, no. 2, 255–260.
46 Dreikurs, R., & Soltz, V. *Children: The Challenge.* New York: Hawthorn/Dutton, 1964, 15.

47 Lingg and Kottman, *op cit*,. p. 256.

48 *Ibid.*, pp. 257–258.

49 Bettner, B. L., & Lew, A. "The Connexions Focusing Technique© for Couple Therapy: A Model for Understanding Lifestyle and Complementarity in Couples." *Individual Psychology 49*, no. 3 & 4 (1993): 372–391.

50 McKay, M., Davis, M., and Fanning. *Thoughts and Feelings: The Art of Cognitive Stress Intervention*. Oakland, CA: New Harbinger Publications, Inc., 1981.

51 Copeland, M. *The Depression Workbook*. Oakland, CA: New Harbinger Publications, Inc., 1992.

52 Ibid. p. 216.

53 Nikelly, A., ed. *Techniques for Behavior Change*. Springfield, IL: Charles C Thomas, 1971.

54 Dreikurs, R. *Social Equality: The Challenge of Today*. Chicago: Regnery, 1971.

55 Allen, T. "Adlerian Interview Strategies for Behavior Change." *The Counseling Psychologist 3*, no. 1 (1971): 40–48.

56 Dreikurs, op. cit.

57 Chandler, C. "Tapping Creative Personal Power." *Individual Psychology 47*, no. 2 (1991): 222–227.

58 Ansbacher, H., and Ansbacher, R., ed. *The Individual Psychology of Alfred Adler*. New York: Harper & Row, 1964, 1967.

59 King. S. M. "Therapeutic Utilization of Client Resistance." *Individual Psychology 48*, no. 2 (1992):165–174.

60 Berne, E. (1964) *Games People Play*. New York: Ballantine.

61 King, op. cit., p. 167.

62 Dreikurs, R. *Psychodynamics, psychotherapy, and counseling*. Chicago: Alfred Adler Institute, 1967.

63 King, op. cit., p. 167.

64 Erickson, M. "The Use of Symptoms as an Integral Part of Therapy." *American Journal of Clinical Hypnosis 8*, 57–65.

65 Adler, A. *Understanding Human Nature*. New York: Fawcett, 1929a: 73.

66 Dreikurs, R. The Technique of Psychotherapy. *Chicago Medical School Quarterly*, 5, 4-7, (1994):35.

67 Adler, A. *Social Interest: A Challenge to Mankind*. London: Faber & Faber, 1938. (Original work published 1933).

68 Carpi, J. *Stress: It's Worse Than You Think*. New York: Sussex Publishers, Inc., 1996.

69 Shulman, B. *A Comparison of Allport's and the Adlerian Concept of Lifestyle*. Chicago: Alfred Adler Institute, 1973.

70 Allen, T. "Adlerian Interview Strategies for Behavior Change." *The Counseling Psychologist 3*, no. 1 (1971): 43.

71 Linden, G. W. "Excuses, Excuses!" *Individual Psychology 49*, no. 1 (1993): 1–12.

72 Ansbacher, H. and Ansbacher, R. (eds). *The Individual Psychology of Alfred Adler*. New York: Basic Books,. 1956, 297.

73 Snyder, C.R. Excuses, excuses. *Psychology Today 18*, no.9 (1984): 53.

74 Ibid., p. 55.

75 Mosak, H. *On purpose*. Chicago: Alfred Adler Institute, 1977, 104.

76 Ibid., 104–105.

77 Dreikurs, op. cit., 229–239.

78 Ibid., p. 223.

79 Ibid., p. 239.

80 Ansbacher and Ansbacher, op.cit., p. 266.

81 Powers, R. and Griffith, J. *Understanding Life Style, the Psycho-Clarity Process*. Chicago: AIAS, (1987), 124–125.

82 Ansbacher and Ansbacher, op. cit., p. 297.

83 Mosak, N. "Adlerian Psychotherapy." In *Current Psychotherapies*, ed. R. Corsini. Itasca, IL: F. E. Peacock, 1979.

84 Carich, M. "Variations of the 'As If' Technique." *Individual Psychology 45*, no. 4 (1989): 538–545.

85 O'Reilly, B., and Edgar, T. "Therapeutic Memoir Technique." *Journal of Individual Psychology 43*, no. 2 (1987): 148–159.

86 Mosak, H. "Interrupting a Depression: The Pushbutton Technique." *Individual Psychologist 41*, no. 2 (1985): 210–214.

87 Baum, L. F. *The Wizard of Oz*. New York: Schocken Books, 1900.

88 Pancner, K., and Pancner, R. "The Quest, Gurus, and the Yellow Brick Road." *Individual Psychology 44*, no. 2 (1988): 159.

89 *Ibid.*, p. 160.

90 *Ibid. ,* pp. 163–165.

91 Lovejoy, A. *Reflections on Human Nature*. Baltimore: Johns Hopkins University Press, 1961.

92 Black, C. "Changing Course." M.A.C. Publishing 1999.

93 Lewin, K. "Quasi-Stationary Social Equilibria and the Problem of Permanent Changes." In *The Planning of Change*, ed. W. G. Beanes, K. D. Benne, and R. Chin. New York: Holt, Rinehart and Winston, 1989.

94 Eckstein, D. *The Encouragement Process in Life-Span Development*. Dubuque, IA: Kendall\Hunt, 1995.

Appendix 1

Alfred Adler was an early associate of Freud in Vienna. Adler's revolutionary and forward-looking theories soon brought him into conflict with Freud, and Adler ended the association to begin his life-long research in understanding people that he called Individual Psychology. This model stresses the centrality of personal freedom, the uniqueness of the individual, the importance of the social interactions and social context for understanding behavior, and the notion of goal-oriented actions. Working with both normal and abnormal behaviors, Adler showed that behavior had both meaning and purpose and was not the result of random forces out of the individual's awareness or control. He applied his philosophical, theoretical, and conceptual model for understanding human development to a wide range of life issues including the development of emotional problems, coping with societal issues, family life, occupational and work areas, and psychotherapy.

Theorists as diverse as Karen Horney, Erich Fromm, Viktor Frankl, Abraham Maslow, Albert Ellis, and Aaron T. Beck credit Adler's work as an important basis for their own contributions. Adler's work was, in fact, the forerunner of modern psychology and has become the basis for most contemporary work including Cognitive Behavior Therapy, Constructivist Psychology, Phenomenology, Ego Psychology, Family Systems, Holistic Psychology, and Solution-Focused Therapy. Adler was one of the earliest theorists to utilize a short-term, active, focused, and problem-oriented approach to psychotherapy. Adler's work is foundational to the professions and practices of School Psychology, Guidance Counseling, the community mental health movement, and parent education.

Individual Psychology terms and concepts such as life style, inferiority complex, and social interest have entered the common vocabulary. Still active and vital, Individual Psychology continues to develop and grow with the changing needs of the times.

What is NASAP?

The North American Society of Adlerian Psychology (NASAP) was founded in 1952 under the leadership of Dr. Rudolf Driekurs. The purpose of NASAP is to advance the understanding and development of Individual Psychological principles as well as to promote the effective approaches to living based on the ideas developed and promulgated by Alfred Adler and his co-workers.

Today, NASAP exists as a meeting place for educational, psychological, psychiatric, counseling, and pastoral care professionals of diverse orientations. In addition, NASAP encourages the active and equal participation of parents, families, and community members. Through its journals, newsletters, annual conference and associated training opportunities, and local affiliate organizations, NASAP promotes Individual Psychology.

NASAP Has as Its Mission

- Encouraging research and scientific inquiry into the application of Individual Psychology.
- Expanding the availability of counseling, psychotherapy, parent education, and family enrichment programs.
- Publishing books, journals, newsletters, and other materials.
- Maintaining an Individual Psychology website (www.alfredadler.org).
- Developing a network of local and regional Individual Psychological organizations throughout the United States and Canada.
- Developing and supporting training centers and educational institutes.
- Providing networking opportunities for members and with other groups, associations, and schools of thought in psychology and education.

Benefits of Membership

- A subscription to the quarterly Journal of Individual Psychology, a scholarly journal with over 500 pages per year of articles on research practice, and applications of Individual Psychology, reports of NASAP programs and business, schedules of training activities, and general information from and about NASAP members and affiliate groups.
- Six bimonthly issues of the NASAP Newsletter, which includes articles about Individual Psychology, reports of NASAP programs and business, schedules of training activities, and general information from and about NASAP members and affiliate groups.
- Discounts on registration at the annual NASAP conference and at other workshops and training activities throughout the year.
- Discounts on NASAP produced audio and videotapes, books, and materials.
- The NASAP membership directory.
- A password for the IP Digest, NASAP's newest publication, an on-line journal that reviews international journals for articles of interest to Individual Psychologists (on-line in 2001).
- Receipt of the Adlerian magazine to be published annually.
- Periodic resource pages that appear as part of the Newsletter, written and compiled by the noted Adlerians, directly applicable to clinical and/or educational practice.
- Eligibility for the Certificate of Study in Individual Psychology after meetings educational requirements.
- Continuing professional education at the conferences and special meetings, and at the NASAP website.
- Access to biennial membership survey data.
- Eligibility to apply for the Diplomate in Adlerian Psychology.

NASAP Special Interest Sections
(Additional to membership dues)

_____ ($10.) Adlerian Counseling and Therapy serves and encourages counselors and therapists by networking and sharing Adlerian ways of working with individuals and communities.

_____ ($10.) Organization Development applies the precepts of Individual Psychology to organizations for the purposes of assessment, understanding, and intervention.

_____ ($10.) Education explores and addresses Individual Psychological theory and techniques to the specific concerns of educators and the educational environment.

_____ ($12.) Family Education provides training and resources in Individual Psychology principles that promote and encourage the development of healthy and productive relationships within family systems.

_____ ($10.) Clinicians encourages the professional development of clinicians; promotes training, knowledge, and the teaching of Individual Psychology in clinical settings; encourages dialogue with related clinical orientations. (Student membership to any division is 1/2 the member's cost)

_____ ($10.) Theory and Research promotes scientific investigation of Individual Psychological approaches to education, therapy, and effective living.

_____ Dues
_____ Section Dues
_____ Certificate
_____ Total amount paid

Office Use Only

New_____ Renewal_____ Returning_____ Student_____ Retired_____ Affiliate_____

Sections_____ ACT B/O Ed FamEd Clin T/R

*Applicants for student membership must have verifying faculty signature.

Institution_____ Faculty_____

Application (Please type or print)

Name _____
Title _____
Address _____
City _____
State/Prov. _____ Zip _____
Telephone (H) _____
Telephone (W) _____
FAX _____
E-mail _____
Occupation _____
Work Setting _____
Education _____ (Degree) _____ (Date) _____
(Institution)
_____
_____

General Membership (dues payable in USD)

	(US)	(Canada)
_____ Individual Member	$125.	$105.
_____ Student Member* **	$25.	$25.
_____ Student Journal	$20.	$20.
_____ Retired Member	$45.	$40.
_____ Family Member	$45.	$40.
_____ Affiliate Organization	$125.	$105.
_____ Associate Members	$25.	$20.
_____ Annual membership certificate	$10.	$8.

** Student membership DOES NOT include The Journal Of Individual Psychology. The Journal subscription is $20.00 (USD) per year.

Method of Payment (U.S. funds only)

_____ Check enclosed _____ Money order _____ Credit Card (see below)

Visa/MC# _____ Expiration date _____

Signature _____

Brochure courtesy of NASAP with permission

Appendix II

Work Style Assessment

Les White, Psy.D., and Linda J. Page, Ph.D.

The Work Style Assessment grew out of frustrations faced by the first author (White) in administering standard assessment tools in a career management setting. For example, instruments such as the Clinical Assessment Questionnaire (CAQ), the Sixteen Personality Factor Questionnaire (16-PF), the Flanagan Industrial Tests, the Career Orientation Placement & Evaluation Survey (COPES), the Jackson Vocational Interest Survey (JVIS), the Edwards Personal Preference Schedule (EPPS), the Occupational Stress Inventory (OSI), and even the popular Myers-Briggs Personality were composed of questions that clients considered impersonal and irrelevant to their situation. By matching clients' answers and scores with thousands of other test takers in various vocations, the purposes of many of these instruments is to narrow down vocational interests and cite job related stressors. However, White found that many of these instruments' scores and summaries were contradictory, especially when computer generated. White found that reports of these scores often confused clients, who then asked, "What does that mean?" Upon being told how their scores related to the scores of others "like them," they had trouble relating this information to the specifics of their own lives.

In hearing of this frustration, the second author (Page) suggested that part of the problem was an exclusive reliance on nomothetic instruments (See "One of a Kind" Introduction, pp. ix–xii) in career assessment. She recommended developing an idiographic assessment based on the principles of Life Style Assessment, incorporating some materials from Page's Life Style Assessment courses plus ideas from Adler,[1] Bettner and Shifron,[2] Bitter,[3] Bruhn,[4] Dreikurs,[5] Eckstein,[6] Kopp,[7] Manaster and Perryman,[8] Shulman and Mosak,[9] Nicholl,[10] Powers and Griffith,[11] Shifron,[12] Walton,[13] and White.[14] White developed and tested the WSA.

The WSA is based on the Adlerian concept of Life Style and represents a specific application of principles found elsewhere in this volume. It is directed toward the challenges presented by the work task and the work place and can be used by individual clinicians, job coaches, career counselors, and appropriately trained human resource and EAP professionals. Supervised practice of the exercises presented in this book should provide an excellent foundation for administering the WSA. The Interview (Part 1) is conducted between the client and the assessment guide[15] and takes between one and two hours to complete. The guide then uses the report templates (Parts 2-6) to organize the information in a form that can be presented to the client.

Introduction to Work Style Assessment (WSA)

---

*"Find something you love to do and
you'll never have to work another day in your life."*
— Alexander Bialywlos White, M.D.[16]

To the client:

If you are like most adults, you spend a good third of your life at work. Yet most training for work teaches you how to fit the job, rather than helping you understand your unique assets and how you may find the job that fits you. The purpose of the Work Style Assessment (WSA) is to help you approach occupation, the workplace, customers, supervisors, subordinates, and peers in ways that suit both you and them. Becoming aware of useful and useless approaches will help you understand job fit, job search, career potential, favorable and unfavorable work relationships, and consequences of behaviors. You may become more aware of your cooperative energy and the power of choice which directs that energy into better relationships with coworkers and managers. If you are in management, you can learn how to cooperate and supervise more respectfully and productively.

The person who is guiding you through this assessment is interested in helping you make more satisfying choices now and in the future. Although some questions in the interview may refer to information from your childhood, this is only to understand what kind of "baggage" you bring to your work. Once you know how your early training connects with your present career issues, you can modify, retain, or completely change it. The choice is yours.

You will first be asked a series of questions about you and how you learned about work life and working with others. Obviously, there are no right or wrong answers because you know your life better than anyone else. For that reason, the person guiding you is considered an expert only on the process of assessment, not on the content of your life. We have found that putting your expertise together with that of your **guide** makes for a very powerful and useful combination.

Between the time you answer the interview questions and your next session, your guide will come up with guesses about your work life based on the information you have given. These remain mere guesses until your second session when the guide tells you what they are and asks for your confirmation. Sometimes, these guesses may make you feel, "Yes, that's right—that's me!" Other times, you may feel nothing. In that case, the guess is probably simply incorrect, and it is your part to tell the guide so.

You might also find yourself feeling uncomfortable when your guide makes a guess. This may be because the guess has some measure of you in it, but the wording or emphasis is not quite right. In this case, please work with the guide to rephrase the guess so it feels right to you.

Discomfort may also come when the guide makes guesses about aspects of your life that you would just as soon not be aware of. It will be up to you to decide if these aspects relate to your work and should be explored despite your discomfort. If you are unwilling to delve into any aspect of your life, your guide will respect that. Please remember that your guide has been trained to focus on your strengths and successes and to set aside any tendency to make judgments or to think that he or she knows best for you. There are enough people in the world who do those things already.

After the second session where you and your guide have met to consult on the interpretation of your Work Style, the guide will organize the material into written summaries and recommendations to present to you at your third session. Even at this stage, your input is vitally important. Just because something appears in writing does not make it true or useful to you. You are invited to work with your guide to make changes in the written reports as you come to understand your work style from a new perspective.

At the end of the written reports, you and your guide will decide what to do with your new understanding. This will result in a specific Action Plan.

Here is your chance to tell your story to someone who is dedicated to helping you use that information to create a more satisfying work life.

WORK STYLE ASSESSMENT—INTERVIEW QUESTIONNAIRE

Make your answers succinct. Rather than ponder answers, it is best to answer with whatever comes quickest to mind. If necessary, use the back of the questionnaire or use other paper:

1. Name: _____

    Phone number: _____

    Address: _____

    _____

    _____

2. Regarding work and the workplace, what do you want to change?

    _____

3. What does your name mean? Or, do you ascribe any meaning to your name?

    _____

4. Do you ascribe any meaning to your birth date?

    _____

5. What did you want to be when you were growing up (i.e., personality style, activities, health, values, discipline)?

    _____

6. Succinctly describe yourself and your siblings: what each of you were like when you were growing up. (Use extra pages)

    _____

    _____

    _____

    _____

7. Siblings' ages, and occupations today:

    _____

    _____

8. Parents' occupations when you were growing up:

    _____

    _____

9. Succinctly describe your parents: what each was like when you were growing up:

_____

_____

10. How did your parents resolve differences? Your role in this?

_____

_____

11. Your partner's age and occupation.

_____

_____

Partner's relationship with his siblings and parents, and their occupations. How do you fit in with your partner's family and/or compare to their work and career values?

_____

_____

_____

_____

12. How was school for you while growing up?

_____

_____

13. What classes did you like? Teachers?

_____

_____

14. What classes did you not like? Teachers?

_____

_____

15. Did you have any role models when you were growing up? Did you form alliances with anyone or with any groups? Was there anyone you did not want to be like?

_____

_____

16. Three Early Recollections (Minimum of):
    a.

    Age: _____

    Most vivid moment: _____

    Feeling (at that moment): _____

    Consequence of this behavior/situation: _____

b.

Age: _____

Most vivid moment: _____

Feeling (at that moment): _____

Consequence of this behavior/situation: _____

c.

Age: _____

Most vivid moment: _____

Feeling (at that moment): _____

Consequence of this behavior/situation: _____

17. Extra Recollection (from any age):

Age: _____

Most vivid moment: _____

Feeling (at that moment): _____

Consequence of this behavior: _____

18. Most Memorable Observation

_____

_____

_____

The following question is modified from Walton's (1998) question regarding parenting style. Here the question is used to get an idea as to whether the client used any conscious "decisions" in forming his/her belief system. As modified, the question asked here respects Frankl's idea that to be fulfilled, man must consciously search for or decide meaning.

It seems very common for each of us to look at our life and draw a conclusion about some aspect of it that appears to be important. Sometimes it is positive, like "I really like this aspect of life. I'd like it to be just this way." Sometimes it is negative, like "I don't like this at all. This is really distasteful. I am going to do everything I can to keep this from occurring." What was it for you? As you think of your life—at any age—what conclusions do you think you drew? They may have been positive, negative, or it may have been both. What conclusion do you think you've drawn—any moments that come back to you?

19. If you did not have the work/career issues or concerns that you currently do, what do you think you would be or could be doing?

WSA Administration and Interpretation

To you who will guide the assessment:

Step I: **Administer WSA Interview Questionnaire**

The interview is comprised of questions that elicit information about the client's values, influences, and evaluations of those influences. Although it is recommended that you ask the questions to the client, the interview questionnaire may be completed by a client on his/her own time. The interview typically takes between one and two hours to complete.

Step II: **Guess meaning of data from interview**

Between the interview and the next appointment, you will examine the data regarding the following themes. Your answers to the questions below represent guesses on your part.[17] To qualify as legitimate, any guess should be supported by at least two data points.[18] Please note that suggested WSA questions are those considered most likely to relate to each theme. However, relevant data may come from any of the other questions.

- **Overall Impressions**, especially WSA questions 2, 3, 4, 18, 19: What meaning does the client give to self, others, and the workplace? What choices have been made or avoided regarding career?

    Example 1: Consider Mr. A, a Caucasian male in his 40s. Despite an Ivy League MBA degree, his work record, mostly in the banking and financial fields, was spotty. He chose these fields because they were the fields the "movers" and shakers" chose, that is, this is what he felt was expected of him. The objective tests showed, perhaps because of his obvious high intelligence, that he was interested in nearly every field offered: sciences, arts, leisure, and so forth. How could the WSA help him? Though he was not working at the time of assessment, he reported (question 2) that what he would like to have changed about his previous assignments was their general lack of social encounters. To question 3 (What does your name mean?), which often reveals the identity one is trying to project, or live up to or "down" to, Mr. A noted that his name reflected his family's heritage, wealth, and "pedigree." In response to question 18 (Most Memorable Observation), which "pulls" for how a client wants life to be or not to be, Mr. A reported a time at summer camp when he was taken with the simplicity of the dwellings and directed others in trying to build one. In response to question 19 (If you did not have the work/career issues or concerns that you currently do, what do you think you would be or could be doing?), Mr. A revealed his desire to explore architectural and design issues. Overall, Mr. A's answers revealed that he feels he must assume a "kingly" stance to be true to his heritage, although he doesn't actually see himself that way. It was suggested that he become a rehabber or developer of homes, directing others in useful pursuit, having contact with clients to discuss artistic, design ideas. Mr. A revealed that he always wanted to follow such a route but considered it not "lofty" enough. The WSA helped him recognize how he could better pursue an occupation that suited him rather than the expectations of others. It helped him decide on a goal to pursue, one that he felt comfortable in pursuing. It provided the support he needed.

    Example 2: Mrs. B perceived herself as a "pleaser." The objective tests reflected that she was "Artistic." She revealed that her name, when translated into English, meant "flower" (question 2). She revealed in questions 6-10 that as a youngest child, not only in her family but in the neighborhood, she was given the grungy, dirty, clean up work. About life, she concluded (question 18) that she expected and didn't dislike this position. Her attitude was that, after all, somebody has to do it. When asked what she could be doing if she were not feeling discouraged in her job as a computer programmer, she revealed her love of gardening. A more useful career for her to pursue might be one that involved horticulture or landscaping: providing beauty and a service for others.

Example 3: Mr. C had trouble keeping a steady job. He had worked mostly in labor intensive but short-term jobs like construction. At the time of his assessment, Mr. C was working in a shipping office of a company that had just declared bankruptcy. Objective vocational instruments revealed that he showed average ability and interest in just about any field. Although he did not ascribe any meaning to his name or to his birth date (question 2), Mr. C admired the history of a wanderlust grandfather from his father's side of the family. As to conclusions he had drawn from life (question 18), he felt that others discouraged him from his true love, fishing and exploring. To question 19 (If you did not have the work/career issues or concerns that you currently do, what do you think you would be or could be doing?), he spoke of his love of athletics and the outdoors. He also related that he admired other members of his family who had gone into the teaching profession, but he did not want to go through all the necessary requirements. He jumped at the idea, based on his WSA-answers, that he consider becoming a camp counselor a wilderness training guide, or a parks employee. He suggested that he would probably like to be a tour guide.

Example 4: Although most clients answer "no" to question 4 (Do you ascribe any meaning to your birth date?), some reveal in this answer the special place they perceive they hold in the universe. A child of a Holocaust survivor, Mr. D was born on the tenth anniversary of Hitler's suicide. The WSA helped him to see himself as an advocate for the disenfranchised.

Example 5: Ms E did not think of her birth date as special at all. She remembered a birthday party at which she received an unwanted gift. She also related that she felt she would never obtain a job that was meaningful to her. Despite two Masters degrees, she was constantly taking low paid, clerk-type assistant's work. She said she had concluded that it was best not to speak up for her rights because others, she felt, did not understand her (question 18—Most Memorable Observation). Always a top student, she revealed that if she could, she would teach English to foreigners (question 19—If you did not have the work/career issues or concerns that you currently do, what do you think you would be or could be doing?). It seemed obvious to the assessment guide that Ms E could happily and ardently pursue teaching English as a foreign language and be useful to others. In this, she could make herself and others be heard and understood. However, the WSA also indicated Ms E's biggest obstacle—the discouragement that she had unwittingly reinforced by looking only for assistant, clerk type roles. It took some encouragement on the assessment guide's part to help her recognize and believe the answer she herself had given!

- **Work Environments and Atmosphere**, especially question 5 through 12: How did the values of the family and early issues regarding learning, performance, and persistence impact the client's choice of careers, career fit, and approaches to the workplace?

  Example 1: Mrs. F rebelled against the family value that saw men as authority figures and women as stay-at-home moms. Consequently, she found it difficult to work in environments she viewed as traditional.

Example 2: Ms G reported that her parents argued all the time. She perceived the family atmosphere as stormy. She would "hide" when she came home from school. Consequently, Ms G perceived most work environments as battle fields similar to her home environment. She preferred to isolate herself from others and evade the work task.

Example 3: Mr. H related that the family tradition meant going into the family business and going along with whatever the oldest male or male authority figure wanted. Consequently, Mr. H was bitter and depressed. He worked at "half-speed," expecting his opinion not to matter.

- **Getting a Sense of Belonging in the Workplace**, especially questions 5 through 12: How does the client's relationships with siblings influence her/his work style and behavior toward coworkers, supervisors, and subordinates? These questions generally refer to how clients made themselves significant or wanted to make themselves significant in their early years, compared to others, and whether they are still able to make such arrangements today. Current successes or failures of clients' siblings, as well as how clients currently view their standing relative to their partners' and partners' family of origin, indicates how close clients are to reaching the goals they set for themselves and whether they see themselves as inferior/discouraged or superior.

  Example 1: Ms I, a middle child, felt she lagged behind the rest of her family. Her mother died when she was a young girl. Her father was a taskmaster. Her siblings outperformed her. They were tops in academics and athletics and discouraged her interests in weaving and dressmaking. Now married, she related that her husband and his siblings were all tops in their scientific fields. She felt that she did not belong anywhere. She drifted from clerk job to clerk job. It was not difficult to encourage Ms I to take classes in fashion design.

  Example 2: Mr. C, the youngest of three boys, modeled what he thought were the best of their behaviors. He did not consider himself a "third wheel." A bass player, he could always be counted on to "keep the rhythm." He found himself discouraged when, in his thirties, he felt he had to lead and prove himself by being a boss. He was better at making sure procedures were followed than at making procedures.

  Example 3: Mr. J grew up as second oldest but only boy in a family of three children. When he was just entering adolescence, his older sister became a drug addict. Mr. J "leapfrogged" over her and became overly responsible to the family value of "do your best." Mr. J developed a pattern of taking on too many responsibilities and consequently "burning out."

- **Planfulness**, especially questions 3, 5, 18, and 19: What are the client's likes, dislikes, and expectations regarding career? Planfulness is based on the concept of "Planful Problem-Solving," which is defined as "deliberate (rational, cognitively-oriented) effort to change or escape the situation"[19] As used in the WSA, planfulness takes into account the Adlerian concepts of self-determination and teleology, especially in the area of career. It is important to consider how clients have "reached" or "not reached" the identities they feel expected to live up to (question 3); their long-standing interests or types of career they saw themselves in (question 5); the conclusions they have drawn about life (question 18); and which sorts of activities they feel could contribute to their feeling more satisfied (question 19). Thus, these questions help to ascertain whether clients have reached their goals or, if not, how far "afield" have they gone in their current occupations or studies. Answers to these questions often give clues as to those activities in which clients encouraged themselves early in their lives, but which were discouraged later by others. Question 5 is especially telling. Asking clients what they wanted to become shows how close or far they are in achieving that dream.

Example 1: Mr. K wanted to be a comedian or actor. His parents were aghast. Such professions offer little stability, they insisted. Indeed, he found that success on the circuit was always just beyond his reach. Though he excelled when poking fun at dating and family foibles, he received rejection notice after rejection notice. He took up his father's advice to try the financial field and became a commodities trader. Despite high intelligence and some success, it was not to his liking. Mr. K was encouraged to pursue theater in his off times and to prepare to become a teacher and/or marriage and family counselor. Teachers are constantly on stage. Counselors are alert to the foibles of others. Audiences composed of students do not leave. His gift for the comic practically ensures his relating to others.

Example 2: Dr. L, an internist, reported having always wanted to be a scientist or a doctor. A survivor of the Holocaust, the only survivor of his family, the war interrupted his education at age 13. After the war, he demonstrated planfulness by trading in his Red Cross rations for tutoring in order to take university entrance exams.

Example 3: Ms E gave up planning for the long term. Her father died when she was a child. She and her mother, a taskmaster, went to live with relatives. She felt that she was always treated as an unwanted guest. She felt that she could not depend on others. Nothing seemed permanent, so why try? Though she was fluent in several languages and had once hoped to be a language teacher—giving voice to others—she pursued temporary jobs. She was encouraged to obtain a teaching certificate in order to teach language.

- **Expectations, Choice, Consequences**, especially questions 16 and 17: Our specific memories from childhood (known as Early Recollections) have the purpose of reminding us what is most important about life. How do these convictions relate to the client's experiences with work, the workplace, coworkers, managers, and subordinates? The WSA asks for three Early Recollections (ERs). Putting a limit on the number of ERs prompts clients to succinctly edit their own lives and relate what is of prime importance. Asking for an "Extra" recollection after eliciting the three "major" ones is useful because sometimes the Extra recollection reflects what the client has been "holding back" and/or how the client has responded or would respond differently to similar stimuli. (Because the three ERs asked for first often "say it all," it is not unusual for a client not to relate an Extra recollection.)

Example 1: Ms E's first three ERs centered on people dying or not attending to her. She showed little confidence in her abilities, expected others to be even less sure of her abilities, despite two Masters degrees. Her work life could best be summed up as "Chicken Little" running from job to job. Her work record was spotty. She felt others made fun of her. She expected to fail and, consistent with her expectations, she did. Temporary jobs ensured instability. In her Extra recollection, she got up the courage to leave her front yard, but "chickened out" at the last moment. This reflected that she had the ability to plan but needed encouragement to grow.

Example 2: Mr. M was unhappy with his work as an attorney. He saw himself as a corporate pawn. High powered and highly paid, he represented large corporations against little, individual shareholders whose law suits he felt often were legitimate but which he was expected to crush. In his ERs, he felt left out and not invited to join the big older boys unless he was in costume (for example, for Halloween). Keeping up appearances and pleasing his high pressured bosses were of prime importance to him. Such actions offered him status. Every one of his ERs took place on a street, the name of which also was the name of an anti-trust monopoly bill. In the only recollection that he evaluated as being happy, he was creating playthings for other children in the neighborhood. Though Mr. M related that he would like to use his knowledge of corporate politics to represent the unfortunate, he feared the loss of prestige and income. He was encouraged to find a powerful firm that helped the little guy.

Example 3: Mr. N related ERs in which women appreciated him for any activity he undertook. Consequently, he found he gets along better with female managers.

Example 4: Dr. O remembered being sickly as a child. Authority figures forced him to undergo painful treatments for his skin rashes. He became a dermatologist.

Example 5: Dr. L recollected that women, especially his mother and grandmother, encouraged his elementary school studies, whereas male teachers debated his ideas. He now finds himself seeking out female assistants and battling male co-workers.

Example 6: Ms P, a nurse, related ERs in which she (1) wondered which door of a house to enter, (2) rode on the handle bars of a bike steered by a male, then (3) wondered why she could not swim one day when she was an expert swimmer. Ms P found that she worked best in highly structured environments.

- **The Creative Self**, especially questions 16, 17, and 18: How has the client used his/her creativity to conform to or rebel against the "status quo"? What strengths does this reveal? Clients' answers often give clues as to activities that they liked, were praised for, felt competent accomplishing or would like to try but perceived discouragement or a loss of status if pursued. Often, a client feels that ideas are not adult-like.

  Example 1: Growing up, Mr. H liked to explore his neighborhood. He gave extremely detailed stories about himself and his family, and his conclusions about life were very visual and documentary-like. He felt an obligation to enter the family's very structured retail business, but reported that he would like to be a photojournalist.

  Example 2: Mr. Q remembered the fascination he had watching bakers bake bread once when he was on vacation. He perceived that his father discouraged him, remembering that his father said that bakers and restaurant owners never have time off. Now, 23, Mr. Q feels he does not have a work identity. He has bounced in and around four different colleges. Friends of his are now graduating. After he related that his favorite pastime was to cook for friends, Mr. Q was encouraged to pursue culinary school.

  Example 3: In Mr. R's recollections, disastrous circumstances—car crashes, deaths, and so forth—happened after playing with his younger siblings, reaching out to others, and swimming. He concluded that he was not allowed to have fun, that he must struggle for any sense of hope or accomplishment. He reported wanting to help others and was encouraged to think about social work in order to be an advocate for those who have suffered losses.

- **Best Fit re: Job, Supervisors, Coworkers**, all questions: How can the client use the knowledge of her/his strengths to determine a "best fit" job, workplace, position, and atmosphere. As evidenced by the examples given, clients often remember or know which activities are encouraging to them and they would like to pursue and which would positively engage others. However, they often are hampered by the idea that they do not measure up. Recognizing when clients felt that they contributed most and were most accepted by others is often the clue to best job fit.

Example 1: Mrs. B, now working with computers, may feel more encouraged if she directed others in helping them design gardens and landscaping.

Example 2: Ms E, who felt that no one listened to her growing up, may feel more of a connection with the human race if she were to teach foreign languages.

Example 3: Mr. A could feel important in contributing his design sense to building or rehabbing homes.

Whereas the objective vocational tests may help narrow down areas of interests, the WSA can help to better pinpoint a goal or goals the client already has the motivation to strive towards.

Step III: Confirm Guesses with Client

In your second meeting with the client, offer the guesses you develop in Step II above.[20] Focus on strengths. Remember that the client is the expert on the content of his or her life. You are in charge only of the process. Work with the client to confirm, reject, or modify any guesses. Only after this process may the guesses be considered valid interpretations. If the client does not wish to explore any aspect of this, please respect her/his wishes.

Step IV: Summarize and Develop Recommendations

Before your third meeting with the client, you will organize the interpretations from Step III into a series of written summaries that comprise the remaining sections of the Work Style Assessment:

WSA Summary 1: Influences, Values, and Mentorship

Roughly corresponding to the Summary of Early Training in a Life Style Inventory, this section includes those values and beliefs that a client has perceived as influential, and which that client might have adopted or questioned. It provides information about how the client has striven to make him/herself significant in connection and comparison to others. Filling in the blanks in the following template may help in preparing this summary:

Client sees self as _____ (leader, communicator, etc.). (Corresponds with birth order, psychological vantage position)

Client expects environment/management to be _____ (what client perceives to be best/worst about the workplace). (Corresponds to family atmosphere, how conflicts tended to be resolved in family-of-origin)

Client expects mentorship and supervision to stress _____.

(Corresponds to masculine and feminine guiding lines)

Client makes self useful or not useful in the workplace by _____. Compared to others, client _____. (Client's Sense of Belonging/Psychological Vantage)

Client's perceptions of others in the workplace is _____. He perceives co-workers as _____. He perceives supervisors as _____. (Sibling Order/Sense of Belonging/Psychological Vantage; co-workers; also mentors and supervision; working relations)

Client perceives ideal occupation and/or work environment as _____. (Role Models/Alliances; ideal occupation; also mentorship, supervision, working relations)

Good occupational fits for client entails _____. (Childhood experiences; School; Early Learning)

Client has thus far answered, or not answered, the question or challenge of work by _____. (Question remaining/Issues still confronting, pressing)

WSA Summary 2: Evaluation of Work and Workplace

As in the Summary of Present-Day Convictions in the Life Style Inventory, this section considers how a client is currently evaluating his/her experiences and, in accordance with these evaluations, how that client is responding to the challenges of work, relationships with others, and expectations of the self. It is future-oriented and shows the client's current direction and/or plan and the stance that the client has been "rehearsing" to meet challenges. The following template may be of assistance in preparing this summary:

Work is be _____. It should be _____.

I tend to approach it/respond to it (by, in, etc.) _____.

Supervisors are/should be _____.

I tend to approach them/respond to them _____.

Coworkers are/should be _____.

I tend to approach them/respond to them by _____.

In order to have a place at work/the world of work/fit in , I tend to _____.

I tend to work best in atmospheres that _____, and worst in atmospheres that _____.

All in all, my role at work tends to be that of the _____ .[21]

WSA Summary 3: Attributes and Misconceptions

Behaviors and perceptions both help and hinder a client in the achievement of positive career goals. Like the Assets and Interfering Ideas of a Life Style Summary, conclusions about life tend to have both positive and negative aspects. In fact, people often create problems for themselves by applying their strengths in situations that are inappropriate. (Example: Insisting on being in control doesn't work in a situation that calls for relaxed sociability and spontaneity, but it is crucial where good organization is required.) Attributes can be capitalized on and misconceptions can be shifted through awareness.

LIST ATTRIBUTES AND MISCONCEPTIONS

This summary may be developed from interpretations of past successes and failures. If you have difficulty listing attributes and misconceptions, or if you wish to check further on the validity of your interpretations, you may find it helpful to guide the client through the following sentence-completion exercise modified from one developed by Leo Lobl. Ask the client to apply the exercise to any problematic response she or he has had at work:

1. The bad part about responding this way is _____.

2. I never thought of this before, but if there is a good part to responding this way, it might be _____.

3. In a paradoxical way, arranging to respond this way protects me in that as long as I am responding this way _____.

4. Maybe I wouldn't respond this way if only _____.

5. What I am becoming aware of as a result of this exercise is _____.

WSA Summary 4: Work Approach

The consequences of the client's convictions result in a particular style of psychological movement. This summary combines a focus on current, pressing issues as well as summarizing how one's style has worked in the past and why now it may not be working to the client's satisfaction now. The following template may be of help in developing this summary:

I expect work/supervisors/co-workers to be _____. However, my experience is that work/supervisors/co-workers are _____. This prompts me to feel _____ , and therefore I _____.

Step V: Deliver Summaries and Recommendations to client

Often, clients find it most effective when you give them a copy of the WSA Summaries and then read them aloud. Remember that, even at this stage, the client may suggest modifications to the Summaries.

WSA Action Plan

This section is completed by the guide and client after the Summaries have been presented and discussed. In order achieve satisfaction, build competence, and enhance self-esteem at work, the client must take action that is informed by his or her new-found understanding. Repeat the following template for as many actions as the client is willing to commit to.

In order to _____ , I will _____ by this date: _____.

The WSA now serves as basis for implementing the Action Plan in a career counseling or management setting or in therapy.

An example of a completed WSA from the first author's practice is presented below:

Work Style Assessment Summaries and Action Plan—Case Example: Mr. Z

1. Influences, Values, and Mentorship Summary

   Client sees self as an ideas man. He seeks recognition by virtue of tradition—that it should be bestowed on him simply because of who he is and how good his ideas are.

   Client expects environment/management to be fun, not rigid—unstructured, exciting, and creative.

   Client expects mentorship and supervision to stress fun, creativity, and be very caring toward him.

   Client makes himself useful or not useful in the workplace by being creative, but also by perceiving that rules do not especially apply to him. Compared to others, client sees himself as being special and above the ordinary details of a job.

   He also feels that he has not found his place in the work arena.

   Client's perception of others in the workplace is that, although he accepts them, they need direction and should serve him. He perceives co-workers as "commoners," followers to carry out the details. He perceives supervisors as rigid, constricting, and pressuring him to achieve.

   Good occupational fits for client include those in which he can feel that he is the "boss," for example, museum administrator/curator, foundation director, fundraiser. The leisure industry may appeal to him, for example as a manager of a hotel or a cruise director.

   Client has thus far answered, or not answered, the "question" or challenge of work by continuing to dream and wonder "what am I going to do when I grow up?" He feels under pressure to take his place as one of the "officers" in society. He may prefer to play the "game" rather than commit to a career from fear that he may not achieve or be as successful as he feels he should be.

2. Evaluation of Work and Workplace Summary

   Work is constricting. It should be exciting, adventurous.

   I tend to approach it/respond to it in "starts and stops," starting, losing interest, and then moving on.

   Supervisors should be fun and not pressuring, "hands off" though catering to my needs. I tend to approach them/respond to them by expecting them to see to my needs.

   Coworkers are/should not only be amusing, interesting, and supportive, they should be the ones to carry out my ideas and plans. I tend to approach them/respond to them by socializing, bringing my ideas to them, and having high expectations of them.

   In order to have a place at work/the world of work/fit in, I tend to show people how refined I am, create things to do. However, currently, I feel "impotent" in this area.

   I tend to work best in atmospheres that are diverse, give me freedom to create and be appreciated, and worst in atmospheres that are repetitive, confining, and demanding.

   All in all, client's role at work tends to be that of the dabbler and "harvester."

3. Attributes and Misconceptions Summary

His role as dabbler and "harvester" means he is flexible and can move quickly from one activity or project to another. It also means he can see and take advantage of opportunities when they present themselves. On the other hand, he may have trouble identifying and concentrating on priorities. He may also be discouraged about contributing to others or to the job at hand.

His attributes include being creative and enjoying creativity and excitement, and wanting being able to engage in a diversity of activity. Client perceives ideal occupation and/or work environment as free-flowing, a place where he can be creative and free of details or rules that will make him feel constricted.

His misconceptions include expecting others to see to his needs. He therefore does not include them in a discussion of his ideas.

Past difficulties with supervisors and coworkers may be related to this aversion to constrictions, as well as to his not seeing himself as contributing to others.

4. Work Approach Summary

Client expects supervisors and coworkers to be fun and supportive of his creativity, no questions asked. However, his experience is that they are constricting and do not see to his needs. Thus, he is prompted to feel angry and to show others how important/superior he is. Inside, however, he feels impotent.

Action Plan

- In order to increase the likelihood of using my creativity and not feel so constricted on a job, I will contact at least one cruise ship company, one tour guide company, and one museum to arrange information interviews by two weeks from today.

- In order to demonstrate to myself that I have something to contribute to others, I will volunteer to help in one Children's Wish Foundation activity by two weeks from today.

Summary

The Work Style Assessment is presented as a useful tool in a career management, human relations, or workplace setting. It represents an idiographic assessment that can lend balance to the nomothetic tools common in such settings. The WSA is also an example of how the principles of Life Style Assessment, once mastered, can be modified and applied to help people in various specific situations identify their strengths, their goals, and how to remove barriers to achieving their full potential.

The authors hope that readers of this volume will consider the WSA to be a work in progress. Questions and comments should be directed to either author.[22]

Authors

Linda J. Page, Ph.D., directs the Adler School of Professional Psychology's M.A. in Counseling Psychology program in Toronto. She is President of Adler Professional Schools Inc. and the Adler School of Professional Coaching Inc. and served as a core doctoral faculty member at the Adler School of Professional Psychology in Chicago from 1992 to 1997. She received her Ph.D. in Sociology, specializing in cultural anthropology and sociolinguistics, from Princeton University in 1973.

She then completed her M.A. in Counseling Psychology at Adler and is a Licensed Clinical Professional Counselor in the State of Illinois. Linda enjoys her grandchildren, her dogs, teaching, and helping students reach their full potential.

Les White received his Psy.D. from the Adler School of Professional Psychology in Chicago. His work with forensic clients, the severely mentally ill, and males who had been discouraged from pursuing their interests and entering the work force prompted his interest in psychological strengths, the creative uses of Life Style, and how individuals approach the challenge of work. His dissertation, "Life Style Variables of Holocaust Survivors Who Became Successful," statistically identified those qualities common to a group of Holocaust survivors who, having faced great hardship, later achieved great success in the workplace. In response to the widely used vocational instruments that clients complained did not capture nor focus on the uniqueness of the individual, White co-developed the WSA (WSAIQ) to provide a more helpful, individual and holistic vocational assessment. In addition to his clinical and research work, White is interested in theater and film. He has taught film and psychology, and is a past recipient of a New York Dramatists Guild award, an Illinois Arts Council grant, a Chicago International Film Festival award, and an Illinois Filmmaker award.

Endnotes

[1] Ansbacher, H. L., & Ansbacher, R. R. (1964). *The Individual Psychology of Alfred Adler*. NY: Harper & Row

[2] Bettner, B. L., & Shifron, R. (1999, August). The crucial "cs", creativity and addictions. Presentation conducted at the International Association of Individual Psychology, 21st International Congress, Chicago, IL.

[3] Bitter, J. (1999, May). Brief Therapy. Presentation conducted at the North American Society of Adlerian Psychology, annual meeting, Atlanta, GA.

[4] Bruhn, A. R. (1990). Earliest childhood memories volume 1: Theory and application to clinical practice. NY: Praeger.

[5] Dreikurs, R. (1995). Dreikurs sayings. Stuttgart: Horizonte Verlag GmbH., Dubuque, IA: Kendall/Hunt.

[6] Eckstein, D., Baruth, L., & Mahrer, D. (1978). Lifestyle: What it is and how to do it. Dubuque, IA: Kendall/Hunt.

[7] Kopp, R. R. (1986). Styles of striving for significance with and without Social Interest: An Adlerian typology. Individual Psychology: The Journal of Adlerian Theory, Research & Practice, 42, 17-25.

[8] Manaster, G. J., & Perryman, T. B. (1974). Early recollections and occupational choice. Journal of Individual Psychology, 30, 232-237.

[9] Shulman, B. H., & Mosak, H. H. (1988). Manual for life style assessment. Bristol, PA: Accelerated Development.

[10] Nicholl, W. G. (1999, May). Brief Therapy. Presentation conducted at the North American Society of Adlerian Psychology, annual meeting, Atlanta, GA.

[11] Powers, R. L., & Griffith, J. (1987). Understanding lifestyle: The psycho-clarity process. Chicago: The Americas Institute of Adlerian Studies, Ltd..

[12] Shifron, R. (1999, August). Early Recollections and Vocational Training. Presented at International Committee of Adlerian Summer Schools and Institutes.

[13] Walton, F. X. (1999). Use of the most memorable observation as a technique for understanding choice of parenting style. The Journal of Individual Psychology, 54, 487-494.

[14] White, L. E. (2001). Life Style Variables of Holocaust Survivors who became Successful. Unpublished doctoral dissertation, Adler School of Professional Psychology, Chicago.

[15] Because the Work Style Assessment is designed to be used widely by career management professionals, workplace coaches, human relations specialists, etc., rather than being limited to clinical psychologists and counselors, the term "assessment guide" is used to refer to the person administering the WSA.

[16] Personal Communication, 2000.

[17] This is consistent with the requirement of triangulation as outlined in the Introduction to this volume (page xi).

[18] Example: Data point 1, from Question 4—Older brother was hardworking. I was fun-loving and social. Data point 2, from Question 10—In school, I was more interested in having friends than doing my homework. Guess: Could it be that you find it easier to work in a relaxed setting where people are friendly rather than in a workplace where you are expected to "drive" yourself?

[19] Suedfeld, P., Krell, R. , Wiebe, R. E., & Steel, G. D. (1997). Coping strategies in the narratives of Holocaust survivors. Anxiety, stress, and coping (pp. 153-179). Amsterdam: Harwood Academic Publishers.

[20] This is consistent with the requirement of iteration as outlined in the Introduction to this volume (pages xi–xii).

²¹ Recognizing that people can achieve the same goal in either encouraged, socially interested ways, or in discouraged, socially useless ways, Richard Kopp developed the following typology (for each goal, the discouraged style is listed first and the socially interested style is listed second):

Goal: Morality, achieved by being either moralizer or conscience.
Goal: Fairness, achieved by being either victim/martyr or advocate.
Goal: Independence, achieved by being either opposer or individualist.
Goal: Knowledge, achieved by being either know-it-all or resource
Goal: Achievement, achieved by being either driver or achiever
Goal: Order, achieved by being either controller or organizer
Goal: Acquisition, achieved by being either getter or harvester
Goal: Evaluation, achieved by being either critic-judge or sounding board
Goal: Peace, achieved by being either pleaser or diplomat

²² 2 Les White: Adler School of Professional Psychology, 65 E. Wacker Place, Suite 2100, Chicago, IL, 60601, telephone 312-201-5900, email lesw@21stcentury.net; Linda J. Page: Adler Professional Schools, 48 St. Clair Ave. W., Suite 1000, Toronto, ON M4V 3B6, telephone 416-923-4419, email ljpage@adler.ca.

Appendix III

Birth Order Studies Bibliography

1. Adams, B. N. (1972). Birth-order: A critical review. *Sociometry, 35,* 411–439.

2. Adler, A. (1964). *Problems of neurosis: A book of case histories.* New York: Harper & Row.

3. Allred, H., & Poduska, B. (1988). Birth order and happiness. *Journal of Individual Psychology, 44(3),* 346–354.

4. Altus, W. D. (1965). Birth order and academic primogeniture. *Journal of Personality and Social Psychology, 2,* 872–876.

5. Altus, W. D. (1966). Birth order and its sequelae. *Science, 151,* 44–49.

6. Altus, W. D. (1967). Birth order and its sequence. *International Journal of Psychiatry, 3,* 23–31.

7. Angelini, H. B. (1969). Family structure and motivation to achieve. *Revista Interamericana de Psicologia, 1,* 115–125.

8. Ansbacher, H. L., & Ansbacher, R. R. (Eds.) (1956). *The Individual Psychology of Alfred Adler.* New York: Basic Books.

9. Babladelis, G. (1972). Birth order and responsiveness to social influence. *Psychological Reports, 30,* 99–104.

10. Bahr, H. M. (1971). Birth order and failure: The evidence from skid row. *Quarterly Journal of Studies on Alcohol, 32,* 669–686.

11. Bakan, D. (1949). The relationship between alcoholism and birth rank. *Quarterly Journal of Studies of Alcohol, 10,* 434–400.

12. Baker, F., & O'Brien, G. M. (1969). Birth order and fraternity affiliation. *Journal of Social Psychology, 78,* 41–43.

13. Barry, H., III, & Barry, H., Jr. (1971). Birth order of psychiatric patients. *Nature, 231,* 57.

14. Barry, H., III, & Barry, H., Jr. (1967). Birth order, family size, and schizophrenia. *Archives of General Psychiatry, 17,* 435–440.

15. Bayer, A. E. (1967). Birth order and attainment of the doctorate: A test of economic hypotheses. *American Journal of Sociology, 72,* 540–550.

16. Becker, S. W., Lerner, M. J., & Carroll, J. (1966). Conformity as a function of birth order and type of group pressure: A verification. *Journal of Personality and Social Psychology, 3,* 242–244.

17. Belmont, L. (1977). Birth order intellectual competence, and psychiatric status. *Journal of Individual Psychology, 33,* 97–104.

18. Belmont, L., & Marolia, F. A. (1973). Birth order, family size, and intelligence. *Science, 182,* 1096–1101.

19. Belmont, L., Stein, Z. A., & Susser, M. W. (1975). Comparison of associations of height with intelligence test score. *Nature, 225,* 54–56.

20. Bigner, J. J. (1972). Sibling influence on sex-role preference. *Journal of Genetic Psychology, 121,* 271–282.

21. Blane, H. T., & Barry, H., III. (1973). Birth order and alcoholism: A review. *Quarterly Journal of Studies on Alcohol, 34,* 837–852.

22. Blane, H. T., & Barry, H., III. (1975). Sex of siblings of male alcoholics. *Archives of General Psychiatry, 32,* 1403–1405.

23. Bliss, W. D. (1970). Birth order of creative writers. *Journal of Individual Psychology, 26,* 200–202.

24. Blossard, J. H. S. (1956). *The large family system: An original study in the sociology of family behavior.* Philadelphia: University of Pennsylvania Press.

25. Breland, H. M. (1974). Birth order, family configuration and verbal achievement. *Child Development, 45,* 1011–1019.

26. Breland, H. M. (1977). Family configuration and intellectual development. *Journal of Individual Psychology, 33,* 86–96.

27. Brink, R., & Matlock, F. (1982). Nightmares and birth order. *Journal of Individual Psychology, 38(1),* 47–49.

28. Bryant, B. (1987). Birth-order as a factor in the development of vocational preference. *Journal of Individual Psychology, 43(1),* 56–58.

29. Burnand, G. (1973). Birth order and autobiography. *Journal of Individual Psychology, 29,* 35–38.

30. Chapman, A. J., & Speck, L. J. (1977). Humorous laughter and relief of anxiety in first-born children. *Journal of Individual Psychology, 33,* 37–41.

31. Chen, E., & Cobb, S. (1960). Family structure in relation to health and disease. *Journal of Chronic Diseases, 12,* 544–567.

32. Claudy, J. G. (1976). *Cognitive characteristics of the only child.* Paper presented at the 84th Annual Convention of the American Psychological Association, Washington, DC.

33. Clausen, J. A. (1966). Family structure, socialization, and personality. In L. W. Hoffman & M. L. Hoffman (Eds.), *Review of child development research.* New York: Russell Sage Foundation.

34. Claxton, R. P. (1994). Empirical relationships between birth order and two types of parental feedback. *The Psychological Record, 44,* 475–487.

35. Collard, R. (1968). Social and play responses of first born and later born infants in an unfamiliar situation. *Child Development, 39,* 325–334.

36. Conners, C. K. (1963). Birth order and needs of affiliation. *Journal of Personality, 31,* 409–416.

37. Coopersmith, S. (1967). *The antecedents of self esteem.* San Francisco: Freeman.

38. Corfield, V. K. (1968). The utilization of guidance clinic facilities in Alberta. *Alberta Psychologist, 9,* 15–45.

39. Curtis, J. M., & Crowell, D. R. (1993). Relation of birth order and scores on measures of pathological narcissism. *Psychological Reports, 72,* 311–315.

40. deLint, J., Blane, H. T., & Barry, H., III. (1974). Birth order and alcoholism. *Quarterly Journal of Studies on Alcohol, 35,* 292–295.

41. Dember, W. N. (1964). Birth order and need affiliation. *Journal of Abnormal and Social Psychology, 68,* 556–557.

42. deSaugy, D. (1962). L'Alcoholique et sa femme. *Hygiene Mentale, 81*–105, 147–201.

43. Dimond, R. E., & Munzz, D. C. (1967). Ordinal position and self- disclosure in high school students. *Psychological Reports, 21,* 829–833.

44. Dubno, P., & Freedman, R. D. (1970). Birth order, educational achievement and managerial attainment. *Personnel Psychology, 24,* 63–70.

45. Eckstein, D. (1978). Leadership, popularity, and birth-order in women. *Journal of Individual Psychology, 34(1),* 63–66.

46. Eckstein, D., & Driscoll, R. (1983). Leadership, popularity, and birth-order in women. *Journal of Individual Psychology, 34(1),* 70–77.

47. Edwards, A. L. (1963). *Edwards Personal Preference Schedule.* New York: Psychological Corporation.

48. Ernst, C., & Angst, J. (1983). *Birth order. Its influence on personality.* Berlin: SpringerVeriag.

49. Falbo, T. (1976). *Folklore and the only child: A reassessment.* Paper presented at the 84th Annual Convention of the American Psychological Association, Washington, DC.

50. Falbo, T., & Polit, D. (1988). The intellectual achievement of only children. *Journal of Biosocial Science, 20(3),* 275–285.

51. Falbo, T. (1977). The only child: A review. *Journal of Individual Psychology, 33(1),* 47–61.

52. Farley, F H., Smart, K. L., & Briftain, C. V. (1974). Birth order, rank and branch of service in the military. *Journal of Individual Psychology, 30,* 227–32.

53. Feeney, F. E., Mindlin, D. F., Minear, V. H., & Short, E. E. (1955). The challenge of the skid row alcoholic. *Quarterly Journal for the Study of Alcohol, 16,* 643.

54. Feinhardt, R. F. (1970).The outstanding jet pilot. *American Journal of Psychiatry, 127,* 732–736.

55. Fischer, E. H., Wells, C. F., & Cohen, S. K. (1968). Birth order and expressed interest in becoming a college professor. *Journal of Counseling Psychology, 15,* 111–116.

56. Forbes, G. B. (1971). Birth order of political success: A study of the 1970 Illinois general election. *Psychological Reports, 29,* 1239–1242.

57. Forer, L. K. (1969). *Birth order and life roles.* Springfield, IL: Charles C Thomas.

58. Forer, L. K. (1976). *The birth order factor* New York: David McKay Co.

59. Forer, L. K. (1977). The use of birth order information in psycho-therapy. *Journal of Individual Psychology, 33,* 105–113.

60. Gallagher, R., & Cowen, E. L. (1977). Birth order and school adjustment problems. *Journal of Individual Psychology, 33,* 70–77.

61. Gebhard, P., Raboch, J., & Giese, H. (1970). *The sexuality of women.* New York: Stein and Day.

62. Greenberg, M. S. (1967). Role playing: An alternative to deception? *Journal of Personality and Social Psychology, 7,* 152–157.

63. Guildford, R. B., & Worcester, D. A. (1930). A comparative study of the only and non-only child. *Journal of Genetic Psychology, 38,* 411–426.

64. Hall, E. (1965). Ordinal position and success in engagement and marriage. *Journal of Individual Psychology, 21,* 154–158.

65. Harris, I. D. (1964). *The promised seed: A comparative study of eminent first and later sons.* London: Free Press of Glencoe.

66. Helmreichl, R., Kulken, D., & Collins, B. (1968). Effects of stress and birth order on attitude change. *Journal of Personality, 36,* 38–44.

67. Herrell, J. M. (1972). Birth order and the military: A review of the Adlerian perspective. *Journal of Individual Psychology, 28,* 38–44.

68. Hetherington, E. M. (1972). Effects of father absence on personality development of adolescent daughters. *Developmental Psychology, 7*, 313–326.

69. Horrock, J. E. (1962). *The psychology of adolescence.* Boston: Houghton and Mifflin.

70. Hough, E. (1932). Some factors in the etiology of maternal over- protection. *Smith College Studies of Social Work, 2*,188–208.

71. Howe, M. G., & Madgett, M. E. (1975). Mental health problems associated with the only child. *Canadian Psychiatric Association Journal, 20*, 189–194.

72. Hoyt, M. P., & Raven, B. H. (1973). Birth order and the 1971 earthquake. *Journal of Personality and Social Psychology, 20*,122–128.

73. Innes, J. M., & Sambrook, J. E. (1969). Paired associate learning as influence by birth order and the presence of others. *Psychonomic Science, 16*, 109–110.

74. Ivancevich, J. M., Matteson, M. T., & Gamble, G.O. (1987). Birth order and the Type A coronary behavior pattern. *Journal of Individual Psychology, 43(1)*, 42–49.

75. Jones, H. E. (I 954). Environmental influence on mental development. In L. Carmichael (Ed.), *Manual of Child Psychology(2nd ed.).* New York: Wiley.

76. Joubert, C. E. (1989). Birth order and narcissism. *Psychological Reports, 64*, 721–722.

77. Kammeyer, K. (1967). Birth order as a research variable. *Social Forces, 46*, 71–80.

78. Kaplan, H.B. (1970). Self-derogation and childhood family structure. *Journal of Nervous and Mental Disease, 151*, 13–23.

79. Kemper, T. D. (1966). Mate selection and marital satisfaction according to sibling type of husband and wife. *Journal of Marriage and the Family*, 346–349.

80. Ko, Y., & Sun, L. (1965). Ordinal position and the behavior of visiting the child guidance clinic. *Acta Psychologia Taiwanica*, 1016–1062.

81. Koenig, F. (1969). Definitions of self and ordinal position of birth. *Journal of Social Psychology*, 287–288.

82. Kosugu, Y., & Tanaka, M. (1967). Parent deprivation, birth order and alcoholism. *Journal of Studies on Alcohol, 37*, 779.

83. Kurth, E., & Schmidt, E. (1964). Multidimensional examinations of stuttering children. *Probleme and Ergebnisse der Psychologie, 12*, 49–58.

84. LaVoie, J. C. (1973). Individual difference in resistance to temptation behavior in adolescents. *Journal of Clinical Psychology, 29*, 20–22.

85. Lees, J. P., & Steward, A. H. (1957). Family or sibship position and scholastic ability: An interpretation. *Sociological Review, 5*, 173–190

86. Lester, D. (I 985). Suicide and sibling position. *Journal of Individual Psychology, 41(3)*, 328–335.

87. Liberman, L., et al. (1985). Scientific revolutions and birth order. *Journal of Individual Psychology, 41(3)*, 328–335.

88. Longstreth, L. E. (1970). Birth Order and avoidance of dangerous activities. *Developmental Psychology, 2*,154.

89. MacDonald, A. P., Jr. (1967). Birth order effects in marriage and parenthood: Affiliation and socialization. *Journal of Marriage and the Family, 29*, 656–661.

90. McCann, S., & Stein, L. (1987). Frightening dreams and birth order. *Journal of Individual Psychology, 43(1)*, 56–58.

91. McCann, S., et al. (1990). Frightening dream frequency and birth order. *Journal of Individual Psychology, 46(3)*, 304–310.

92. McGhee, P. E. (1973). Birth order and social facilitation of humor. *Psychological Reports, 33,* 105–106.

93. McGurk, H., & Lewis, M. (1972). Birth order: A phenomenon in search of an explanation. *Developmental Psychology, 7,* 336.

94. Melillo, D. (1983). Birth order, perceived birth order, and family position of academic women. *Journal of Individual Psychology, 39(1),* 57–62.

95. Miller, N., & Maruyama, G. (1976). Ordinal position and peer popularity. *Journal of Personality and Social Psychology, 33,* 123–131.

96. Murdock, P. H. (1966). Birth order and age at marriage. *British Journal of Social and Clinical Psychology, 5,* 24–29.

97. Nisbett, R. E. (1968). Birth order and participation in dangerous sports. *Journal of Personality and Social Psychology, 9,* 352–353.

98. Nowicki, S. (1971). Ordinal position, approval motivation and inter- personal attraction. *Journal of Consulting and Clinical Psychology, 36,* 65–267.

99. Oberiander, M., & Jenkins, N. (1967). Birth order and academic achievement. *Journal of Individual Psychology, 23,* 103–109

100. Oberiander, M., Frauenfelder, K. J., & Heath, H. (1971). The relationship of ordinal position and sex to interest patterns. *Journal of Genetic Psychology, 119,* 29–36.

101. Ogburn, W. F. (1930). The changing family with regard to the child. *Annals of the American Academy of Political and Social Science, 151,* 20–24.

102. Payne, D. L. (1971). Birth order, personality and performance at the Air Force Academy. *Journal of Individual Psychology, 27,* 185–187.

103. Perlin, M., & Grater. (1984). The relationship between birth order and reported interpersonal behavior. *Journal of Individual Psychology, 401(1),* 2–28.

104. Peven, D., & Shulman, B. (1983). The psychodynamics of bipolar affective disorder. *Journal of Individual Psychology, 39(1),* 2–15.

105. Phillips, A. S., & Phillips, C. R. (1994). Birth order and achievement attributions. *Journal of Individual Psychology, 501(1),* 119–124.

106. Phillips, A., et al. (I 988). Birth-order and selected work-related personality variables. *Journal of Individual Psychology, 44(4),* 492–499.

107. Phillips, A., Long, R. G.,& Bedeian, A.G. (1990). Type A status: Birth order and gender effects. *Journal of Individual Psychology, 46(3),* 365–373.

108. Pilkington, L. R., White, J., & Matheny, K. B. (1997). Perceived coping resources and psychological birth order in school-aged children. *Journal of Individual Psychology,* 43–53.

109. Pulakos, J. (1987). The effects of birth order on perceived family roles. *Journal of Individual Psychology, 43(3),* 319–328.

110. Rapoport, R. N., & Rapoport, R. (1971). Early and later experiences as determinants of adult behavior, married women's family and career patterns. *British Joumal of Sociology, 22,* 16–30.

111. Rieth, E. (1973). Soziologische und psychologische ursachen der sucht frauen. *Quarterly Journal of Studies on Alcohol, 34,* 613.

112. Roe, A. A. (1953). Psychological study of eminent.psychologist and anthropologist and a comparison with biological and physical scientist. *Psychological Monographs, 67.*

113. Rosen, B. C. (1961). Family structure and achievement motivation. *American Sociological Review, 28,* 574–585.

114. Rosen, B., & Andrade, R. C. T. (1959). The psychosocial origins of achievement motivation. *Sociometry, 22,* 185–218.

115. Rosenberg, M. (1965). *Society and the adolescent self-image.* Princeton University Press.

116. Rosenfeld, H. (1966). Relationships of ordinal position to affiliation and achievement motives: Direction and generality. *Journal of Personality, 34,* 467–479.

117. Runco, M. A., & Bahleda, M. D. (1987). Birth order and divergent thinking. *Journal of Genetic Psychology, 148(1),* 119–125.

118. Sampson, E. E. (1962). Birth order, need achievement and conformity. *Journal of Abnormal Psychology, 64,*155–159.

119. Sampson, E. E., & Hancock, F. R. (1967). An examination of the relationship between ordinal position, personality and conformity: An extension, replication and partial verification. *Journal of Personality and Social Psychology, 5,* 398–407.

120. Schachter, S. (1963). Birth order, eminence and higher education. *American Sociological Review, 28,* 757–768.

121. Schachter, S. (1959). *The psychology of affiliation: Experimental studies of the sources of gregariousness.* Stanford, CA: Stanford University Press.

122. Schooler, C. (1972). Birth order effects: Not here, not now! *Psychological Review, 78,* 161–175.

123. Schubert, D. S. P., Wagner, M. E., & Schubert, H. J. P. (1977). Family and creativity. *Journal of Psychology, 96,* 144–149.

124. Searcy, M. L., Cowen, E. L., &Terrell, D. L. (I 977). School adjustment problems of children from small vs. large families. *Journal of Community Psychology, 5,* 178–182.

125. Sells, S. B., & Roff, M. (1963). Peer acceptance-rejection and birth order. *American Psychologist, 18,* 355.

126. Shulman, B. H., & Mosak, H. M. (1977). Birth order and ordinal position: Two Adlerian views. *Journal of Individual Psychology,33,* 114–121.

127. Skouholt, T., Moore, E., & Wellman, F. (1973). Birth order and academic behavior in first grade. *Psychological Reports, 32,* 395–398.

128. Smith, E. E., & Goodchilds, J. D. (1963). Some personality and behavioral factors related to birth order. *Journal of Applied Psychology, 47,* 300–303.

129. Snell, W., et al. (1986). Birth order and achievement motivation con- figurations in women and men. *Journal of Individual Psychology, 42(3),* 32–38.

130. Stein, S., et al. (1988). Birth order, substance abuse, and criminality. *Journal of Individual Psychology, 44(4),* 500–506.

131. Stotiand, E., Sherman, S. E., & Shaver, K. G. (1971). *Empathy and birth orders: Some experimental explorations.* Lincoln: University of Nebraska Press.

132. Strumpfer, D. J. W. (1970). Fear and affiliation during a disaster. *Journal of Social Psychology, 83,* 263–268.

133. Sulloway, Frank 1. (1966). *Born to rebel.* New York: Pantheon Books.

134. Sutton-Smith, B., & Rosenberg, B. G. (1968). Sibling consensus on

135. power tactics. *Journal of Genetic Psychology, 112,* 63–72.

136. Sutton-Smith, B., & Rosenberg, B. G. (1970). *The sibling.* New York: Holt, Rinehart, and Winston, Inc.

137. Sutton-Smith, B., Roberts, J. M., & Rosenberg, B. G. (1966). The dramatic sibling. *Perceptual and Motor Skills, 22,* 993–994.

138. Thompson, V. D. (1974). Family Size: Implicit policies and assumed psychological outcomes. *Journal of Social Issues, 30,* 9–124.

139. Tobacyk, J., & Eckstein, D. (1979). Ordinal position and death concerns. *Psychological Report, 44,* 967–971.

140. Toman, W., & Toman, E. (1970). Sibling positions of a sample of distinguished persons. *Perceptual and Motor Skills, 31,* 825–826.

141. Touhey, J. C. (1971). Birth order and virginity. *Psychological Reports, 28,* 894.

142. Tuckman, J., & Regan, R. A. (1967). Size of family and behavioral problems in children. *Journal of Genetic Psychology, 111,* 151–160.

143. Very, P. S., Goldblatt, R. B., & Monacelli, V. (1973). Birth order, personality development and vocational choice of becoming a Carmelite nun. *Journal of Psychology, 85,* 75–80.

144. Wagner, M. E., & Schubert, H. J. P. (1974). Sibship variables and United States presidents. *Journal of Individual Psychology, 30,* 221–226.

145. Wark, D. M., Swanson, E. O., & Mack, J. (1974). More on birth order: Intelligence and college plans. *Journal of Individual Psychology, 30,* 221–226.

146. Winterbottom, M. R. (1958). The relation of need for achievement to learning experiences in independence and mastery. In J. W. Atkinson (Ed.), *Motives in fantasy, action, and society,* 15–16. New Jersey: Van Nostrand.

147. Wrightsman, L. S., Jr. (1960). Effects of waiting with other on changes in level of felt anxiety. *Journal of Abnormal Social Psychology, 61,* 216–222.

148. Zajonc, R. B. (1976). Family configuration and intelligence. *Science, 192,* 227–236.

149. Zajonc, R. B., & Markus, G. B. (1975). Birth order and intellectual development. *Psychological Review, 82,* 74–88.

150. Zimbardo, P., & Formica, R. (1963). Emotional comparisons and self esteem as determinants of affiliation. *Journal of Personality, 31,* 141–162.

151. Zweigenhaft, R. L. (1975). Birth order, approval-seeking and membership in Congress. *Journal of Individual Psychology, 31,* 204–210.

Authors' Biographies

Daniel Eckstein, Ph.D., is president of Encouraging Leadership, Inc., Scottsdale, Arizona. He is also an adjunct professor for Capella University, Minneapolis, Minnesota; and the Adler School for Professional Psychology, Toronto, Canada. He previously played two years of professional football with the Green Bay Packers, the Miami Dolphins, and the Hamilton (Ontario) Tiger-Cats.

Dr. Eckstein has authored or co-authored twelve books, including *Raising Respectful Kids in a Rude World* and *Leadership by Encouragement*. Since 1976 he has also published the following books with Kendall/Hunt Publishers:

Life Style: What It Is and How To Do It
The Theory and Practice of Life-Style Assessment
The ABC's of Classroom Discipline
Life-Style: Theory, Practice, and Research
Leadership by Encouragement
The Encouragement Process in Life Span Development
Relationship Repair: "Fix It" Activities for Couples and Families

He has diplomates in Counseling Psychology from the American Board of Professional Psychologists and the North America Society of Adlerian Psychology.

Roy Kern, Ed.D. is a professor in the department of counseling and psychological services, and is a faculty member for the executive e-commerce MBA program and center for professional education programs in the business school at Georgia State University. He has been a faculty member for an international summer school for fourteen years. He is a licensed marriage and family therapist, professional counselor, and approved supervisor for the American Association of Marriage and Family Therapy.

His professional writings include books on couples therapy and exam taking. He is the author and coauthor of the Lifestyle Questionnaire Inventory, Kern Lifestyle Scale, and the Basic Adlerian Scales for Interpersonal Success (BASIS-A).

His editorial credentials include serving as editor of *The Journal of Individual Psychology* and column editor for *The family journal: counseling and therapy for couples and families*. He has devoted his professional writing and research career to researching the lifestyle construct from an empirical perspective. To date he has published fifty articles and supervised twenty-three doctoral students in the investigation of some aspect of the lifestyle construct. He has created several courses within the department of counseling and psychological services at Georgia State University devoted to the application the lifestyle technique with clients, families, and teachers in the classroom.